Nervous Conditions

and Related Readings

McDougal Littell
A HOUGHTON MIFFLIN COMPANY

Evanston, Illinois   *Boston*   *Dallas*

Acknowledgments

Seal Press: *Nervous Conditions* by Tsitsi Dangarembga. Copyright © 1988 by Tsitsi Dangarembga. Published by permission of Seal Press.

Harcourt Brace and Company, Random House UK, and the estate of Virginia Woolf: "Professions for Women," from *The Death of the Moth and Other Essays* by Virginia Woolf. Copyright 1942 by Harcourt Brace & Company and renewed 1970 by Marjorie T. Parsons, Executrix. Reprinted by permission of Harcourt Brace & Company; Chatto & Windows, an imprint of Random House UK; and the estate of the author.

International Creative Management, Inc.: "Back to School" by Andrea Lee, from *The New Yorker*, April 29 and May 6, 1996. Copyright © 1996 by Andrea Lee. Reprinted by permission of International Creative Management, Inc.

Continued on page 321.

The editors have made every effort to trace the ownership of all copyrighted selections found in this book and to make full acknowledgment for their use. Omissions brought to our attention will be corrected in a subsequent edition.

Cover Illustration by Linda Montgomery.
Author Photo: The Women's Press, U.K.

Printed in China

Copyright © 1997 by McDougal Littell, a division of Houghton Mifflin Company. All rights reserved.

ISBN-13: 978-0-395-77560-8
ISBN-10: 0-395-77560-4

9 10 11 12 NPC 09 08 07 06

Contents

Nervous Conditions

Tsitsi Dangarembga

The condition of native is a nervous condition.

From an introduction to Fanon's *The Wretched of the Earth*.

Chapter 1

I was not sorry when my brother died. Nor am I apologising for my callousness, as you may define it, my lack of feeling. For it is not that at all. I feel many things these days, much more than I was able to feel in the days when I was young and my brother died, and there are reasons for this more than the mere consequence of age. Therefore I shall not apologise but begin by recalling the facts as I remember them that led up to my brother's death, the events that put me in a position to write this account. For though the event of my brother's passing and the events of my story cannot be separated, my story is not after all about death, but about my escape and Lucia's; about my mother's and Maiguru's entrapment; and about Nyasha's rebellion—Nyasha, far-minded and isolated, my uncle's daughter, whose rebellion may not in the end have been successful.

I was thirteen years old when my brother died. It happened in 1968. It was the end of term and we were expecting him home by the afternoon bus that passed through our village at three o'clock. My brother went to school at the mission where my uncle was headmaster and which was some twenty miles away from the village, to the west, in the direction of Umtali town. Sometimes, when my uncle was not too busy with reports and administration at the end of the school term, he was able to come away from his office at three o'clock in the afternoon, sacrificing the remaining hours in the day in order to bring Nhamo home. This was what Nhamo preferred. He did not like travelling by bus because, he said, it was too slow. Moreover, the women smelt of unhealthy reproductive odours, the children were inclined to relieve their upset bowels on the floor, and the men gave off strong aromas of productive labour. He did not like sharing the vehicle with various kinds of produce in suspicious stages of freshness, with frightened hens, with the occasional rich-smelling goat. "We should have a special bus," he complained, "like they have for students who live in Fort Victoria and in Salisbury," quite forgetting that these were towns, autonomous urban centres, whereas our home was in the communal lands that surround Umtali, and that since my uncle's mission was considered to be in Umtali, there was no need to hire a bus in order to ferry him and the other pupils who lived in our area home.

Even so, hiring a bus would not have made the end of term comfortable enough for my brother. The bus terminus—which is also the market, with pale dirty tuckshops, dark and dingy inside, which we call *magrosa*, and women under msasa trees selling hard-boiled eggs, vegetables, seasonal fruit, boiled chicken which is sometimes curried and sometimes not, and anything else that the villagers or travellers might like to buy—is at least two miles distance from our homestead. Had a bus been hired or not my brother would still have had to walk the two miles home. This walk was another aspect of his homeward journey that my brother wished not to have to endure.

I, not having had to make the journey regularly each end of term and each beginning of a new term, could not understand why my brother disliked walking so much, especially after being cramped in an airless bus for such a long time: the bus-journey to the mission took nearly an hour. Besides the relief of being able to stretch your legs after such a long journey, the walk home from the bus terminus was not a long walk when you had nowhere to hurry to. The road wound down by the fields where there were always some people with whom to pass ten minutes of the day—enquiring about their health and the health of their family, admiring the broad-leafed abundance of the maize crop when it was good, predicting how many bags the field would yield or wondering whether the plants had tasselled too early or too late. And although the stretch of road between the fields and the terminus was exposed to the sun and was, from September to April, except when it rained, harsh and scorching so that the glare from the sand scratched at your eyes, there was always shade by the fields where clumps of trees were deliberately left standing to shelter us when we ate our meals or rested between cultivating strips of the land.

From the fields the road grew shadier with shrubs and trees. Acacia, lantana, msasa and mopani, clustered about on either side. If you had time you could run off the road into more wooded areas to look for matamba and matunduru. Sweet and sour. Delicious. From this woody section the road rolled down into a shallow ravine, a river valley thoughtfully appointed along its floor with smooth, flat-topped boulders which made exciting equipment for all sorts of our childhood games. Across and around the lowest of these boulders, the river flowed sparsely in a dry season, but deeply enough in places when the rains were heavy to cover a child's head and to engulf me to my nipples. We learnt to avoid these places when the river flowed violently, but in most seasons it flowed placidly enough to permit bathing along most of its length. As children we were not restricted. We could play where we pleased. But the women had their own spot for bathing and the men their own too. Where the women washed the river was shallow, seldom reaching above my knees, and the rocks were lower and flatter there than in other places, covering most of the riverbed. The women liked their spot because it was sensibly architectured for doing the laundry. But we were apprehensive about growing so big that we would have to wash there with the women and no longer be able to swim in the deeper, cooler, more interesting pools.

The river, the trees, the fruit and the fields. This was how it was in the beginning. This is how I remember it in my earliest memories, but it did not stay like that. While I was still quite young, to enable administration of our area, the Government built its District Council Houses less than a mile away from the places where we washed. Thus it became necessary for all the inhabitants of the dozen or so homesteads that made up our village to cross Nyamarira, as our river is called, whenever we went on business to the Council Houses. It was not long before the entrepreneurial among us, noticing that there were always more people gathered at the Council Houses than anywhere else in the village (except at church on Sundays and on other days in places where beer was being drunk), built their little tuckshops which sold the groceries we needed—bread, tea, sugar, jam, salt, cooking oil, matches, candles, paraffin and soap—there beside the Council Houses. I do not remember the exact sequence of this development, whether the place became a bus terminus before or after the tuckshops were built, but soon buses were stopping there too. Idle, the less industrious youth of the village began to loiter around the tuckshops, buying each other when they could afford to, which was not often, Fanta and Coca-Cola and perfume that smelt of vanilla essence, cheap at a tickey a bottle. An enterprising owner of one of the tuckshops, taking advantage of this, introduced a gramophone into his shop so that the youth could entertain themselves with music and dancing. They played the new rumba that, as popular music will, pointed unsystematic fingers at the conditions of the times: "I'll beat you up if you keep asking for your money," "Father, I am jobless, give me money for *roora*," "My love, why have you taken a second wife?" There was swaying of hips, stamping of feet to the pulse of these social facts. There was solidarity. The authorities became alarmed. Seeing how enterprising our community had been, they rewarded us for our efforts by building us a beer-hall, painted dark blue like the Council Houses, where "native beer" and "clear beer" were sold cheaply every day of the week. Thus our washing places became thoroughfares for people going to *magrosa* for all sorts of reasons. In the interests of decency bathing was relegated to further up the river. Nevertheless, when I was feeling brave, which was before my breasts grew too large, I would listen from the top of the ravine and, when I was sure I had felt no one coming, run down to the river, slip off my frock, which was usually all that I was wearing, and swim blissfully for as long as I dared in the old deep places.

This was the walk that my brother detested! Truly, I could continue endlessly describing the possibilities that were in that walk, so I could not understand why he was so resentful of it. Yet resentful he was, and most of the time he managed to avoid it by staying at the mission after the end of term on one pretext or another until my uncle, who is my father's brother and the eldest child in their family, decided that he would pay us a visit. My uncle visited us often.

It had been my uncle's idea that Nhamo should go to school at the mission. Nhamo, if given the chance, my uncle said, would distinguish himself academically, at least sufficiently to enter a decent profession. With the money earned in this way, my uncle said, Nhamo would lift our branch of the family out of the squalor in which we were living. Thus my uncle's gesture was oceanic, and my father, who liked hyperbole, did not need much persuading to see the sense of this plan. After only the mildest of polite hesitations, during which he reminded my uncle that Nhamo's departure would result in more work on the homestead for the rest of us, he agreed to let my brother go. This happened when my brother was in Standard Three, which was in 1965, the year of my uncle's return from England. By that time, the end of 1965, my brother had already begun to distinguish himself by coming top of the class in his first two years of primary school and staying in the top five thereafter. It was this tendency that my uncle, who had been excited by it, wished to develop. "If I had your brains," my father used to say to Nhamo by way of encouragement during my brother's early school years, his formative years, "I would have been a teacher by now. Or maybe even a doctor. Ya! Maybe even a doctor. Do you think we would be living the way we are? No! In a brick house with running water, hot and cold, and lights, just like Mukoma. It would have been good, if only I had the brains." Nhamo, who believed in filial obedience, used to agree with my father that indeed it would have been good and to reassure my father that the intelligence he had been blessed with would not be abused. I was different. I wanted to find out the truth. Did my father mean that Babamukuru was sharp at his lessons? I asked one day, overhearing one of these conversations.

"Not exactly that," my father replied. "I wouldn't say Mukoma was sharp. No. Not exactly sharp. But he used to read. Ha! Mukoma used to read. Whatever he touched he pushed, that's the way he was. I-i-h! Mukoma used to read," he concluded, opening his mouth in a wide grimace, wrinkling his forehead in awe-filled tribute to my uncle's perseverance. And then, realising the trap he had set for himself and fallen into, he was obliged to excuse himself. "But

Mukoma was lucky. He got the chance. He went to the mission at an early age. The missionaries looked after him so well, you know, that the books, ha-a-a, the books came naturally."

Whether Babamukuru was sharp or industrious or merely lucky, Nhamo was usually able to cajole his uncle into driving him home. How Nhamo managed this is a mystery to me, because Babamukuru has never been the sort of person who is easily cajoled. Nevertheless, Nhamo could usually manage. But this time, this particular end of term that I am talking about in November 1968, when Nhamo had just completed his Standard Six and therefore finished early, Babamukuru was attending a meeting in town. Nhamo was obliged to take the bus. Actually I think Babamukuru had decided that it would be good for Nhamo to take the bus for a change. I think my uncle had begun to worry about the way in which my brother was developing. Certainly, all of us at home who were old enough to worry, all of us except my father that is, had begun to worry about Nhamo's development.

Very soon after going to the mission my brother stopped coming home to stay during the short vacations. Although he did visit occasionally with my uncle, he came back home to stay only once a year when the school year ended and the maize year began. During the April and August holidays Nhamo refused to come home, saying it was necessary to read his books ceaselessly in order to pass his examinations at the end of each year. This was a good argument. It enabled him to avoid the uncomfortable tasks of pulling down and stacking the maize and stripping the cobs of their leaves. We used to itch viciously at the end of each day during the maize harvest and run straight to the river from the fields to wash the itching away. It was not surprising that Nhamo did not like the harvest. None of us found it a pleasant task. It was just one of those things that had to be done. September and October were different. At this time the land was prepared for the new crop. In the beginning people used to dig the land with hoes, which was hard work but not uncomfortable and therefore not unenjoyable. Then, just before Babamukuru went to England in 1960, he bought my father an ox-plough, so that by the time I was old enough to help in the fields the work was reduced to planting the maize in the years that my father or any visiting male relative who was strong enough found time to use the ox-plough. In the years that they did not find the time, it was digging and planting as usual. After the planting, after the crop had germinated, all through the rainy season until the plants were tall and sturdy, we weeded, using our hands and our hoes. Sometimes it was not only maize but mhunga and rukweza as well. The beginning of the crop year was a busy time. My uncle insisted that Nhamo be home for it on the grounds that there were no examinations pending to justify his staying at the mission. Thus Nhamo was forced once a year to return to his squalid homestead, where he washed in cold water in an enamel basin or a flowing river, not in a bathtub with taps gushing hot water and cold; where he ate *sadza* regularly with his fingers and meat hardly at all, never with a knife and fork; where there was no light beyond the flickering yellow of candles and home-made paraffin lamps to enable him to escape into his books when the rest of us had gone to bed.

All this poverty began to offend him, or at the very least to embarrass him after he went to the mission, in a way that it had not done before. Before he went to the mission, we had been able to agree that although our squalor was brutal, it was uncompromisingly ours; that the burden of dispelling it was, as a result, ours too. But then something that he saw at the mission turned his mind to thinking that our homestead no longer had any claim upon him, so that when he did come home for his vacations, it was as if he had not: he was not very sociable. Helping in the fields or with the livestock or the firewood, any of the tasks he used to do willingly before he went to the mission, became a bad joke. When the rains came early at the end of his first year at the mission, he pointed out that most of the work had already been done and we had coped very well; when the rains came late, as they did at the end of his second year there, he reminded us that we had managed without him in the previous year. The only times that he would expend any energy to help around the homestead were the times when Babamukuru sent word that he was coming to visit. On such days Nhamo would rise at dawn with the rest of us, working so hard that the dirt ingrained itself into the skin of his hands and the sweat ran down his bare back, leaving him smelling and looking for all the world like an archetypal labourer. His strategy was perfect. He never returned to the homestead, no matter how tedious and heavy the tasks at hand, until Babamukuru, having arrived home and found it deserted, drove down to the fields.

Sometimes Babamukuru wore shorts when he came to visit. If we were all at the fields on such an occasion he would take a hoe and join us for a while in our labours before driving back to the homestead with my father and Nhamo to listen to my father's progress report concerning how far behind we were with the sowing, the cultivating or the harvest; how the neighbours' cattle were plundering our fields; how Babamukuru should provide a barbed-wire fence to keep out the baboons as well as the cattle. When Babamukuru was not wearing shorts they would return to the homestead immediately. My mother, lips pressed tight, would hitch little Rambanai more securely on her back and continue silently at her labours. The ferocious swings of her arms as she grabbed and stripped a maize stalk restrained Netsai and me from making the slightest murmur of rebellion. We imagined those ferocious movements of our mother's arm sending a switch whistling down on our legs and this thought made us very diligent. Netsai turned on what I thought was an excessive amount of steam when mother grew silently ferocious. She would have outstripped me by an indecent number of yards, an embarrassingly high quota of cobs, if I hadn't been ashamed to lose face by letting my younger sister out-work me. We would follow in the tracks of my uncle's car when the sun began to set, herding the cattle back to their kraal as we went since there was no other young man in our family besides Nhamo to attend to this chore. We would travel as briskly as we could so that we would not be late in preparing the evening meal. Personally, I did not like to see Babamukuru in shorts, because in his mission clothes he was a dignified figure and that was how I liked to imagine him.

On the days that Babamukuru came to visit we killed a cock. Or rather, we killed a cock if there was one to spare, otherwise just a hen. We also killed a fowl on the occasions that Nhamo came home, whether he came with Babamukuru or whether he came alone. Netsai and I would corner the bird and catch it, eventually, after much frustrated grasping of air and feathers, encouraged in the chase by squeals of delight from little Rambanai, who often ended up crying when the bird flew away from us into her face.

On this particular November afternoon that we were expecting Nhamo home, my mother decided to water her vegetables—rape, *covo*, tomatoes, *derere* and onions—which she grew on a plot that had been my grandmother's, quite close to the homestead although still a quarter of an hour's walk away. We walked from the fields together, my mother and I, with the cattle, until we reached the vegetable garden, where we parted, she to her watering, I to the homestead, the cattle-whip in my hand but unused because the animals were as eager to be home as I was. Our shadows had already elongated thinly eastwards as the sun sank behind the hills. It was well past six o'clock. Being this late I was sure I would find Nhamo at home when I arrived, but when I walked up from the cattle kraal I saw only Rambanai and Netsai playing in the sandy yard around the kitchen. They were playing *nhodo*, which is to say that Netsai was playing and Rambanai, when it was her turn, was simply throwing the stone into the air and protesting loudly when Netsai resumed her turn. Rambanai was too young to throw a stone up into the air and pick up several other stones and then catch the first stone as it fell. Netsai knew this very well but enjoyed beating Rambanai at *nhodo* all the same.

As soon as Rambanai saw me she came running, complaining vehemently about Netsai's unfairness in her unintelligible language, so that it was only the look on her face that told me what she was saying.

"Hush, now," I soothed, picking her up and settling her on my hip. "I'll play *nhodo* with you. We'll have a good game. Did Nhamo send you for his luggage?" I asked Netsai.

"No, Sisi Tambu," she answered. "Mukoma Nhamo has not yet come."

"He hasn't yet come?" I was not worried because the three o'clock bus was often a four o'clock or even a five o'clock bus. I was relieved too. I would not have to kill the cock. "Then maybe tomorrow, when Babamukuru will be able to give him a lift."

Knowing Nhamo as I did, I knew he would not

arrive home that late in the day on foot, for that would entail carrying his own luggage. Not that there was much of it, since he left his trunk at Babamukuru's. He usually carried no more than a small bag containing his books plus one or two pairs of old khaki shorts, which were the only clothes he had that he was not afraid to spoil by wearing at home. Sometimes he carried a plastic bag as well, containing odds and ends like sugar and tea, and soap, toothbrush and toothpaste. The sugar and tea were more often than not a gift from my aunt to my mother although Nhamo kept them for himself. He would drink sweet black tea while he read his books and we went about our chores. This used to amuse my mother. When she caught him at it she would scold him off to herd the cattle, but when she related the incident she would laugh. "That boy and his books! He'll make a fine teacher one of these days with all that reading!"

At any rate, Nhamo's luggage was never too cumbersome for him to carry. All the same, he would not carry it all himself. Instead, he would leave something, a few books, a plastic bag, anything as long as there was something, at the shops at the bus terminus, for he was on friendly terms with everybody, so that he could send Netsai to fetch them as soon as he arrived home. When he was feeling gracious he would offer to mind Rambanai, who was still toddling, while Netsai ran the errand. When he was being himself he would smirk that minding children was not a man's duty and Netsai, who was young although big for her age, would strap the baby to her back in order to fetch the luggage. Once or twice, because there was too much for her to manage on her own, I went with her. Knowing that he did not need help, that he only wanted to demonstrate to us and himself that he had the power, the authority to make us do things for him, I hated fetching my brother's luggage. Because I was almost as big as he was and when I was angry could push a log from the fire into his face, he did not bully me too much, but Netsai compensated for whatever I got away with. Nhamo enjoyed taking a stick to her at the slightest excuse. To keep the peace I would accompany Netsai when she needed help, all the way to the shops muttering and fuming to both of us about our brother's laziness. You may wonder why I did not stand up for my sister, tell my brother to carry his own luggage. I did on the first occasion that he made Netsai run the errand. He agreed to go himself, then, when I had gone back into the kitchen, took Netsai out of earshot and gave her a sound whipping about the legs with a slender peach branch. Poor Netsai! She told me she ran all the way to the shops. And then she asked me why I had not let her go in the first place! At first I thought it was the beating that was making her ask such a silly question, but later I realised that she really did not mind carrying Nhamo's luggage if there wasn't too much of it. She was a sweet child, the type that will make a sweet, sad wife. As for Nhamo, he was very capable of convincing himself that Netsai would not carry the luggage if there was too much for her. So I did not mind helping her when necessary.

This was not all that was unpleasant about our brother. That Nhamo of ours had hundreds of unreasonable ideas. Even after all these years I still think that our home was healthier when he was away. I certainly thought so at the time. I remember feeling quite relieved on that November afternoon. Since I no longer had to kill a cock and prepare it, only the *sadza* and vegetables needed attention. This was no task at all, giving me the option of going back to the garden to help my mother. The thought of my mother working so hard, so alone, always distressed me, but in the end I decided to prepare the evening meal so that she would be able to rest when she returned. For I knew that if there was still work to be done when she finished her watering, she would tire herself further to do it.

"What is wrong, Sisi Tambu?" asked Netsai, bringing me out of my thoughts. Shifting Rambanai on to my left hip I found that my right knee had locked.

"Wrong, Si' Tam'?" queried Rambanai.

So typical of Netsai to ask a question I could not answer. I could not cold-bloodedly inform my sisters that I had been thinking of how much I disliked our brother. I felt guilty about it. As he was our brother, he ought to be liked, which made disliking him all the more difficult. That I still managed to do so meant I must dislike him very much indeed!

"It will be good," I observed in an attempt to convince myself, "when Mukoma Nhamo comes home."

"Why?" Netsai was puzzled. "What will he do?"

"What do?" echoed Rambanai, allowing me to laugh at her and so avoid answering. Putting her down I went to the *dara* to fill the enamel basin with water and to take the pots and plates I would need for my cooking. The *dara* was depressing. Termites had determinedly chewed their way right through one leg, so it stood tilted at an insolent angle, constantly letting things fall off it. As if that wasn't enough, several of the bark thongs that tied the crossplanks together had rotted. The planks had shifted, leaving large gaps between them, so that when things did not fall off the *dara* they fell through it.

It must be fixed; I must fix it, I thought as I had thought a dozen times before, promising myself that I would make the time. I bent down to pull the ten-gallon drum that we used for storing water from under the *dara*, fervently hoping that there was enough water in it for the night.

Netsai was watching me. "It's full," she smiled. "We used the tins. We only had to go three times to the river."

"Go river," agreed Rambanai.

"You are a good worker," I told my sister, touched by her concern. Her pretty little face lit up from the inside. We smiled at each other and Rambanai chortled.

The *covo* was crisp and large-leafed, not requiring much washing. The pots were all clean, further evidence of Netsai's considerate nature. I enjoyed preparing the food when the messier aspects had been taken care of. I hummed as I shredded the *covo* into the pot, was pleased when the chickens came to peck up the stray pieces, cleaning up the place without the threat of being caught and prepared themselves! How I hated the whole process of enlisting Netsai's help to head off the bird's escape, growing irritable as I lunged for its wings and clutched empty air until finally I caught it, protesting and cackling in its strident voice until, sensing the inevitable, it was quiet. Nor could I bear the smell of blood that threatened to suffocate when boiling water was poured over the headless bird to loosen its feathers. Next time, I thought naïvely, Nhamo will catch it himself. If he wants to eat chicken, he will catch it and kill it. I will pluck it and cook it. This seemed a fair division of labour.

I thought naïvely. Netsai's beating because of the luggage should have made it clear to me that Nhamo was not interested in being fair. Maybe to other people, but certainly not to his sisters, his younger sisters for that matter. Perhaps I am being unfair to him, laying all this blame on him posthumously, when he cannot defend himself and when I have seen enough to know that blame does not come in neatly packaged parcels. Perhaps I am making it seem as though Nhamo simply decided to be obnoxious and turned out to be good at it, when in reality that was not the case; when in reality he was doing no more than behave, perhaps extremely, in the expected manner. The needs and sensibilities of the women in my family were not considered a priority, or even legitimate. That was why I was in Standard Three in the year that Nhamo died, instead of in Standard Five, as I should have been by that age. In those days I felt the injustice of my situation every time I thought about it, which I could not help but do often since children are always talking about their age. Thinking about it, feeling the injustice of it, this is how I came to dislike my brother, and not only my brother: my father, my mother—in fact everybody.

Chapter 2

Nhamo began school in the year that he turned seven. This was the age at which the Government had declared that African children were sufficiently developed cognitively to be able to understand the abstractions of numbers and letters: 1 + 1 = 2; k-i-t-s-i = kitsi. Nhamo was one of the youngest pupils in his class. Perhaps other parents, believing that we really were a retarded lot, thought it best to let their children's abilities mature a little before exposing them to the rigours of formal education. And, of course, there was the question of fees. Whatever the reason, many of us did not begin school until we were eight or even nine years old, but the precedent of early entry had been set for our family by Babamukuru, who had obtained a Bachelor's Degree in South Africa and consequently knew a lot about education. "They should go early," Babamukuru told my father, "while their minds are still malleable." Inevitably, therefore, Nhamo began school in the year he turned seven and I followed the next since I was a year younger than him.

Now, for some reason that I do not ever remember understanding since we had fair rains that year, our crops were poor in the year that I began school. Although we harvested enough maize to keep us from starving, there was nothing left over to sell. This meant there was no money in the house. No money meant no school fees. No school fees meant no school. Nor was there any hope of procuring money since Babamukuru had left the mission to go to England to study more about education.

I was only five when Babamukuru went to England.

Consequently, all I can remember about the circumstances surrounding his going is that everybody was very excited and very impressed by the event. Since then, in order to find out what really happened at that time so that I can understand what followed, I have asked many people—Maiguru and Babamukuru, my father, my mother, Nyasha and Chido—to tell me what they recollect. I have discovered, as is not surprising, that there were debates and conflicts and tensions surrounding the departure that as a young child I could not have been aware of.

Babamukuru did not want to leave the mission. He did not want to go far from home again because he had already left his mother once, to go to South Africa, and had not been back long enough to see that she was settled and comfortable in her old age. In addition to this, he now had a family of his own. Although the missionaries who had offered him the scholarship to study in England had offered Maiguru a scholarship as well (so anxious were they that this intelligent, disciplined young couple be trained to become useful to their people), there was the question of the children. The debate and the tensions surrounding Babamukuru's departure centered not so much on the question of his going as on what to do with the children. Babamukuru was appreciative of the opportunity that had been offered; and further, to decline would have been a form of suicide. The missionaries would have been annoyed by his ingratitude. He would have fallen from grace with them and they would have taken under their wings another promising young African in his place. Unable to obtain the necessary qualifications at home, he had no alternative but to uproot himself for a period of five years in order to retain the position that would enable him, in due course, to remove himself and both his families from the mercy of nature and charitable missionaries. My grandmother thought the children would be better off at home, where our ways were familiar and they would be at ease in the family environment. But Babamukuru, remembering how difficult life was on the homestead, did not want his children to experience the want and hardship that he had experienced as a young child. In addition, he preferred to have his children with him so he could supervise essential things such as their education and their development. Therefore Chido and Nyasha were taken to England. My father, of course, thinking that five years without his brother to provide for him was a long time in which to be obliged to provide for himself, consoled himself with the knowledge that on Babamukuru's return with his high qualifications, he would be provided for more abundantly than before. My mother was hopeful. She thought my father would at last grow responsible.

I remember discussing the phenomenon of Babamukuru's education with Nhamo. Nhamo was very impressed by the sheer amount of education that was possible. He told me that the kind of education Babamukuru had gone to get must have been of a very important sort to make him go all that way for it. "England," he told me with weighty authority, "is very far away. It is much further away than South Africa." How did he know?

Nhamo knew a lot of things in those days. He knew more then than he did when he died. For instance, he knew that when he grew up he was going to study for many degrees like Babamukuru and become a headmaster like Babamukuru. He knew that it would be up to him to make sure that his younger sisters were educated, or look after us if we were not, just as Babamukuru had done and was doing for his own brothers and sister. He knew that he had to help in the fields and with the cattle and be pleasant to people.

Above all, he knew that he had to work hard at school and keep coming top of the class. This latter he did diligently in Sub A and Sub B. He was particularly pleased with his Sub B result because he had beaten the next boy by only two marks. Then, having done so well, he was told he could not go to school any longer because there was no money for the fees. He cried.

Fortunately, my mother was determined in that year. She began to boil eggs, which she carried to the bus terminus and sold to passengers passing through. (This meant that we could not eat them.) She also took vegetables —rape, onions and tomatoes—extending her garden so that there was more to sell. Business was fair, and good during public holidays, when visitors from as far as Salisbury, Fort Victoria, Mount Darwin and Wankie would be tempted to buy a little extra to take home with them. In this way she scraped together enough money to keep my brother in school. I understood that selling vegetables was not a lucrative business. I understood that there was not enough money for my fees. Yes, I did understand why I could not go back to school, but I loved going to school and I was good at it. Therefore, my circumstances affected me badly.

My father thought I should not mind. "Is that anything to worry about? Ha-a-a, it's nothing," he reassured me, with his usual ability to jump whichever way was easiest. "Can you cook books and feed them to your husband? Stay at home with your mother. Learn to cook and clean. Grow vegetables."

His intention was to soothe me with comforting, sensible words, but I could not see the sense. This was often the case when my father spoke, but there had not before been such concrete cause to question his theories. This time, though, I had evidence. Maiguru was educated, and did she serve Babamukuru books for dinner? I discovered to my unhappy relief that my father was not sensible.

I complained to my mother. "Baba says I do not need to be educated," I told her scornfully. "He says I must learn to be a good wife. Look at Maiguru," I continued, unaware how viciously. "She is a better wife than you!"

My mother was too old to be disturbed by my childish nonsense. She tried to diffuse some of it by telling me many things, by explaining that my father was right because even Maiguru knew how to cook and clean and grow vegetables. "This business of womanhood is a heavy burden," she said. "How could it not be? Aren't we the ones who bear children? When it is like that you can't just decide today I want to do this, tomorrow I want to do that, the next day I want to be educated! When there are sacrifices to be made, you are the one who has to make them. And these things are not easy; you have to start learning them early, from a very early age. The earlier the better so that it is easy later on. Easy! As if it is ever easy. And these days it is worse, with the poverty of blackness on one side and the weight of womanhood on the other. Aiwa! What will help you, my child, is to learn to carry your burdens with strength."

I thought about this for several days, during which I began to fear that I was not as intelligent as my Sub A performance had led me to believe, because, as with my father, I could not follow the sense of my mother's words. My mother said being black was a burden because it made you poor, but Babamukuru was not poor. My mother said being a woman was a burden because you had to bear children and look after them and the husband. But I did not think this was true. Maiguru was well looked after by Babamukuru, in a big house on the mission which I had not seen but of which I had heard rumours concerning its vastness and elegance. Maiguru was driven about in a car, looked well-kempt and fresh, clean all the time. She was altogether a different kind of woman from my mother. I decided it was better to be like Maiguru, who was not poor and had not been crushed by the weight of womanhood.

"I shall go to school again," I announced to my parents.

My father was sharp with me, thinking that I expected him to obtain the money somehow, perhaps by working. "Your nonsense, you are about to begin it! I can tell. You know your Babamukuru will not be home for a while yet!"

"I will earn the fees," I reassured him, laying out my plan for him as I had laid it out in my own mind. "If you will give me some seed, I will clear my own field and grow my own maize. Not much. Just enough for the fees."

My father was greatly tickled by this. He annoyed me tremendously by laughing and laughing in an unpleasantly adult way. "Just enough for the fees! Can you see her there?" he chuckled to my mother. "Such a little shrub, but already making ripe plans! Can you tell your daughter, Ma'Shingayi, that there is no money. There is no money. That's all."

My mother, of course, knew me better. "And did she ask for money?" she enquired. "Listen to your child. She is asking for seed. That we can give. Let her try. Let her see for herself that some things cannot be done."

My father agreed. A little seed was not a large price to pay to keep me quiet. I began my project the next day, a day in December 1962. The next January my brother entered Standard One. I worked on the homestead, in the family fields and on my own plot. How I mumbled adoring, reverent prayers to my grandmother in those early days of my market gardening. My grandmother, who had been an inexorable cultivator of land, sower of seeds and reaper of rich harvests until, literally until, her very last moment. When I was too small to be anything more than a hindrance in the family fields, I used to spend many productive hours working with my grandmother on the plot of land she called her garden. We hoed side by side strips of land defined by the row of maize plants each carried, I obstinately insisting I could keep pace with her, she weeding three strips to my one so that I could. Praising my predisposition towards working, she consolidated it in me as a desirable habit.

She gave me history lessons as well. History that could not be found in the textbooks; a stint in the field and a rest, the beginning of the story, a pause. "What happened after, Mbuya, what happened?" "More work, my child, before you hear more story." Slowly, methodically, throughout the day the field would be cultivated, the episodes of my grandmother's own portion of history strung together from beginning to end.

"Your family did not always live here, did not move to this place until after the time that I was married to your grandfather. We lived up in Chipinge, where the soil is ripe and your great-grandfather was a rich man in the currency of those days, having many fat herd of cattle, large fields and four wives who worked hard to produce bountiful harvests. All this he could exchange for cloth and beads and axes and a gun, even a gun, from the traders. They did not come to stay in those days; they passed through and left. Your great-grandfather had sons enough to fill a kraal, all big, strong, hardworking men. And me, I was beautiful in those days," her eyes twinkling at me so that I was ashamed of examining her so closely to find the woman she described. Why did she tell me this? She was not beautiful now, but I loved her, so I was ashamed that she saw me search for the lost beauty. "I wasn't always this old, with wrinkles and grey hair, without teeth. At one time I was as small and pretty and plump as you, and when I grew into a woman I was a fine woman with hair so long you could plait it into a single row down the middle of my head. I had heavy, strong hips." This is where she usually ended the first episode. I was on tenterhooks. The princess and the prince. What happened? What happened?

Wizards well versed in treachery and black magic came from the south and forced the people from the land. On donkey, on foot, on horse, on ox-cart, the people looked for a place to live. But the wizards were avaricious and grasping; there was less and less land for the people. At last the people came upon the grey, sandy soil of the homestead, so stony and barren that the wizards would not use it. There they built a home. But the third-born son, my grandfather, lured by the wizards' whispers of riches and luxury and driven by the harshness of the homestead, took himself and his family to one of their wizards' farms. Yuwi! Only to find that they had been enticed into slavery. But one day my grandfather managed to escape to glittering gold mines in the south, where good men were said to be quickly made rich. The white wizard had no use for women and children. He threw my grandmother and her children off his farm. Destitute, they travelled back to the homestead, where my great-grandfather, although he had not regained his former standard of living, had managed to keep the family together. And then my great-grandfather died and the family broke up, and it turned out that my grandfather had not been a good man, for he was killed in the mines, and my grandmother was left with six children to support. And then she heard that beings similar in appearance to the wizards but not of them, for these were holy, had set up a mission not too far from the homestead. She walked, with my uncle, with Babamukuru, who was nine years old and wearing a loin cloth, to the mission, where the holy wizards took him in. They set him to work in their farm by day. By night he was educated in their wizardry. For my grandmother, being sagacious and having foresight, had begged them to prepare him for life in their world.

It was truly a romantic story to my ears, a fairy-tale of reward and punishment, of cause and effect. It had a moral too, a tantalising moral that increased your aspirations, but not beyond a manageable level.

My uncle was not afraid of hard work, having grown used to it from an early age on the farm and on the homestead. He surprised the missionaries by performing exceptionally well at school, in spite of putting in a full day's work on the farm. He was diligent, he was industrious, he was respectful. They thought he was a good boy, cultivatable, in the way that land is, to yield harvests that sustain the cultivator. When he completed his Standards on the mission, they arranged for him to go to secondary school. This only became possible when a secondary school for people like my uncle had been built, which meant that he had to wait for some years in between. During this time and during his secondary-school years they gave him odd jobs at the mission so that he could pay his fees and help his family. Then the Government took over with a scholarship to South Africa. My uncle became prosperous and respected, well enough salaried to reduce a little the meagerness of his family's existence. This indicated that life could be lived with a modicum of dignity in any circumstances if you worked hard enough and obeyed the rules. Yes, it was a romantic story, the way my grandmother told it. The suffering was not minimised but the message was clear: endure and obey, for there is no other way. She was so proud of her eldest son, who had done exactly this.

When she died, which she did peacefully as she took a rest from her work on a day that I was not with her, my mother took over the plot and made it her vegetable garden. It was a big plot. My mother did not need the whole of it, so that half an acre or so lay fallow. This was the plot I chose for my field.

That year I grew older, stronger and sturdier than any eight year old can usefully grow. More often than not I woke up before dawn, the first lifting of the darkness occurring while I was sweeping the yard. Before it was fully light I would be on my way to the river and then returning along the footpath through the trees and past other homesteads, where the women were just waking, my water-drum balanced on my head-pad of leaves and green twigs, and the drum not quite full because when it was full it was too heavy for me to lift on to my head without help. While the cocks were crowing and the hens were shaking the sleep out of their feathers, I made the fire, swept the kitchen and boiled water for washing and for tea. By the time the sun rose I was in my field, in the first days hoeing and clearing; then digging holes thirty inches apart, with a single swing of the hoe, as we had been taught in our garden periods at school; then dropping the seeds into them, two or three at a time, and covering them with one or two sweeps of my foot; then waiting for the seeds to germinate and cultivating and waiting for the weeds to grow and cultivating again. At about ten o'clock, which I judged by the height and heat of the sun, I would go to the family fields to work with my mother, sometimes my father and, in the afternoons after school, my brother.

I think my mother admired my tenacity, and also felt sorry for me because of it. She began to prepare me for disappointment long before I would have been forced to face up to it. To prepare me she began to discourage me. "And do you think you are so different, so much better than the rest of us? Accept your lot and enjoy what you can of it. There is nothing else to be done." I wanted support, I wanted encouragement; warnings if necessary, but constructive ones. On the day that she discouraged me once too often I decided she had been listening too devoutly to my father. Ceasing to pay attention to her, I sought solidarity with Nhamo instead, but he could not help because he was going to school.

"Why do you bother?" he asked, his eyes twinkling maliciously. "Don't you know I am the one who has to go to school?"

"You said you would take care of me. Help me in my field."

"How can you ask when you see I am so busy?"

This was true. With the herd staying in the kraal until he came home from school in the afternoon to take them out to graze and to water before joining us in the fields; with milking before school and after when a cow was in milk; with his books; with my father in the busy times insisting that he help us all day, so that sometimes he missed as much as a week of school at a time; with all these tasks and odd jobs here and there he was very busy. I opened my mouth to say I would take over the milking and the grazing, but self-preservation was stronger than compassion. I closed my mouth without saying the words. Still, I had to do something about my brother's plight.

"Will he concentrate if he is so busy?" I asked my father.

"Why not, if he wants to?"

My mother was right. Some things could not be done.

Nhamo laughed when I related my story. "So what! I don't care what he says," he shrugged, shocking me with this disrespectful language that I had not heard before. "I'm at school, aren't I? It doesn't worry me what he says about me. So what's your problem? It doesn't even affect you."

"But you can't study."

"Who says? I should know. I go to school. You go nowhere."

"But I want to go to school."

"Wanting won't help."

"Why not?"

He hesitated, then shrugged. "It's the same everywhere. Because you are a girl." It was out. "That's what Baba said, remember?" I was no longer listening. My concern for my brother died an unobtrusive death.

By February my maize was dark green, taller than me and still growing. I strutted about as I inspected my crop as though I owned a hundred-hectare farm. Nor was I over-tired these days, because the fields no longer needed much attention. It was a fine feeling. A fine crop. All that remained was to wait for the harvest—cultivate once or twice, but really, wait for the harvest to harvest my fine little crop. Fine little crop. I had to be careful in thinking about the harvest in case I was discouraged. I had to push away the knowledge that I could not earn much from my crop.

A few weeks later, when the cobs were ripe for eating, they began to disappear.

"What did you expect?" Nhamo said. "Did you really think you could send yourself to school?"

The Sunday after my mealies began to be stolen I decided to go to church. Sunday was hardly ever a day of rest with us, and even more rarely a day of worship. Often my mother, not daring to sin as grotesquely as going to the field, would nevertheless work her garden on a Sunday. Or if there was little enough work to allow her to stay at home with a clear conscience, she was too tired to clean herself up and walk the two and a half miles to church. During the year in which I had gone to school I had found myself going to church more and more frequently, because children who had not attended Sunday School were caned on Monday, or put to work in the teacher's gardens. Without the prospect of caning to push me, I had hardly been to church since I left school. But this particular Sunday, the Sunday after my mealies began to disappear, I craved for the games we played at Sunday School. I desperately needed the laughter, the light-heartedness and the camaraderie. I went to the river, washed myself carefully and changed into my good dress, which had holes nowhere except under the armpits and there only because I had grown too big for it. I rubbed a lot of vaseline on to my legs, my arms, my face and into my hair. Then I was sorry for the waste, because it only meant I would get very dusty very quickly. By the time I arrived at Rutivi School, my old school, where the services were held, the games had already begun. The girls were already at *pada* in the road where a stick would scratch the boxes into the dust, and the boys were energetically kicking about a football made of plastic and newspaper on the meagerly grassed football pitch. The girls were pleased to see me, to have me with them again. It was just like the old days. I had a turn immediately.

"We think of you," said Nyari, who had been my best friend, as I threw my *pada*. "Especially when Nhamo gives us mealies," she said with a sigh. "They are fun to roast after class. If only you were here."

The blood prickled under my skin. I hopped precariously into square number eight.

"You are out," said Chitsva. "You did not kick the *pada*."

"Nhamo gave you maize?" I asked on one leg in square number eight.

"Lots of times," Nyari assented.

They told me I took off from the *pada* game like a dog after a buck. I remember at one moment playing *pada*, the next Nhamo and I rolling about in the dirt of the football pitch, a group of excited peers egging us on. They said I went straight for my brother and brought him down in a single charge. The element of surprise was on my side. I sat on top of him, banged his head into the ground, screamed and spat and cursed. Nhamo heaved. I fell off him. He pinned me to the ground, not striking, only holding me there, the malicious twinkle back in his eye. "What's the matter with you?" he drawled. "Have you gone mad?" The crowd laughed.

"Why talk?" a footballer shouted. "Just hit. That's what they hear."

I hissed and spat and screamed and cursed some more, and kicked and broke free, backing away into the crowd, which parted to let me through. I charged again, intending this time to kill, and instead found myself struggling in mid-air at the end of an adult arm.

Mr. Matimba was very cross with everybody. "I am ashamed of you," he shouted above my screams, "of all of you. Nhamo, if you are going to fight your sister, who will look after her? And you, Tambudzai, must also behave better. The rest of you, the rest of you stand there clapping as though you were at a football game. What's wrong with you?"

"She started it," Nhamo said lazily, watchfully.

"Yes," chorused everybody. "She charged. We saw it. She just charged for no reason at all."

I screamed out my reasons at the top of my lungs.

"What is she saying?" asked Nyari, who was looking serious. "Does she want mealies?"

"If I ever see anything like this again," continued Mr. Matimba, "I will whip you, every one of you. A stick will break about each person's legs. Now go, all of you. Sunday School is over." They melted away;

Mr. Matimba was known not to speak in vain. "And you, child," he said sternly, "what were you doing causing such a scene?"

A warm liquid trickled down my leg. I might have wet myself, but it was red and sticky on the outside of the leg, not colourless and watery on the inside. I could not feel the cut. Tears of impotent rage threatened to decompose me. I blinked them back and told Mr. Matimba that Nhamo had stolen my mealies.

"What mealies are these?" asked Mr. Matimba, patient if puzzled. I told him the whole story, how I was going to come back to school the following year, how I was going to earn the money by selling my crop. Mr. Matimba listened attentively. At some point during my speech, which was long because it was not very coherent and Mr. Matimba had to keep asking me questions, we began to walk around the football pitch. Mr. Matimba listened hard, inclining his whole person towards me; and I talked to him as though he were just another person and not an adult and a teacher. I felt myself recoalesce.

"You would do better to sell them green," Mr. Matimba suggested when I had finished. "It would fetch you more money."

"But everybody has green maize to eat," I objected. "Ho-o-o! You are saying I should go to the bus-stop?"

"That is possible," answered Mr. Matimba, "but I was thinking that you should sell to the Whites. When the cobs are fat and heavy, they buy them for as much as sixpence each."

I did not believe him. Nobody had that much money, not even Babamukuru.

"If you took your green mealies to town," continued Mr. Matimba, "you might make enough for a couple of term's fees. After that, we would have to see."

"But I cannot get to town," I pointed out. I

shrugged. "I shall take my mealies to *magrosa*."

"Perhaps you will not have to," Mr. Matimba said, smiling in a conspiratorial way. "On Tuesdays I take the school truck into town for school business. If you come to my house at eleven o'clock on Tuesday, I will take you there and we will see what can be done. But make sure to ask your father for permission."

My father said Mr. Matimba was behaving irresponsibly and interfering in matters that did not concern him. "Does he think he is your father?" he enquired. "He thinks that because he has chewed more letters than I have, he can take over my children. And you, you think he is better than me. He wants somebody to work in his garden, that's what he wants. I forbid you to go."

"But I must sell my maize," I insisted.

"Were you intending all this time to go and sell it in town, ha? Is that it?" my father asked sarcastically, hurtfully. "Ma'Shingayi," he ordered my mother, "tell this child of yours she cannot go to town with that man."

"And why should I tell her such things?" my mother asked. "The girl must have a chance to do something for herself, to fail for herself. Do you think I have not told her her efforts will come to nothing? You know your daughter. She is wilful and head-strong. She won't listen to me. I am tired of telling her things to which she pays no attention," she whined. "She must see these things for herself. If you forbid her to go, she will always think you prevented her from helping herself," she continued, recovering her sense of direction. "She will never forget it, never forgive you."

Words like "always" and "never" were meaningful to my father, who thought in absolutes and whose mind consequently made great leaps in antagonistic directions when it leapt at all. "Then let her go," he said.

That is how on the Tuesday I kept my appointment with Mr. Matimba. I climbed into the school truck beside him. My basket of maize was on my lap, neatly covered with brown paper. The other children, who had finished their lessons, watched me, envy written so clearly on their faces that I felt I had scored a significant victory even if I did not sell any maize.

"Bye-bye." I waved as we drove off. "Next year I will not be able to go to town because I will be with you behind the desk!" Mr. Matimba laughed at me more nicely than most adults can. I laughed too, because his laugh was infectious and because I was excited about the trip and pleased with him and pleased with myself.

I had never ridden in a motor vehicle before. I was inundated by new sensations: the soft plastic seat that made me sweat, sticking my dress to my buttocks; the bumps in the road that were worse than they were when Nyari's father's ox-cart rolled over them. I asked Mr. Matimba about this:

"Why are the roads for cars so bumpy? The roads for carts are not so bad."

"The roads are equally bumpy," he explained. "But a car moves more quickly than an ox-cart, so we feel the bumps more when we are in a car."

So the bumps were the same! Were they really?

I was concerned when we came to the river. "How will the car swim?"

"The wheels will move on the bottom of the river," Mr. Matimba explained affably. "It is just like the way you walk across when the river is not too deep." I was intrigued by all these new ideas.

The tarmac road with the white stripes down the middle was another wonder to be explained.

"Why do you stay on one side when there is the whole road?" I asked Mr. Matimba. A dairy truck roared towards us and past us in the opposite direction. "I know, I know," without waiting for his answer. "Cars that are going to town use this side. Cars that are coming from town use the other side. That's so they don't bump into each other!" Mr. Matimba complimented me. He said I was sharp. I felt that I was, but did not say so.

"Umtali is on the other side of these mountains," Mr. Matimba said as we approached the intersection of the Inyanga Highway with the Umtali Road. "The mountains around here are some of the highest mountains in Rhodesia. All the high mountains are found here in the eastern part of our country. These are things you will learn about when you come back to school."

The road began to climb upwards on the shoulder of the hill. The truck faltered, and changed its voice and moved more slowly.

"The white people must be very strong to build such a wide road so high up," I observed.

Mr. Matimba did not think so. "We did the building," he told me. "It was a terrible job. We did many terrible jobs. Now we are approaching the top of Christmas Pass," he said, changing the subject. "Look down when we get to the other side and you will see something worth seeing."

I looked and saw, neatly laid out below us, a very small town with rows of small houses which grew smaller and smaller as they stretched to the north-west.

"That is Umtali," Mr. Matimba said, "Rhodesia's third largest town. Only Salisbury, which is the capital city, and Bulawayo are larger than Umtali. These are more things that you will learn. One day I will bring you here at night. Then it is very beautiful, because the lights of the town are like hundreds of stars below you instead of above."

Stars below instead of above! I wanted to see them straight away. I prayed for a miracle, for the sun to set.

We rumbled down the pass. There were many more cars now in different shapes and sizes and colours, some in front of us, some behind and some beside us. Some were going into town like we were, others were going back up the pass. Then the road split up, branching into every direction, and the cars came and went in all directions too. I became quite frightened that one of them would move off in the wrong direction and come crashing into us, but Mr. Matimba was quite relaxed. How clever of him to make the car go where he wanted it to when there were so many confusing ways it might take.

"We will go to a place where there are many large shops and a place where the white people leave their cars," he told me as we moved slowly up the road. "I will stay with you for a little while to show you what to do, then I will leave you for some time to do my own business." I would have been frightened of being alone if I had thought about it.

We drove up the wide street curiously guarded by lights on a pole. When the top light was burning all the cars stopped. When the bottom light came on, we all moved again! I wondered how the lights knew to switch themselves on and off.

"They are controlled by machines," Mr. Matimba said, less precise than he had been in answering my questions until now. "You will learn about them in Standard One, when you read about Ben and Betty in Town and Country."

It became evident to me that I had no alternative but to sell my maize and go back to school.

Mr. Matimba stopped the truck at the corner of the street beyond the lights. We dismounted and walked to the side of a large shop mainly made out of glass.

"Keep well back against the wall so that you don't get into anyone's way," Mr. Matimba instructed me. "Now," he continued, "try to make your mealies look appetising. Take off the brown paper."

I did as I was told and was inspired to take out half a dozen cobs, which I arranged around my basket, propping them against the rim.

"Excuse me, Madam," Mr. Matimba said in English, in the softest, slipperiest voice I had ever heard him use, speaking to an old white woman who walked arm in arm with her husband. "Excuse me, Madam, we are selling green mealies, very soft, very fresh, very sweet."

Smiling brightly I held two cobs out while my stomach rolled itself into tight, nervous knots. I did not like the way they looked, with their skin hanging in papery folds from their bones, malignant-looking brown spots on their hands, a musty, dusty, sweetish odour clinging around the woman like a haze. Making sure not to wrinkle my nose, because these were the people who had the money that I needed to go back to school, I smiled more broadly, showing all my teeth, and said, "Nice maize, good maize." "Nice, good," I repeated, because I had no more English adjectives with which to describe my produce.

The old woman looked at me shaking her head. "Ts-ts-ts-ts!" she clicked.

"Come, Doris," the man said, anxiously grasping her elbow. "We don't need any mealies."

"Shocking, simply shocking," protested Doris. "I'd be shocking myself if I walked by and didn't say anything, George! Oi, young man, yes you!" she said, raising her voice to address Mr. Matimba. "Is she your little girl?" Without waiting for an answer she gave him a piece of her mind. "Child labour. Slavery! That's what it is. And I'm sure you don't need to make the poor mite work. You are natty enough, but look at the mite, all rags and tears."

Doris' husband turned down the corners of his mouth at Mr. Matimba, apologetically, embarrassed, annoyed.

"Come now, Doris, it's none of our business."

This appeared to be the opinion of the other Whites in the street. They crossed over before they reached us. Some did walk by, but I think they did not speak English; in fact no one spoke at all except for one beefy youth.

"What's the matter, lady? The munt being cheeky?"

A crowd of black people gathered. "What's the matter with the old ones?" asked a young man in sunglasses and a tweed cap irrepressibly set over one eye. He spiked the beefy youth with a vigilant eye. I was obliged to tell him that I did not know because I did not speak English. But, I assured him, I was going to learn English when I went back to school.

Doris would not keep quiet. "The child ought to be in school, learning her tables and keeping out of mischief," she railed. "Now, don't tell me there aren't any schools, young man, because I know the Governor is doing a lot for the natives in the way of education."

"They're kaffirs," interjected the youth. "They don't want to learn anything. Too much like hard work."

"Speak up for yourself, now," Doris commanded Mr. Matimba.

Mr. Matimba did speak for himself. He spoke most sorrowfully and most beseechingly. Doris darkened like a chameleon. Money changed hands, paper money from Doris' hands to Mr. Matimba's. The beefy youth was disgusted. "That's more than two crates of *shumba*. Wasted on a kaffir!" Doris allowed her husband to lead her away. I offered my basket, repeating my slogan, for her to choose the biggest cobs. She patted my head and called me a plucky piccannin.

Some of the crowd cheered, saying she was more human than most of her kind. Others muttered that white people could afford to be, in fact ought to be, generous.

"What is good is not given," warned the man in the cap. "What will she do when the money runs out? Look for another old White?" He spat on the pavement. I did not know why he was so angry, but Mr. Matimba was smiling conspiratorially, so I knew that everything was all right.

"There is no reason to stay," he said. "Pack the maize and we will go." I did as I was told, although I was worried that we had not sold any maize. In the truck Mr. Matimba explained what had happened, how Doris had accused him of making me work instead of sending me to school and how he had told her that I was an orphan, taken in by my father's brother but, being the thirteenth child under their roof, had not been sent to school for lack of fees. He had said that I was very clever, very hardworking and was selling mealies to raise my school fees with his assistance. He told me that Doris had commended him for trying to help me, had donated ten pounds towards my school fees. He showed me the money, the crisp clean note. Ten pounds. We never even talked about that much money at home. Now here I was holding it in my hands! The money, the money, no thought for the method.

"It is a lot of money," Mr. Matimba agreed. "What will you do with it?"

"I will take it home and keep it, and then I will use it to pay my school fees, next year and the year after and the year after."

Mr. Matimba was dubious. "Money is a difficult thing to keep, especially when it is scarce. We must arrange something. I think you will give the money to the headmaster. He will give you a receipt, which I will keep for you, and then from the first term of next year onwards he will deduct your school fees from the money until it is finished."

That is what happened. My parents did not believe

me when I told them how much money I had in the headmaster's keeping. Nor did my brother. He thought I was making it up. "Lies won't get you to school," he mocked.

My father was more active in his disapproval, although, of course, I did not know why he disapproved. He went to see the headmaster, who confirmed my story.

"Then you have taken my money," my father told the headmaster. "That money belongs to me. Tambudzai is my daughter, is she not? So isn't it my money?" This was a difficult problem for the headmaster, who was an honest man. Eventually he showed my father the receipt.

"I have not stolen your money," he said. "See, your daughter's name is on the receipt. It is her money, not mine. The school is only keeping it for her."

The argument grew so heated that Mr. Matimba was called in, to give evidence and also to be prosecuted.

"He is the real thief," said my father. "He is the one who influenced my daughter to pay the money to you."

"You forget," Mr. Matimba reminded him, "that I was the one who was given the money by the white woman and that it was given to me so that your daughter's fees could be paid. If you do not see this, it is a matter for the Sabhuku to settle."

My father was intimidated but not appeased. "This is only ten pounds that we are quarelling over," Mr. Matimba continued. "What good can it do you besides wetting your throat with a few pots of *masese*? But one day, when Tambudzai has done well in her studies, she will earn more than ten pounds a month."

"Have you ever heard of a woman who remains in her father's house?" growled my father. "She will meet a young man and I will have lost everything."

But the receipt remained in the headmaster's office. That year there were plenty of green mealies to boil and roast and eat as we pleased.

I went back to school the following year, although I had to go back into Sub A. I came first that year and people said it was because I had been repeating, which might have been true. I was top of my class again the next year in Sub B. That time people said it was because I was older. My brother took particular pains to point this out to me, because in that year, when he was in Standard Three, he only managed to come fourth. For all his nonchalance, I knew he was upset, so I reminded him that fourth was a very good position to take.

Babamukuru and his family returned from England when I was in Sub B, the year that my brother came fourth in Standard Three. My father had always been ingratiating in Babamukuru's presence. Even so, the performance he staged on the occasion of my uncle's return was magnificent by anybody's standards. Money was found, I expect through begging since this was something that my father had developed an aptitude for, having had to do it often. He was very good at it by that time. "*Vakomana, vakomana,*" he must have said, holding his head in his hands and shaking it, possibly even striking his forehead with the flat of his palm. "Did you ever see the like of the things that are happening here at your home? I would never have thought it possible myself. That Mukoma could actually pack his things and leave the mission to go to overseas, stay there for five years and come back with a degree, with a degree, to find nothing, not even a goat, on his return! Tsha—a! I didn't think it could happen! It shames me truly, it shames me.

"Look, see how your home is. We impress people around here. Who built the first baked-brick house in this area? Who has such a bright corrugated-iron roof that it can be seen twinkling as far as the main road? *Mukoma!* Let me tell you, *Mukoma* did this for us. We impress people because of *Mukoma*. And we can't even kill a goat for him. See, *hama dzangu*, how poverty degrades us. It stops us welcoming our own flesh and blood. Ts-hm-m!" he must have sighed nasally, "we cannot manage celebrations and *Mukoma* will arrive at an empty airport—I don't even have bus fare to Salisbury." There would have been a pause then. "*Hama dzangu*, can you not help me? I have forgotten about the goat, but five bob, just *five* bob for the bus? *Mukoma* will give you your money when he comes." My father is the sort of person to whom people decide not to lend money only after they have already done so. I can imagine the ferreting about in old mattresses, the furtive unblocking by moonlight of small holes in the mud-brick walls, the unearthing at dusk of shallowly buried coffee tins that this speech caused. However it came about, ultimately the money was acquired. Babamukuru was to be welcomed at the airport.

My brother was to accompany my father on the trip and exaggerated his anticipation of the event for my benefit by asking rhetorically in my presence very silly questions. Was the roar of an aeroplane so loud it would deafen? Was it in fact a leonine roar or did it sound more like a giant bee-fly? How did an aeroplane flap its wings when it was close to the ground? Naturally, I would not answer.

They were to take the night train from Umtali to Salisbury, travelling, uncomfortably, in fifth class. Although the most practical, for there was nowhere to stay in Salisbury, this itinerary added an entire extra day to the trip. The problem was to get to the railway station in time for the train's departure, which happened between eight o'clock and nine o'clock in the evening. This should have been straightforward enough, but the buses to town passed through the village irregularly and according to an unreliable timetable. As a result trips had to be planned by the day rather than by the hour. For these reasons my father and Nhamo decided to travel to Umtali by the early morning bus, which was scheduled to, but did not often, stop at our bus terminus at half past six every morning. When it did arrive at all, it would arrive randomly an hour later or earlier than scheduled, and even then it was likely to be filled to capacity: you could tell because the inside looked black even at a distance of, say, twenty yards. Therefore, the logistics of the journey had to be carefully planned. There was a long and loose-ended debate about whether to spend the night at home, which necessitated an early start in the morning, or to sleep at my aunt's homestead since she lived nearer to the terminus than we did. Baba and Nhamo were, of course, in favour of the latter arrangement, but my mother irrationally pointed out that though my aunt would feed them well while they were at her homestead, she could not be expected to provide for the journey as generously as my mother would. They should not blame her, my mother said, if they slept at my aunt's homestead only to die of hunger on the train. The point was taken. Father and Nhamo decided to bivouac at my aunt's the night before their departure, and have me take them the provisions that my mother would have prepared in the morning. They agreed that I would take the provisions to the bus-stop rather than to my aunt's home in case I was slow on the way and reached my aunt's home after they had departed.

My mother had miscalculated. She had hoped that by seeming to dissuade them from spending an extra night away from home, she would ensure that they did so and thus be free of them for a while longer. This she had achieved, but she also landed herself with the impracticable and strenuous task of finding the provisions. They wanted cornbread, because white bread from the shops did not remain long in the stomach while yesterday's *sadza* stayed there too long, and sweet potatoes and chicken. My mother was offended. "But these men don't think," she complained. "They know very well that no corn was planted, so where does the cornmeal come from? And sweet potatoes, which I finished putting down only yesterday because I planted single-handed! As for their chicken, if they really want it, what will they cook for Babamukuru when he comes?"

The crisis was resolved in the usual manner. I fetched cornmeal from my aunt's, having first tried the neighbours and found none, though when I explained to them why the cornmeal was needed they gave me peanuts instead. The sweet potatoes did not ripen in time, but the day before the trip news reached us by telephone message via the Council Houses that Babamukuru had sent money for a goat. Thus Baba and Nhamo were, in effect, able to have their chicken and eat it.

It was a very complicated journey that my father and Nhamo were undertaking. Complicated, therefore exciting. I wanted to be part of it. I wanted to juggle with transport timetables as well. I wanted to eat fresh cornbread, ashy roast peanuts and salty boiled chicken on the train at midnight too. Above all, I wanted to be as deafened as anyone by the roar and the buzz (was it a roar or a buzz?) of the aeroplanes. My yearning to go must have shown, probably on my face as I listened to them make their plans and undo them and make them again, because my father called me aside to implore me to curb my unnatural inclinations: it was natural for me to stay at home and prepare for the homecoming.

My father's idea of what was natural had begun to irritate me a long time ago, at the time that I had had to leave school. I used to try to avoid having it explained to me by maintaining a sullen silence, which according to my father was also unnatural: "Now that the mouth is shut, the heart is proud." He would threaten to beat me but, preferring to be lazy, never bothered to catch me when I ran.

I was fortunate that my father was so obviously impossible, otherwise I would have been confused. Under the circumstances the situation was clear: there was no way of pleasing my father, nor was there any reason to. Relieved, I set about pleasing myself, which antagonised him even further. He did not like to see me over-absorbed in intellectual pursuits. He became very agitated after he had found me several times reading the sheet of newspaper in which the bread from *magrosa* had been wrapped as I waited for the *sadza* to thicken. He thought I was emulating my brother, that the things I read would fill my mind with impractical ideas, making me quite useless for the real tasks of feminine living. It was a difficult time for him because Mr. Matimba had shown him that in terms of cash my education was an investment, but then in terms of cattle so was my conformity. In frustration he resorted to absolutes. Ignoring Babamukuru's imminent homecoming, he threatened to take me out of school again. It was a thoughtless threat: how could he have done that? Not having the power, he left me alone. We co-existed in peaceful detachment.

Chapter 3

Babamukuru came home in a cavalcade of motor vehicles, sighted four miles away on the main road by three jubilant pairs of eyes. Netsai and I and little Shupikai, whose mother was one of the relatives gathered to celebrate the occasion of Babamukuru's return, watched as the cavalcade progressed, distressingly slowly, now disappearing behind clumps of trees, now reappearing hours later, or so it seemed, no more than a few hundred yards nearer. The vigil lasted twenty minutes. We watched from a rock on the hill behind the homestead until the cars disappeared for the last time into the home-stretch. Then we went wild. We slid off our rock, skinning elbows and knees on the way, scrambled oblivious through bushes that scratched our legs, dashed out on to the road and ran on. "Ba-ba-mu-ku-ru! Ba-ba-mu-ku-ru!" we chanted, running and jumping and waving our skinny arms about all at the same time, skirts swirling, bottoms jutting as we capered. Shupikai, several yards behind, started to cry, still tottering along and chanting through her sobs, because we had left her behind and because she was excited. Her crisis was so inconvenient. I considered ignoring her, which could not be done. Dashing back, I snatched her up to continue the mad welcome with her perched on my hip.

My aunt Gladys, the one who is my father's womb-sister, older than him but younger than Babamukuru, came first, her husband behind the wheel of a gallant if rickety old Austin. They hooted long and loud. We waved and shouted and danced. Then came Babamukuru, his car large and impressive, all sparkling metal and polished dark green. It was too much for me. I could have clambered on to the bonnet but, with Shupi in my arms, had to be content with a song: "*Mauya, mauya. Mauya, mauya. Mauya, Babamukuru!*" Netsai picked up the melody. Our vocal cords vibrating through wide arcs, we made an unbelievable racket. Singing and dancing we ushered Babamukuru on to the homestead, hardly noticing Babamunini Thomas, who brought up the rear, not noticing Mainini Patience, who was with him, at all.

Slowly the cavalcade progressed towards the yard, which by now was full of rejoicing relatives. My father jumped out of Babamukuru's car and, brandishing a staff like a victory spear, bounded over the bumpy road, leaping into the air and landing on one knee, to get up and leap again and pose like a warrior inflicting a death wound. "*Hezvo!*" he cried. "Do you see him? Our returning prince. Do you see him? Observe him well. He has returned. Our father and benefactor has returned appeased, having devoured English letters with a ferocious appetite! Did you think degrees were indigestible? If so, look at my brother. He has digested them! If you want to see an educated man, look at my brother, big brother to us all!" The spear aimed high and low, thrust to the right, to the left. All was conquered.

The cars rolled to a stop beneath the mango trees. Tete Gladys disembarked with difficulty, with false starts and strenuous breathing; because she was so large, it was not altogether clear how she had managed to insert herself into her car in the first place. But her mass was not frivolous. It had a ponderous presence which rendered any situation, even her attempts to remove herself from her car, weighty and serious. We did not giggle, did not think of it. On her feet at last, Tete straightened herself, planted herself firmly, feet astride, in the dust. Clenched fists settling on hips, elbows jutting aggressively, she defied any contradiction of my father's eulogy. "Do you hear?" she demanded, "what Jeremiah is saying? If you have not heard, listen well. It is the truth he is speaking! Truly our prince has returned today! Full of knowledge. Knowledge that will benefit us all! Purururu!" she ululated, shuffling with small gracious jumps to embrace my mother. "Purururu!" they ululated. "He has returned. Our prince has returned!"

Babamukuru stepped out of his car, paused behind its open door, removed his hat to smile graciously, joyfully, at us all. Indeed, my Babamukuru had returned. I saw him only for a moment. The next minute he was drowned in a sea of bodies belonging to uncles, aunts and nephews; grandmothers, grandfathers and nieces; brothers and sisters of the womb and not of the womb. The clan had gathered to welcome its returning hero. His hand was shaken, his head was rubbed, his legs were embraced. I was there too, wanting to touch Babamukuru, to talk, to tell him I was glad that he had returned. Babamukuru made his fair-sized form as expansive as possible, holding his arms out and bending low so that we all could be embraced, could embrace him. He was happy. He was smiling. "Yes, yes," he kept saying. "It is good, it is good." We moved, dancing and ululating and kicking up a fine dust-storm from our stamping feet, to the house.

Babamukuru stepped inside, followed by a retinue of grandfathers, uncles and brothers. Various paternal aunts, who could join them by virtue of their patriarchal status and were not too shy to do so, mingled with the men. Behind them danced female relatives of the lower strata. Maiguru entered last and alone, except for her two children, smiling quietly and inconspicuously. Dressed in flat brown shoes and a pleated polyester dress very much like the one

Babamukuru bought for my mother the Christmas before he left, she did not look as though she had been to England. My cousin Nyasha, pretty bright Nyasha, on the other hand, obviously had. There was no other explanation for the tiny little dress she wore, hardly enough of it to cover her thighs. She was self-conscious though, constantly clasping her hands behind her buttocks to prevent her dress from riding up, and observing everybody through veiled vigilant eyes to see what we were thinking. Catching me examining her, she smiled slightly and shrugged. "I shouldn't have worn it," her eyes seemed to say. Unfortunately, she had worn it. I could not condone her lack of decorum. I would not give my approval. I turned away.

I remember disapproving of my cousin Chido as well as Nyasha that day, although I do not know why I disapproved of Chido, who was innocuously if smartly dressed in shorts and shoes and socks. I think it was not anything to do with him as a person, but with the fact that he was Nyasha's brother. As for my own brother, I was thoroughly disgusted with him. Nhamo took after my father in the way that he could effuse over anything that was necessary, over many things at the same time if that was necessary too. Therefore I was not surprised when he suddenly stopped leaping in the central regions of Baba-mukuru's domain in order to stake his claim on our clean, kempt cousins. He had an awful lot to say to them, but I was sure that the English he was using was broken. This was probably why he did not succeed very well in his attempts to draw them into conversation. The girl, while not actually ignoring him, did not respond to him, casting at intervals probing glances over the gathering and including my brother in her surveillance. Chido tried to smile, but the smile was too narrow to dispel the apprehension in his eyes. He was incapable of any communication more meaningful than an occasional nod of his head. Every time that Chido smiled at him, Nhamo smirked at me, managing, as he intended, to irritate me intensely.

Yes, I was very irritable on that occasion, the occasion of my uncle's return, which should have been for me, as it was for everyone else, a sublime occasion. It was spoiled for me because I could not help thinking that had I been allowed, had I been able to welcome Babamukuru at the airport, I would have been there too, with Nhamo and my cousins, rejoicing, re-establishing the relationship that had been cut off when my cousins went away. Not going to the airport, not being able to resume my relationships with my cousins, these events coalesced formlessly in my mind to an incipient understanding of the burdens my mother had talked of. Whereas before I had believed with childish confidence that burdens were only burdens in so far as you chose to bear them, now I began to see that the disappointing events surrounding Babamukuru's return were serious consequences of the same general laws that had almost brought my education to an abrupt, predictable end. It was frightening. I did not want my life to be predicted by such improper relations. I decided I would just have to make up my mind not to let it happen. Curling my lip at Nhamo and my cousins, I departed, flouncing surlily, pointedly, out of the house to the kitchen; there, thrusting a log into the hearth so viciously that the three-legged pot that on normal days contained *sadza*, but today was full of meat, splashed half its juices into the embers.

A piece of meat fell out too. I picked it out of the ashes and ate it, and then felt sick because I was still thinking about Nhamo and the cousins, and being cross with Nhamo for excluding me from their circle in spite of the fact that I did not approve of any of them. I considered the situation. Had I approved of my cousins before they went to England? Most definitely I had; I had loved them. When they visited the homestead we had played long, exciting games. Why did I no longer like them? I could not be sure. Did I like anybody? What about Babamukuru? Had the change to do with me or had it to do with them? These were complex, dangerous thoughts that I was stirring up, not the kind that you can ponder safely but the kind that become autonomous and malignant if you let them. If I continued in this way, I would soon be itching to beat Nhamo up because his smirking had brought the matter to a head. But I could not have the satisfaction of indulging my frustration in this way. Nhamo and I had stopped beating each other up a long time ago, at the time that I went back to school, more because we had developed so differently that we no longer had enough common ground in which to fight than out of mutual respect or affection. Besides, I was reluctantly aware that beating up Nhamo would not help: my discontent had to do with more than my brother's annoying manners. Sensing how unwise it was to think too deeply about these things in case I manoeuvred myself into a blind alley at the end of which I would have to confront unconfrontable issues, I busied myself with housework.

The housework was agreeable when it did not have to be done. Today, because of Babamukuru's home-coming, there were so many young aunts and nieces and cousins present that I could cook or not cook as I chose. Consequently I took great pains with the stew, letting the meat fry gently in its own fat until it was deliciously brown, adding enough chopped tomato and onion to make a rich gravy. It smelt good. I was pleased with my efforts, but they had lasted less than half an hour. To kill more time I made sausages out of the tripe and the small intestine of Babamukuru's goat. When I had finished I cooked the vegetables.

The women were pleased with me when they came to prepare supper. "You are quite a little worker," they said. "All that is left is to prepare the *sadza*." Their praise made me feel better. It made me feel good. My confidence returned: Nyasha would not, I was sure, be able to prepare such a fine stew, certainly not at an open hearth. This idea made me feel so superior, so wholesome and earthy, like home-baked cornbread instead of the insubstantial loaves you buy in the shops, that I helped to cook the *sadza* as well. We did this outside in large drums, using sticks as thick as my arm for stirring. Chatting to aunts and cousins as we waited for the *sadza* to thicken, pouring in more mealie-meal when it had, I stopped feeling excluded and, since I no longer had need of them, my feelings of superiority disappeared as well. Exclusion held dreadful horrors for me at that time because it suggested superfluity. Exclusion whispered that my existence was not necessary, making me no more than an unfortunate by-product of some inexorable natural process. Or else it mocked that the process had gone wrong and produced me instead of another Nhamo, another Chido, another Babamukuru-to-be. I often felt superfluous in those days, but there in the camaraderie of the cooking, it was comfortable to occupy the corner that that same natural process had carved out for me. It was comfortable to recognise myself as solid, utilitarian me.

We cooked two five-gallon drums of good, smooth *sadza* using finely pounded, well winnowed and sieved *mutwiwa*, but there was no rice, and this was serious. On occasions such as this there should have been rice. But since Babamukuru had not been there to provide it, there was none. Maiguru had had the foresight to bring a few packets with her, but a few packets were not enough to feed the multitudes, so my mother was cooking Maiguru's rice on Maiguru's Dover Stove behind the house to make sure that it was reserved for the right people. When it was done she came down to help us dish out—mounds of steaming *sadza* into one set of dishes, great hunks of meat wallowing in gravy in another, vegetables in a third. These we carried to the house, where my mother had already set out the rice.

I had a special task. I had to carry the water-dish in which people would wash their hands. I did not like doing this because you had to be very sure of the relative status of everybody present or else it was easy to make mistakes, especially when there were so many people. Today it was doubly tricky because although Babamukuru was the guest of honour, there were male relatives present of higher status than he. Making a considered and perhaps biased decision, I knelt first in front of Babamukuru, which was a mistake because he wanted me to let his uncle Isaiah, our eldest surviving grandfather, wash first. I knelt and rose and knelt and rose in front of my male relatives in descending order of seniority, and lastly in front of my grandmothers and aunts, offering them the water-dish and towel. The situation deteriorated after my grandfathers and Babamukuru had washed because after that the hierarchy was not clear. This uncle was that uncle's *tezvara* by virtue of his marriage to that one's sister, but also his brother because their mothers were sisters, albeit not of the womb. When this happened each of the parties insisted that the other was the superior and therefore ought to wash first. It was very complicated and confusing. I made more mistakes, which made people laugh and ask why I did not know the ways in which we were all related. At one point, having knelt for several minutes in front of one disclaiming uncle, I grew tired and let some water slop out of the dish on to his feet (apologising profusely) to encourage him to wash without further discussion. Nyasha indicated her solidarity with the ghost of a smile and a twitch of her eye, which I thought was insulting and so ignored her. Eventually the last younger aunt washed her hands and I rose to depart, whereupon my father asked me why I had neglected to offer Chido the water, so I went down on my knees in front of him. Naturally Nhamo took advantage of the situation to wash his hands too. Then I had to let Nyasha wash as well. Feeling fractious and put upon because I thought all three of them should have been eating with us in the kitchen, I offered Nyasha the water. Babamukuru said grace. The meal began with much clapping of hands, praising of the gods for their providence and of us for our hard work.

In the kitchen we dished out what was left in the pots for ourselves and the children. My aunt Mavis, Shupikai's mother, in her joy over Babamukuru's return, had been unrestrained in dishing out the meat for the house so that there was not enough left in the pot to make a meal for those of us who were not dining there. As a result the youngest of us had only gravy and vegetables to go with our *sadza*. But the gravy was good and there was plenty of it. We, who rarely tasted meat, found no reason to complain.

By the time the eating was over and we went to the house to collect the plates, the elders were in an absolute delirium of happiness. It was truly remarkable to see them so transported without so much as a pot of *masese* between them to encourage them to forget themselves. My father took great pleasure in his *masese*, as did the majority of my male relatives, and my grandmothers and older aunts as well, but Babamukuru was strictly abstinent, so uncompromisingly temperate that he could detect alcohol on your breath at five yards in a strong wind. Beer was therefore taboo at this gathering, and the company was having to make do with *mahewu*, left to stand as long as possible without actually letting the mash ferment. Naturally there were mutterings of discontent, particularly from young uncles who were not closely related to Babamukuru and so did not adequately appreciate his authority. In spite of the absence of anything more lively than *mahewu* no gaiety had been lost from the gathering. Tete Gladys, arms swinging, dress swishing, was on her feet, swirling dizzily left and right to the tempo of "Amazing Grace," executing an exuberant low bow at the end of each bar: "Da-a-i (bow) ndi-i-ne (bow) ma-pa-aa-piro (bow), Nda-a-i (bow) bhu-u-ru (bow) -ru-ka (bow)"! Meanwhile aunts and uncles and cousins uproariously improvised what they would do on account of Babamukuru's return had they only the wherewithal.

In the yard, unmarried uncles, cousins and aunts began on the drums and *hosho* in a circle, dancing and singing while individuals freestyled in the centre. It was almost like a wedding with music and movement pulsing through the night to make your skin crawl and tingle, your armpits prickle, your body impatient to be up and concerned with the beat. My early childhood had been a prime time for dancing. Then I had used to amuse everybody by dropping my scholarly seriousness to twist and turn, and clap almost in time to the music. As I had grown older and the music had begun to speak to me more clearly, my movements had grown stronger, more rhythmical and luxuriant; but people had not found it amusing anymore, so that in the end I realised that there were bad implications in the way I enjoyed the rhythm. My dancing compressed itself into rigid, tentative gestures. I did not stop completely, but gatherings were much less fun after that and made me feel terribly self-conscious.

"We are dancing," I invited Nyasha, who took a long time to understand.

"They don't understand Shona very well anymore," her mother explained. "They have been speaking nothing but English for so long that most of their Shona has gone."

What Maiguru said was bewildering, bewildering and offending. I had not expected my cousins to have changed, certainly not so radically, simply because they had been away for a while. Besides, Shona was our language. What did people mean when they forgot it? Standing there, trying to digest these thoughts, I remembered speaking to my cousins freely and fluently before they went away, eating wild fruits with them, making clay pots and swimming in Nyamarira. Now they had turned into strangers. I stopped being offended and was sad instead.

"Ask them, Maiguru," I urged. "Even if they don't understand, they wouldn't refuse, would they? Things like that," I continued vaguely but earnestly, "would bring their speech back more quickly." The singers were becoming inspired, the drums more and more animated. I could see Nyasha listening, tapping her fingers on her crossed knees in time to the drums. She talked to her mother eagerly in an English whose accent was so strange I could not understand a word of it, co-opting Chido into the discussion and talking in very definite tones. I was sure that my cousins wanted to join the merry-making but Maiguru was not encouraging. I could tell from her voice, which was flat and passive, and from the odd word that I picked up like "dirty" and "sleep." It was odd that Maiguru preferred her children not to dance. If they could not enjoy themselves with us, there was no reason for them to have come home. I think Nyasha was saying similar things to Maiguru because in the end her irritation became so open that my aunts stopped their lively conversations to find out what was going on.

"Now, what is the problem, Maiguru?" asked Tete Gladys. "You are not forbidding your children to join the others, are you?"

"Why should I do that, Tete?" Maiguru replied evenly. "I am only saying they should rest. You know, a flight is very tiring. But if you say they should dance, they shall. Tete has told you to go to the dance," she informed her children in her uninflected voice.

Chido declined politely ("It's all right, Mum, I'm a bit tired anyway.") Nyasha clicked her tongue scornfully and switched herself off. It was very abrupt the way she did it. One minute she was taking in everything that was happening, the next she would not have heard you even if you had spoken to her. I went outside, trying very hard not to let the episode spoil the rest of the evening. It was difficult though. I had been looking forward to having my cousins back so that things would be fun and friendly and warm as they had been in the old days, but it was not happening that way. So deep was my disappointment that I was not comforted when Nhamo, seduced by our unrestrained voices and the throb of the drum, came out to join us. I thought he was fickle, that he wanted to eat his chicken and have eggs as well.

Babamukuru stayed with us for only one night at that time, the time of his return, because he was to assume his old duties as headmaster and new duties as Academic Director of the Church's Manicaland Region immediately. There was not much time to discuss all the things that had needed to be discussed but had had to wait while he was away, so Babamukuru and his brothers and sister talked together far into the night and the early hours of morning. Babamukuru was concerned about the way in which the family was developing, pointing out that as an individual he had done what he could for the family's status by obtaining a Master's Degree; that he hoped his children would do as much again, if not more; that he was pleased that he was in a position to provide his children with a fine start in that direction. His branch of the family was able to hold its head high in whatever company it found itself, but, he accurately indicated, the same could not be said for all the other branches. He had come to the conclusion on the basis of the news he had received from Jeremiah and others while he was in England, that the future did not look comfortable for the family as a whole. Now that he had returned, he said, it was time for the members to put their heads together to think of means of ensuring the prosperity of each branch of the family.

When Babamukuru speechified, which as head of the family he had to do often, he had a way of doing it that was calm and mild and so sensible that while you listened you couldn't help being overwhelmed by the good sense of his words and resolving to do exactly as he suggested, whatever that happened to be. Babamukuru was inspiring. He inspired confidence and obedience. He carried with him an aura from which emanated wisdom and foresight. There was sighing in acknowledgment of the family's difficulties, murmurs of agreement with Babamukuru's analysis.

"Er—what I see," said Babamukuru, clearing his throat and removing pieces of meat that had stuck between his teeth with the slim blade of his multiple-blade penknife, "is that what needs to be done is this." He leant back in his chair at the head of the dining-table. "We need to ensure that at least one member from each family is educated, at least to Form Four standard, because after that he will be in a position to take a course. Although this is not to say, of course, that, if it is possible, it would not be a good thing for this member to continue up to Form Six and even to university level after that."

"It would be good," agreed Tete Gladys. "A graduate in each family! We would be proud."

"Not just one!" expanded my father. "Why shouldn't they all graduate? Why not?"

"Jeremiah," reprimanded Babamukuru, "that is not a useful contribution. We must look for useful solutions. We cannot afford to dream."

"Quite right, Mukoma, quite right," agreed my father affably. "Who can afford to dream these days? Aiwa! You can't dream! You can't dream!"

"Looking at the family as it stands today," continued Babamukuru, "I see that the main problem is with Jeremiah. Tete here is all right—her husband is able to take care of her and her children. Thomas is also in no trouble—he may not have a degree, but his teacher training is a solid qualification. The family does not go hungry. They live in a comfortable home. They wear decent clothes. When the children are of school-going age they will be able to go to school. These children who can go to school today are the ones whose families will prosper tomorrow. So Tete's branch and Thomas' branch are provided for. The real worry is your branch, Jeremiah." Tete pursed her lips and nodded in regretful agreement. Babamunini Thomas, modestly lowering his head, said nothing out of deference to his unfortunate elder brother.

"I remember," Babamukuru went on, "that the year after my family and I arrived in England, you wrote to us, Jeremiah—no, it must have been the second year after we arrived. Yes, the second after we arrived, because we went there in 1960 and you wrote this particular letter, the one I am talking about, in 1962. It was dated 16 November 1962. I remember it very well, because when I was tired and discouraged and feeling so low I used to read that letter. I read that letter very many times. That letter made me see that even more than myself my whole family needed my qualification. That is how I was able to carry on even when things were very bad. That letter made me say to myself, 'Come what may, I will succeed.' Yes, Jeremiah, I remember we received news from you saying that there was no money for school fees. We sent you what we could. We knew it was not much, but we were very pleased to hear that you were able to send both children back to school as a result of receiving that money we had sent."

"Things were tough, Mukoma, things were tough," acknowledged my father, grimacing strenuously to show just how tough. "Would we have survived if it hadn't been for you? Aiwa, we would not. Never!"

"It is true, Mukoma," endorsed Tete. "Our Jeremiah could have died. He and his whole family. Matters were that bad. Truly, *muera bonga*, you did a great deed."

"A great deed, a very great deed," murmured Babamunini Thomas.

"My wife and I were very surprised," said Babamukuru, "that the crops had failed, because other people were telling us that there had been good harvests. Anyway, that is another matter. When we heard that both Nhamo and heyo—er, this girl—er, Tambudzai—had returned to school, we were very pleased that you had used the money sensibly, Jeremiah." Babamukuru put his penknife away and sat tall in his chair. His presence became grave and weighty. As though giving way beneath its weight, my father, Babamunini Thomas and Tete inclined themselves attentively towards their brother.

"What I have been thinking," Babamukuru began again after a lengthy pause, which made it evident that indeed he had been thinking deeply and effectively about the matter in hand. "What I have been thinking is this: providing money for school fees is good but it is not all that must be done to ensure a child's success in school. A child must also be provided with the correct atmosphere which will encourage his mind to develop even when he is not in the classroom."

"True, Mukoma, you speak the truth," sighed my father, having gauged and approved the direction of Babamukuru's speech. "Look at our Nhamo. I have never seen a child who loves his books the way he does, that Nhamo of ours. But how can he study when there is no electricity? How can he read when there are no books? Even going to school, how can he do that everyday when there is so much work to be done on the homestead? I feel sorry for the boy but he— does he say anything? No. He just keeps quiet and works hard here and at school. I was blessed when I was given that son. Truly, I was blessed." He shook his head in sorrow and sympathy for his son's suffering.

"You are right, Jeremiah. I have observed that Nhamo is a promising scholar," agreed Babamukuru. "What we must do is to let Nhamo stay with us at the mission, let him go to school there. He must come at once, because the sooner he is given the best, the sooner will the best be returned. He is finishing Standard Three so there will be no problem with the transfer. I will come to fetch him a few days before the new school year begins. Meanwhile I will have him registered for Standard Four at the mission."

My aunt was on her feet before Babamukuru had finished speaking. "Purururu!" she shrilled as his last word dropped benevolently into the room. "Thank you, *muera bonga. Muera bonga*, we thank you. Would we, could we survive without you! Truly, we could not! Jeremiah," she commanded, turning to my father, "tell me plainly, you. Would you survive without your brother? For one day, just one day, could you do it? Kneel down! Kneel down properly. Thank God for giving you a saint for a brother. Thank your ancestors, Jeremiah, thank them well for giving you a brother who looks after you." She sank to the floor in front of Babamukuru, clapping her hands. Bo-bo-bo-bo-bo. "A great deed has been done, *muera bonga*." Bo-bo-bo. "Truly, you have done a great deed." My father and Uncle Thomas magnified Tete's praise with their own eulogies, my father going down on one knee to do homage. Babamukuru belched magnanimously.

"Do not thank me, do not thank me!" he disclaimed modestly. "There is nothing surprising here. When there is a duty to do, it has to be done, that is all."

My father informed Nhamo of these developments the next day, after Babamukuru had gone. They remained cloistered together in my parents' room in the house for an hour, and this was only possible because most of the guests, living nearby and so being able to pop in at any time, had departed. Tete Gladys and Babamunini Thomas stayed with us for a week because they lived far away, in Mtoko and Selukwe, and so did not visit often.

Nhamo was exultant, so puffed up with his own importance that it was uncomfortable and necessary for him to let off steam without delay. Unable to wait until I came home to begin bragging, he came to the vegetable garden, where he sat on a log and congratulated himself while I diverted one of Nyamarira's smaller tributaries into the beds of onions and rape. It was a bounteous story, the way he told it, holding much more promise than Babamukuru had in fact indicated.

"You know," drawled my brother, twiddling a stalk of grass in the gap between his front teeth,

"Babamukuru wants a clever person, somebody who deserves the chance. That's why he wants me. He knows I've been doing very well at school. Who else is there for him to take?"

Nhamo, Nhamo, sneaky Nhamo! He did not speak more plainly than this because to have done so would have been blatantly nasty. Nhamo was seldom obviously offensive in case you confronted him with it and took him to task. His sins were mainly sins of omission. But on the occasions that he did do something actively nasty, he was satanically good at insinuating himself so sneakily into your most sensitive spots that if you did not know him well you could end up thinking you were being unfair to him when he annoyed you.

"Babamukuru says I am so bright I must be taken away to a good school and be given a good chance in life. So I shall go and live with Babamukuru at the mission. I shall no longer be Jeremiah's son," he boasted, speaking my father's name in such derogatory tones that for once I was up in arms on my father's behalf. "I shall wear shoes and socks, and shorts with no holes in them, all brand new, bought for me by Babamukuru. He has the money. I will even have underwear—a vest and pants. I shall have a jersey in winter, and probably a blazer too. I shall stop using my hands to eat. I will use a knife and fork."

I think a little jealousy was permissible, even healthy under the circumstances. Unfortunately, since I had stopped reacting to Nhamo a long time ago, so that all the annoying things he did had been building up for a long time, and since this time the irritation was too persistent to ignore, I was more than a little, less than healthily jealous. This was untactical of me because Nhamo carried on in the way that he did, describing himself in unqualified superlatives and suggesting that his good fortune was unquestionably deserved, a natural consequence of the fact that he was Nhamo, only in order to bait me. And eventually, my composure of the past few years, dating from the time we had fought on the football pitch at Sunday School, disintegrated into so many fine particles. I rose magnificently to the bait.

"Ha! You are so stupid," I jeered. "If you are going to the mission to use a knife and fork, you will be disappointed. Didn't you see Babamukuru eat with his hands? All of them—Maiguru and those proud children. They all ate with their hands."

"Did you want them to embarrass us?" he retorted. "If they had wanted knives and forks, where would we have taken them from? But in their own home they use them. Each one has his own plate with his own portion of food and his knife and fork. I saw it. That's what happened when we went to eat in Salisbury at Maiguru's brother's house, the one who is a medical doctor. I asked Chido if they eat like that at home and he said yes."

I could not argue with such concrete evidence so I attacked from another position. "You will still be our father's son. You will still be my brother. And Netsai's. Even if you don't like it. So you had better stop being proud for nothing and be grateful to Babamukuru for helping you."

"And you had better stop being jealous. Why are you jealous anyway?" he retaliated, free to use all his ammunition now because I had begun the engagement. "Did you ever hear of a girl being taken away to school? You are lucky you even managed to go back to Rutivi. With me it's different. I was meant to be educated."

"I'm glad you are going," I said. "Your voice makes noise. It hurts my ears."

"And you have eyes like a chameleon! I can see you are getting angry. You are going dark like one. Be careful, otherwise you will stay that way and people will run away from you in case you bite them. Be careful, be careful! In case you bite!"

I picked up a rock and flung it at him. Nhamo sat unperturbed, following the missile's trajectory with exaggerated movements of his head. It landed harmlessly in the grass. He laughed. I dived for him, but he was up and running lightly towards the cattle kraal, laughing and chanting "Du-du-muduri, kache! Rwavi muduri kache! Tambu muduri, kache! Pound well while I am eating potatoes at the mission!"

I considered running after him to give him the thrashing he deserved, but judging his head-start, saw that I would not catch him. Besides, we were so evenly matched these days that he might have won a fight or I might have, but I had not fought for a long time and I was out of practice. Today it was better not to fight than not to win. I let him go, still very cross with him for saying such silly things.

I was quite sure at the time that Nhamo knew as well as I did that the things he had said were not reasonable, but in the years that have passed since then I have met so many men who consider themselves responsible adults and therefore ought to know better, who still subscribe to the fundamental principles of my brother's budding elitism, that to be fair to him I must conclude that he was sincere in his bigotry. But in those days I took a rosy view of male nature. After an episode like that a grotesque and sad picture of my father and Nhamo in relation to Babamukuru and my cousin would come to my mind. I wanted my father and Nhamo to stand up straight like Babamukuru, but they always looked as though they were cringing. That picture was frightening. I used to suppose that they saw it too and that it troubled them so much that they had to bully whoever they could to stay in the picture at all. For from my grandmother's history lessons, I knew that my father and brother suffered painfully under the evil wizards' spell.

Babamukuru, I knew, was different. He hadn't cringed under the weight of his poverty. Boldly, Babamukuru had defied it. Through hard work and determination he had broken the evil wizards' spell. Babamukuru was now a person to be reckoned with in his own right. He didn't need to bully anybody any more. Especially not Maiguru, who was so fragile and small she looked as though a breath of wind would carry her away. Nor could I see him bullying Nyasha. My cousin was pretty and bold and sharp. You never thought about Babamukuru as being handsome or ugly, but he was completely dignified. He didn't need to be bold any more because he had made himself plenty of power. Plenty of power. Plenty of money. A lot of education. Plenty of everything.

When you have a lot of anything it makes you feel good to give a bit of it away. I knew that because when I had a tickey from Babamukuru I could buy six *fet koeks* at break. I felt like a saint when I gave my friend Nyari two. That was why Babamukuru was always so kind and generous. That was why he bought his wife and his daughter pretty clothes and always made sure that there was money for Nyasha's education. That was why he did all he could for everybody and in this case had singled out Nhamo for special promotion, as he had been singled out by the good wizards at the mission. I understood that Nhamo was older than I and much more advanced academically. I understood that that made him the logical choice for Babamukuru's project. If he had not insisted that there were other criteria that disqualified me at the outset, I might have been happy for him. But he did insist, and I was very angry indeed.

It cost me a lot of energy to bury that incident with Nhamo so deeply that it would not interfere with the business of living. As it turned out, I was not altogether successful, because I could no longer bring myself to speak to my brother. Not that I consciously decided to ignore him. It just happened. Try as I would, I simply could not open my mouth to talk to him. My mother, who was in the first part of the pregnancy that resulted in Rambanai, was very distressed by all this.

"Now what evil spirits have arisen between you two?" she scolded. "If you have been bewitched, then tell us so that something can be done. But if it is your own madness, stop it straight away!" She was anxious, my poor mother, because four babies, three of them sons, had died in infancy between my birth and this pregnancy. There was talk that somebody had tied her and she was afraid that it might get so bad she would begin to miscarry, or not conceive at all. The rumours were vicious. One or two particularly bad people who knew a little about my mother's family predicted that my mother's younger sister, Lucia, was the culprit because Lucia was passing her prime but was still unmarried and it would be useful for her to be called in to be a second child-bearer for my father. Seeing how badly my mother was taking our quarrel, I nearly called a truce with Nhamo, but when he told me that I would be better off with less thinking and more respect, I was glad I had stood my ground. Towards the end my anger disappeared and I would have talked to him if it had not meant losing face. So when Babamukuru came to fetch Nhamo, I was very relieved, first because he had gone, secondly because I would be free to talk to whomever I wished.

Another advantage of my brother's absence was that he was not there to interfere with my attempts to be friends with Nyasha. Babamukuru came to visit us often, at least every other weekend, and sometimes two weekends in a row and during the week as well.

Maiguru usually accompanied him. Sometimes Nyasha came too. On very rare occasions everyone came, including Nhamo and Chido. I did my best to talk to Nyasha when she came. I racked my brains for odd English words that I could slip into my sentences to help her understand what I was saying, but it was no use. She did not talk beyond a quick stuttered greeting. Nor did she smile any more at all. Most of the time, much to Babamukuru's irritation, she stayed close to Maiguru, refusing my invitations to play *pada* or pound maize or take a trip to Nyamarira. When she did venture away from her mother, our games were strained and silent. In the end I felt stupid and humiliated for making such a fuss over my cousin, but it was difficult to leave her alone. I missed the bold, ebullient companion I had had who had gone to England but not returned from there. Yet each time she came I could see that she had grown a little duller and dimmer, the expression in her eyes a little more complex, as though she were directing more and more of her energy inwards to commune with herself about issues that she alone had seen.

One day she behaved very badly indeed. They arrived at eleven o'clock in the morning, in a season when there was very little in the garden in the way of vegetables. However, there was a cow in milk, so my mother was relieved when Nyasha, having been asked whether she would have milk or vegetables, said she would have milk. Unfortunately, when lunchtime came, Nyasha tucked into the vegetables with the rest of us. When my mother offered her the sour milk she had asked for, she became very morose. She refused to eat anything, although by this time everybody was very concerned and sympathetic and saying she could have whatever she wanted. My parents thought she was a miserable child. They made no secret of saying so when Babamukuru and Maiguru had returned to the mission. Everytime my relatives came from the mission I stayed near Nyasha, and watched her. In this way I saw her observing us all. She said little, but sometimes her lips would move to rehearse the words when someone used complicated language. She was silent and watchful, observing us all with that complex expression of hers—what we said, what we did, how we said it, how we did it—with an intensity that made me uncomfortable.

Then when Nhamo came home at the end of his first year with Babamukuru, you could see he too was no longer the same person. The change in his appearance was dramatic. He had added several inches to his height and many to his width, so that he was not little and scrawny any more but fit and muscular. Vitamins had nourished his skin to a shiny smoothness, several tones lighter in complexion than it used to be. His hair was no longer arranged in rows of dusty, wild cucumber tufts but was black, shiny with oil and smoothly combed. All this was good, but there was one terrible change. He had forgotten how to speak Shona. A few words escaped haltingly, ungrammatically and strangely accented when he spoke to my mother, but he did not speak to her very often any more. He talked most fluently with my father. They had long conversations in English, which Nhamo broke into small, irregular syllables and which my father chopped into smaller and even rougher phonemes. Father was pleased with Nhamo's command of the English language. He said it was the first step in the family's emancipation since we could all improve our language by practising on Nhamo. But he was the only one who was impressed by this inexplicable state my brother had developed. The rest of us spoke to Nhamo in Shona, to which, when he did answer, he answered in English, making a point of speaking slowly, deliberately, enunciating each syllable clearly so that we could understand. This restricted our communication to mundane insignificant matters.

But the situation was not entirely hopeless. When a significant issue did arise so that it was necessary to discuss matters in depth, Nhamo's Shona—grammar, vocabulary, accent and all—would miraculously return for the duration of the discussion, only to disappear again mysteriously once the issue was settled. The more time Nhamo spent at Babamukuru's, the more aphasic he became and the more my father was convinced that he was being educated. My mother was alarmed. She knew that the mission was a Christian place. Nevertheless she maintained that the people there were ordinary people. She thought someone on the mission was bewitching her son and was all for making an appointment with the medium. My father reassured her: "How will the boy remember his English without speaking it? Doesn't he speak with us when he wants? He is dedicated to his studies. Like Mukoma. Dedicated. That's all." Mother did not say anything against Nhamo's language after that, but she was still unhappy. She did want him to be educated, she confided to me, but even more, she wanted to talk to him.

This Nhamo I have described is the Nhamo we were expecting home that November afternoon in 1968. These things I have recounted are the reasons why I was not disappointed when he did not arrive. Mother, as usual, was upset. "That son of mine!" she sighed. "If he could avoid it, he would never come home." Spitefully, I agreed.

We had finished eating and were agreeing that it was too late for Babamukuru to bring Nhamo home when a car rumbled into the yard, its headlights lighting up our smoky kitchen through the door left open for fresh air and coolness. Netsai, who is very loving, was ecstatic. "Mukoma Nhamo has come, Mukoma Nhamo has come," she sang, skipping out into the yard. My father, smiling, puffing up a little, followed. We were all in the yard by the time Babamukuru climbed out of his car. He looked haggard and tired and old. Maiguru, just as distraught, alighted on the other side. For a moment no word was spoken, Babamukuru not even noticing Netsai, who embraced him asking, "Mukoma Nhamo, Babamukuru, where is Mukoma Nhamo?"

Without warning my mother keened shrilly through the dark silence. "Go back!" she wailed. "Go back! Why do you come all this way to tell me what I already know!" She collapsed on to the car bonnet, slipped to the ground, picked herself up and collapsed again. Maiguru came to my mother to hold her, but my mother pushed her violently away. "You want to hold me, you," she hissed. "Now, when it is too late, that is when you are concerned. You pretend. You are a pretender, you. First you took his tongue so that he could not speak to me and now you have taken everything, taken everything for good. Why are you keeping quiet! Why are you not speaking! Because it is true. You bewitched him and now he is dead. Pthu!" She spat at Maiguru's feet. "And you too, Babamukuru! Pthu! I spit at you! You and your education have killed my son." This time when she fell to the ground she did not pick herself up, but rolled there, tearing her hair and her clothes and grinding sand between her teeth. Netsai began to cry.

"Hold her, Jeremiah," said Babamukuru in a heavy, empty voice. "It is true. We do not bring good news."

Maiguru, keening softly, helped my father to coax my mother, now quiet and limp and bewildered, to the kitchen.

Keening. I remember keening that seemed to go on all through the night: shrill, sharp, shiny, needles of sound piercing cleanly and deeply to let the anguish in, not out.

In the kitchen Babamukuru spoke. "There is nothing to be done but to tell you what has happened. The boy complained of a pain in his neck, a slight pain, a few days ago."

"He first told me he was not well on Tuesday," said Maiguru.

"Yes, it was on Tuesday," continued Babamukuru. "On Wednesday he was not feeling better, so we took him to our clinic there at the mission. The doctor thought the boy might have been suffering from mumps. Now, we did not know whether the departed had suffered from mumps or not, so we could not give the doctor useful information on that point. Anyway, the doctor was not sure, but he said if it was mumps, it could get worse, so he decided to keep the boy under observation. That was on Wednesday night. On Thursday morning we went to see him. He did not look bad. In fact he looked much brighter. He even said he wanted to come out of the hospital, but the doctor was not satisfied with his progress. He wanted to keep him for at least another day. I left a telephone message at the Council Offices for you, Jeremiah, saying Nhamo had been admitted to the clinic and that I would pick you up to take you there this evening. Weren't you at the shops today? Didn't you receive that message?"

My father's shoulders were shaking. He could not speak.

"Anyway," Babamukuru resumed, "he did not look bad at that time. I went to a meeting in town. While I was there, my wife received a telephone call from the clinic saying that the boy had grown worse and they were moving him to the hospital in town, the General Hospital. My wife hurried to the clinic. She wanted to accompany him in the ambulance, but when she got there he was already fading. He passed away before they could put him into the ambulance. This was the news I received when I arrived home at some time past eight. I came straight away."

Babamukuru grasped my father's hands in both of his. "My heart cries with yours, but we cannot understand the plans of the heavens," he said, moving on to hold my mother's hands, "but there is One who knows. He will keep you and comfort you even when evil strikes against you."

"Ho-o-re!" groaned my father. "You speak the truth, Mukoma, but today we are overwhelmed by jealous spirits. The boy was bright, doing well. Why should he go unless something was sent to take him? Ha! I did not think such things would happen!" He put his face in his hands. "What else can I say, Mukoma? It is difficult to know what to say at these times. But I know you looked after the boy as if he were yours. Those in the heavens know why he was taken. We can only accept that it has happened." He stood up. "I will go down the road to Samhungu's homestead. They will carry the news to the others." Tears wet his face. He did not wipe them away.

Seeing my father cry, seeing my mother moan and rock in Maiguru's arms, hearing Netsai cry in fear as well as in grief, and Rambanai, waking, whimper and whine, a little of my armour cracked. I was sad for them rather than anguished over any loss of mine, because my brother had become a stranger to me. I was not sorry that he had died, but I was sorry for him because, according to his standards, his life had been thoroughly worth living.

"There is nothing to be done," my aunt was saying to my mother, "except to bear the pain until it passes. You must endure the pain of his passing as you endured the pain of his coming."

"I cannot endure it," my mother moaned. "Maiguru, hold me. I too am going to die."

The body was fetched the next day from the mission and buried in the family burial ground beside my grandmother and other ancestors. After a decent length of time had passed, Babamukuru again raised the question of the emancipation of my father's branch of the family. "It is unfortunate," he said, "that there is no male child to take this duty, to take this job of raising the family from hunger and need, Jeremiah."

"It is as you say," my father agreed. "Tambudzai's sharpness with her books is no use because in the end it will benefit strangers."

"You are correct, Jeremiah," observed my uncle, "but I will not feel that I have done my duty if I neglect the family for that reason. Er—this girl—heyo, Tambudzai—must be given the opportunity to do what she can for the family before she goes into her husband's home."

"Exactly!" agreed my father. "She must be given the opportunity."

My mother was grief stricken when my father told her what he and Babamukuru had decided.

"You, Jeremiah," she said, and she called him Jeremiah infrequently. "You, Jeremiah, are you mad? Have you eaten some wild shrub that has gone to your head? I think so, otherwise how could you stand there and tell me to send my child to a place of death, the place where my first living child died! Today you are raving! She will not go. Unless you want me to die too. The anxiety will kill me. I will not let her go."

"But what will she do?" persuaded my father. "She has finished her Standard Three. Tell me, is there a Standard Four at Rutivi? Kuedza is too far to walk. Where will she do her Standard Four?"

"Don't try to make a fool out of me," my mother

retorted. "Do you think I haven't heard that they are starting the Standard Four at that school? Enrol her at Rutivi, Jeremiah, because I am telling you, I will not let her go."

My father did not pursue the matter, but I went to the mission all the same. My mother's anxiety was real. In the week before I left she ate hardly anything, not for lack of trying, and when she was able to swallow something it lay heavy in her stomach. By the time I left she was so haggard and gaunt she could hardly walk to the fields, let alone work in them.

"Is Mother ill?" whispered Netsai, frightened. "Is she going to die too?"

Netsai was frightened. I, I was triumphant. Babamukuru had approved of my direction. I was vindicated!

Chapter 4

How can I describe the sensations that swamped me when Babamukuru started his car, with me in the front seat beside him, on the day I left my home? It was relief, but more than that. It was more than excitement and anticipation. What I experienced that day was a short cut, a rerouting of everything I had ever defined as me into fast lanes that would speedily lead me to my destination. My horizons were saturated with me, my leaving, my going. There was no room for what I left behind. My father, as affably, shallowly agreeable as ever, was insignificant. My mother, my anxious mother, was no more than another piece of surplus scenery to be maintained, of course to be maintained, but all the same superfluous, an obstacle in the path of my departure. As for my sisters, well, they were there. They were watching me climb into Babamukuru's car to be whisked away to limitless horizons. It was up to them to learn the important lesson that circumstances were not immutable, no burden so binding that it could not be dropped. The honour for teaching them this emancipating lesson was mine. I claimed it all, for here I was, living proof of the moral. There was no doubt in my mind that this was the case.

When I stepped into Babamukuru's car I was a peasant. You could see that at a glance in my tight, faded frock that immodestly defined my budding breasts, and in my broad-toed feet that had grown thick-skinned through daily contact with the ground in all weathers. You could see it from the way the keratin had reacted by thickening and, having thickened, had hardened and cracked so that the dirt ground its way in but could not be washed out. It was evident from the corrugated black callouses on my knees, the scales on my skin that were due to lack of oil, the short, dull tufts of malnourished hair. This was the person I was leaving behind. At Babamukuru's I expected to find another self, a clean, well-groomed, genteel self who could not have been bred, could not have survived, on the homestead. At Babamukuru's I would have the leisure, be encouraged to consider questions that had to do with survival of the spirit, the creation of consciousness, rather than mere sustenance of the body. This new me would not be enervated by smoky kitchens that left eyes smarting and chests permanently bronchitic. This new me would not be frustrated by wood fires that either flamed so furiously that the *sadza* burned, or so indifferently that it became *mbodza*. Nor would there be trips to Nyamarira, Nyamarira which I loved to bathe in and watch cascade through the narrow outlet of the fall where we drew our water. Leaving this Nyamarira, my flowing, tumbling, musical play-ground, was difficult. But I could not pretend to be sorry to be leaving the water-drums whose weight compressed your neck into your spine, were heavy on the head even after you had grown used to them and were constantly in need of refilling. I was not sorry to be leaving the tedious task of coaxing Nyamarira's little tributary in and out of the vegetable beds. Of course, my emancipation from these aspects of my existence was, for the foreseeable future, temporary and not continuous, but that was not the point. The point was this: I was going to be developed in the way that Babamukuru saw fit, which in the language I understood at the time meant well. Having developed well I did not foresee that there would be reason to regress on the occasions that I returned to the homestead.

Without so much going on inside me I would have enjoyed that ride to the mission, remembering how the only other time I had crossed Nyamarira in a vehicle, rolled down my side of the Inyanga Highway and seen Christmas Pass loom up in the distance, was when Mr. Matimba took me to town to sell my green mealies. A-a-h, those green mealies! The hope of selling them had occupied my attention on that first trip, but today I was thinking of more concrete things.

There were many practical issues about my transplantation that I had to think about, all of them mixed up with each other and needing to be sorted out into discrete, manageable portions. There was great pleasure in wondering where I would sleep, since this would certainly not be in a smoky kitchen where people relaxed in the evenings so that you had to wait for everybody else to retire before you could comfortably put yourself to bed. But if not in the kitchen, then where? If Nhamo had been telling the truth, which was as likely as it was not, he had had a whole room to himself at Babamukuru's. A whole room to myself was asking for a lot, expecting too much, and besides, I was not sure that I would enjoy sleeping by myself with nobody to giggle with before falling asleep or whose presence would be comforting when dreams were disturbing. Yet it would be strenuous, disturbing too, to have to share a room with Nyasha, who was morose and taciturn, who made me feel uncomfortable because something had extinguished the sparkle in her eyes. Besides, I still disapproved of her. I thought she had no right to be so unhappy when she was Babamukuru's daughter—that was a blessing in itself. And she wore pretty clothes. She had not been obliged to adjourn her education so that now, although she was the same age as I was, she was already in Form Two. If for no other reason, her eyes should have shone vigorously with gratitude for these blessings, but she was not sensible enough to understand this. She remained ungrateful, awkward, and ill-mannered. The thought of sleeping with Anna, who was Maiguru's housegirl and had come home at the time of Nhamo's funeral to help with the chores, was much more relaxing although not without its problems. Anna could talk and talk and talk about everything and nothing. This was useful when you didn't want to concentrate on depressing things like death and grief, but what would happen when there were serious matters of permanent import like mathematics and history to think about? Still, these were minor concerns. Wherever I slept, I was sure, I would have more than one blanket to cover me. And since Babamukuru's possessions had been disciplined into retaining their newness, these blankets would be thick and fleecy enough to keep the cold out even in the worst June nights. I would not have to get up to sweep the yard and draw water before I set off for school, although on the mission it would not have mattered even if I had had to do these things, since school was close by and getting there did not mean forty minutes at a trot every morning. Nor would I, I thought, openly smiling with the pleasure of it, nor would I need to worry any more about my books becoming embellished with grime and grease-spots in their corner of the *chikuwa*, where I kept them at home. At Babamukuru's I would have a bookcase. My books would live in a bookcase. It would keep them clean. My clothes would be clean too, without fields and smoke and soot to mess them. Nor would keeping them clean entail a walk to the river, twenty minutes away, washing them on rocks, spreading them on boulders and waiting until they dried before I could go home again. I would be able to keep myself clean too, without too much trouble. According to Nhamo, there were taps right inside the house. Not only outside the kitchen like at the headmaster's house at Rutivi School, but right inside the house, where they ran hot water and cold into a tub large enough to sit in with your legs stretched straight out in front of you! And all you had to do to empty the tub was pull out a stopper and the water gurgled away into the earth through a network of pipes laid under the ground. Now, although Nhamo had not been above resorting to fantasy in order to impress, he did prefer facts when they were available. These details seemed factual enough. I could not wait to enjoy these comforts that Nhamo had described to me in patient, important detail. I could not wait to enjoy these consequences of having acquired an education on Babamukuru's part, of being in the process of acquiring one in my case.

Nhamo had had a refrain with which he had punctuated his enthusiastic and reverent descriptions of the luxury and comfort of Babamukuru's house. "Not even the Whites," he had used to carol in an impressionable descant, "not even the Whites themselves could afford it!" I should have been prepared then for the splendour of that house or the mission, but I was not. Having not had the experience with which to improve my imagination, not even my brother's diligent descriptions were able to create for me a true image of my uncle's house.

The grounds were very large, as large as our yard at home. In them stood a single building, Babamukuru's house, if you did not count the outlying constructions, which turned out to be a shed, a garage and the servants' quarters. At home our yard contained many buildings which all had a specific purpose for our day to day living: the pole and *dagga* kitchen, which was about the same size as my uncle's little shed, only round; the *tsapi*, which was small, maybe half as large as Babamukuru's shed; the *hozi*, where Nhamo had slept during the holidays that he did come home; and the House, which was built of red brick, had glass windows and a corrugated-iron roof. We considered the house a very fine house, not only because of the red brick, the glass windows and the corrugated-iron, which made their own emphatic statements about who we were, but also because it had a living-room large enough to hold a dining-table, four matching chairs, and a sofa and two armchairs besides. It was a very fine house, because it had two bedrooms opening off from the living-room which were well furnished with a single bedstead and *koya* mattress, and wardrobes with mirrors that had once been reliable but had now grown so cloudy with age that they threatened to show you images of artful and ancient spirits when you looked into them, instead of your own face. My parents slept in one of the bedrooms, the one on the left as you entered the living-room. The bed and its mattress belonged to my father. My mother was supposed to sleep on the reed mat on the floor with her babies before they were old enough to join me in the kitchen, although she hardly ever did. Usually she fell asleep in the kitchen and could not be bothered to rouse herself to go up to the house. All the women in the family—Mother, Netsai and myself—preferred it this way, and though my father did not, there was not much he could do about it without making a scene. This he did not often have the energy to do.

The other bedroom in the house was spare. This was where Babamukuru and his family used to sleep when they came to visit before they went to England. But now that the children had grown up, Baba and Maiguru slept there alone. In the circles I had moved in until my transfer to the mission, our house on the homestead had been obviously, definitely, a fine, refined home. With that house as my standard it was not easy to grasp that the mansion standing at the top of the drive marked "14, HEADMASTER'S HOUSE" was truly my uncle's very own. Luckily the sign was there, so that by the time we were half-way up the drive I was looking forward to living in such a distinguished home. All the same, had I been writing these things at the time that they happened, there would have been many references to "palace" and "mansion" and "castle" in this section. Their absence is not to say that I have forgotten what it was like. That first impression of grandeur was too exotic ever to fade, but I have learnt, in the years that have passed since then, to curb excesses and flights of fancy. The point has been made: I can now refer to my uncle's house as no more than that—a house.

It was painted white. This was one of the less beautiful aspects of that house, one of the less sensible aspects too. There seemed to be no good reason for wasting time and effort, to say nothing of paint, on painting the cheerful red brick that I had seen elsewhere on the mission as we drove up to Babamukuru's house this clinical, antiseptic white. Naturally, though, there was a reason. I found out from Nyasha, who knew all sorts of things, or glued together facts for herself when knowledge was lacking, that this particular house, the headmaster's house, had been built in the early days of the mission. She said that was around the turn of the nineteenth century at a time when the missionaries believed that only white houses were cool enough to be comfortably lived in. Diligently this belief was translated into action. White houses sprang up all over the mission. All those white houses must have been very uninspiring for people whose function was to inspire. Besides, natives were said to respond to colour, so after a while the missionaries began to believe that houses would not overheat, even when they were not painted white, as long as pastel shades were used. They began to paint their houses cream, pale pink, pale blue, pale green. Nyasha liked to embellish this point. "Imagine," she used to say, "how *pretty* it must have looked. All those pinks and blues gleaming away among the white. It must have been so sweet, so very appealing."

Later, much later, as late as the time that I came to the mission, there was a lot of construction going on. Houses had to be built to shelter the new crop of educated Africans that had been sown in so many Sub A and Sub B night-school classes and was now being abundantly reaped as old boys returned to the mission to contribute by becoming teachers in their turn. Possibly because there was no time for finesse, possibly because the aim was to shelter as many people as quickly as possible, these houses that accommodated the returning teachers remained dark and ruddy.

Nyasha taught me this history with a mischievous glint in her eye. I was like a vacuum then, taking in everything, storing it all in its original state for future inspection. Today I am content that this little paragraph of history as written by Nyasha makes a good story, as likely if not more so than the chapters those very same missionaries were dishing out to us in those mission schools.

At the time that I arrived at the mission, missionaries were living in white houses and in the pale painted houses, but not in the red brick ones. My uncle was the only African living in a white house. We were all very proud of this fact. No, that is not quite right. We were all proud, except Nyasha, who had an egalitarian nature and had taken seriously the lessons about oppression and discrimination that she had learnt first-hand in England.

As the car slowed down to turn into the drive, the

pace of my life increased. I packed a lot of living into the few minutes that it took to creep up the drive to the garage. First was the elation from realising that the elegant house ahead of me was indeed my uncle's. Then there was a disappointment. There was a building almost as long as the house if not as high, so that it could very well have been a little house itself and I thought I had made a mistake. I thought I was not going to live in a mansion after all and my spirits went plunging down. But even then there were plenty of things to be happy about. The smooth, stoneless drive ran between squat, robust conifers on one side and a blaze of canna lilies burning scarlet and amber on the other. Plants like that had belonged to the cities. They had belonged to the pages of my language reader, to the yards of Ben and Betty's uncle in town. Now, having seen it for myself because of my Babamukuru's kindness, I too could think of planting things for merrier reasons than the chore of keeping breath in the body. I wrote it down in my head: I would ask Maiguru for some bulbs and plant a bed of those gay lilies on the homestead. In front of the house. Our home would answer well to being cheered up by such lively flowers. Bright and cheery, they had been planted for joy. What a strange idea that was. It was a liberation, the first of many that followed from my transition to the mission.

Then I discovered that Nhamo had not been lying. Babamukuru was indeed a man of consequence however you measured him. The old building that had disappointed me turned out to be a garage. It was built to shelter cars, not people! And this garage sheltered two cars. Not one, but two cars. Nhamo's chorus sang in my head and now it sounded ominous. Its phrases told me something I did not want to know, that my Babamukuru was not the person I had thought he was. He was wealthier than I had thought possible. He was educated beyond books. And he had done it alone. He had pushed up from under the weight of the white man with no strong relative to help him. How had he done it? Having done it, what had he become? A deep valley cracked open. There was no bridge; at the bottom, spiked crags as sharp as spears. I felt separated forever from my uncle.

It all became very depressing and confusing. At first I had been disappointed because I thought the garage was Babamukuru's house. Now I was worried because it wasn't. For the first time I caught sight of endings to my flight from the homestead that were not all happy. I scolded myself severely for having dared this far in the first place. Hadn't I known, I asked myself, that Babamukuru was a big-hearted man? That didn't make me anything special. Or even deserving. I didn't have anything to do with my uncle's kindness. He would have taken in any poor, needy relative, and to prove it I was only here because my brother had died.

Had I really thought, I continued callously, that these other-worldly relations of mine could live with anyone as ignorant and dirty as myself? I, who was so ignorant that I had not been able to read the signs in their clothes which dared not deteriorate or grow too tight in spite of their well-fleshed bodies, or in the accents of their speech, which were poised and smooth and dropped like foreign gemstones from their tongues. All these signs stated very matter-of-factly that we were not of a kind. I deserved to suffer, I threatened myself, for having been too proud to see that Babamukuru could only be so charitable to our branch of the family because we were so low. He was kind because of the difference.

With a sigh I slid into a swamp of self-pity. My finely tuned survival system set off its alarm at once, warning me to avoid that trap, but I was lost. I could see no path of escape except the one that led back to the homestead. But that, I knew, would do me no good because I was burning up with wanting to escape from there. I did make an effort to improve my state of mind. I scolded myself strongly for not appreciating Babamukuru's concern for my family and me. I tried to call up my courage by imagining the fine grades I would make, which was what mattered, why I had come to the mission in the first place. I must have been much more frightened by the strangeness and awesomeness of my new position than I knew, because none of these tactics worked. I climbed out of the car much less hopefully than I had climbed into it, and followed Babamukuru uneasily as he walked towards the house.

A huge, hairy hound appeared in front of me from nowhere. It leapt out of thin air and scared me to death. Its black lips wrinkled up to show piercing incisors spiking out of gums that were even blacker than its lips. Its ears flattened themselves so far back on its head that its eyes stretched upwards in a demonic squint. Its sudden appearance made it seem all the more sinister. I could not help it. I yelped, which annoyed the beast and set it barking to summon its pink-eyed companion. That albino hound was even more unsettling. Everything about it was either pink or white. So pink were its gums that it took very little for my unhappy mind to conjure up blood and have it seep through the animal's skin to stain its pale teeth red. I was in a bad state or else I would have noticed the chains that bound them to their kennel and the fence that enclosed them in their pen. To me they were loose, ferocious guardians of the gates to this kingdom, this kingdom that I should not have been entering. Their lust for my blood was justified: they knew I did not belong.

Anna came to my rescue. "If they were loose," she called cheerfully, coming round the back of the house to greet me, "they would have chewed you to pieces by now. Welcome, Tambu, welcome. It's good to see you again. That's why they are tied, these dogs. They aren't dogs to play about with, these."

Tied . . . Tied . . . Ah, yes, they were tied! Perspective restored itself. I saw the chains and the fence. My knees calcified again, speech returned. I laughed nervously and tried to tell Anna how silly I had been not to realise that I was safe, but one did not need to do much talking when Anna was around. "What about luggage? Where is it?" she chattered on. "But sometimes they aren't tied—just think!—because they go off and we can't find them. When that happens, ha-a!, you don't catch me outside, not even to hang the laundry. But it's good you have come. I've been thinking of you. Enter, enter," she invited pleasantly, holding the back door open for me.

I was not half-way through the door before Nyasha was on me with a big hug, which I understood, and a kiss on both cheeks, which I did not. She was excited to see me, she was pleased she said. I was surprised to see her in such high spirits, pleasantly surprised, since this was not the cousin I had been steeling myself to meet. Believing my words, I hugged her back and told her that I too had been looking forward to her company.

Nyasha had a lot to say, during which time Anna disappeared to tell Maiguru that I had arrived. Nyasha was baking a cake, she said, for her brother, who was going back to his boarding school next day. The cake was ready to go into the oven, the weather was hot: the cake would rise in the mixing-bowl and flop in the baking-tin if it was not put to bake immediately. Anna would show me where to go. Nyasha disappeared back into the kitchen, taking with her some of the security that had settled on me with her warm welcome. I grew disapproving again of my cousin's bad manners and hoped that she would not carry on like that, because in the few minutes of our conversation I had seen that here at the mission at least I might have my old friend back.

She was very busy, dextrously greasing and flouring a cake tin and pouring in the batter. Not wanting to impose I busied myself with inspecting the kitchen. It looked very sophisticated to me at the time. But looking back, I remember that the cooker had only three plates, none of which was a ring; that the kettle was not electric; that the refrigerator was a bulky paraffin-powered affair. The linoleum was old, its blue and white pattern fading to patches of red where the paint had worn off and patches of black where feet had scuffed up the old flooring at its seams and water had dripped from hands and vegetables and crockery to create a stubborn black scum. The kitchen window was not curtained; a pane of glass was missing. This missing pane caused many problems because through the hole a draught blew, mischievously lowering temperatures in the oven so that buns and cakes were never quite light unless you could close the kitchen door and stop anybody from opening it, blocking the draught in its path. The broken window, the draught and its consequences were particularly annoying to Maiguru.

"It surprises me!" she used to mutter whenever she battled with oven temperatures. "You'd think people would find time to fix windows in their own homes. Yet they don't. Ts! It surprises me."

Later, as experience sharpened my perception of such things, I saw too that the colours were not coordinated. The green and pink walls—it was the fashion to have one wall a different colour from the others—contrasted harshly with each other and with the lino. It pleased me, though, to see that the kitchen was clean. What dirt that could be removed from the lino was removed regularly by thorough scrubbing with a strong ammonia cleaner, which was efficient but chapped your hands much more roughly than ash dissolved in water from Nyamarira ever did. The enamel of the cooker and the plastic of the fridge, although not shining, were white, and the kitchen sink gleamed greyly. This lack of brilliance was due, I discovered years later when television came to the mission, to the use of scouring powders which, though they sterilised 99 per cent of a household, were harsh and scratched fine surfaces. When I found this out, I realised that Maiguru, who had watched television in England, must have known about the dulling effects of these scourers and about the brilliance that could be achieved by using the more gentle alternatives. By that time I knew something about budgets as well, notably their inelasticity. It dawned on me then that Maiguru's dull sink was not a consequence of slovenliness, as the advertisers would have had us believe, but a necessity.

Anna came back with the news that Maiguru was resting. She would be with me in the time that it took to get out of bed and dressed. She would show me to the living-room, where I was to wait for my aunt.

Hoping that it was not illness that had put my aunt in bed at that time of the day, I followed Anna to the living-room, where I made myself comfortable on a sofa. It was impossible not to notice that this sofa was twice as long and deep and soft as the one in the house at home. I took stock of my surroundings, noting the type, texture and shape of the furniture, its colours and its arrangement. My education had already begun, and it was with a pragmatic eye that I surveyed Maiguru's sitting-room: I would own a home like this one day; I would need to know how to furnish it.

Since I had entered my uncle's house through the back door, and so had moved up a gradient of glamour from the kitchen, through the dining-room to the living-room, I did not benefit from the full impact of the elegance of that living-room, with its fitted carpet of deep, green pile, tastefully mottled with brown and gold, and chosen to match the pale green walls (one slightly lighter than the other three according to the fashion). The heavy gold curtains flowing voluptuously to the floor, the four-piece lounge suite upholstered in glowing brown velvet, the lamps with their tasselled shades, the sleek bookcases full of leather-bound and hard-covered volumes of erudition, lost a little, but only a very little, of their effect.

Had I entered from the driveway, through the verandah and the front door, as visitors whom it was necessary to impress would enter, the taste and muted elegance of that room would have taken my breath away. As it was, having seen the kitchen, and the dining-room, which was much smarter than the kitchen, with shiny new linoleum covering every square inch of floor and so expertly laid that the seams between the strips were practically invisible, I was a little better prepared for what came next. This was not altogether a bad thing, because the full force of that opulent living-room would have been too much for me. I remember feeling slightly intimidated by the dining-room, with its large, oval table spacious enough to seat eight people taking up the centre of the room. That table, its shape and size, had a lot of say about the amount, the calorie content, the complement of vitamins and minerals, the relative proportions of fat, carbohydrate and protein of the food that would be consumed at it. No one who ate from such a table could fail to grow fat and healthy. Pushed up against a window, and there were several windows flanked by plain, sensible sun-filters and sombre, blue cotton curtains, was a display cabinet. Glossy and dark as the table, it displayed on greenish glass shelves the daintiest, most delicate china I had ever seen—fine, translucent cups and saucers, teapots and jugs and bowls, all covered in roses. Pink on white, gold on white, red on white. Roses. Old English, Tea, Old Country. Roses. These tea-sets looked so delicate it was obvious they would disintegrate the minute you so much as poured the tea into a cup or weighted a plate down with a bun. No wonder they had been shut away. I fervently hoped I would not be expected to eat or drink from them. I was relieved to find out in due course that everyone was a bit afraid of those charmingly expensive and fragile tea-sets, so they were only ever admired and shown off to guests.

If I was daunted by Maiguru's dainty porcelain cups, the living-room, as I have said, would have finished me off had I not been inoculated by the gradient I have talked of, although calling it a glamour gradient is not really the right way to describe it. This increase in comfort from kitchen to living-room was a common feature of all the teachers' houses at the mission. It had more to do with means and priorities than taste. Babamukuru's taste was excellent, so that where he could afford to indulge it, the results were striking. The opulence of his living-room was very strong stuff, overwhelming to someone who had first crawled and then toddled and finally walked over dung floors. Comfortable it was, but overwhelming nevertheless. Some strategy had to be devised to prevent all this splendour from distracting me in the way that my brother had been distracted. Usually in such dire straits I used my thinking strategy. I was very proud of my thinking strategy. It was meant to put me above the irrational levels of my character and enable me to proceed from pure, rational premises. Today, though, it did not work.

Every corner of Babamukuru's house—every shiny surface, every soft contour and fold—whispered its own insistent message of comfort and ease and rest so tantalisingly, so seductively, that to pay any attention to it, to think about it at all, would have been my downfall. The only alternative was to ignore it. I remained as aloof and unimpressed as possible.

This was not easy, because my aunt took a long time to come from her bedroom. I put this interval to good use in building up my defences. I had only to think of my mother, with Netsai and Rambanai superimposed in the background, to remember why and how I had come to be at the mission. And having seen how easily it could happen, I judged my brother less harshly. Instead, I became more aware of how necessary it was to remain steadfast. Then, to make sure that I was not being soft and sentimental in revising my opinion of Nhamo, I had to survey my surroundings again to see whether they really were potent enough to have had such a devastating effect on him, thus exposing myself again to all the possible consequences. I triumphed. I was not seduced.

You might think that there was no real danger. You might think that, after all, these were only rooms decorated with the sort of accessories that the local interpretations of British interior-decor magazines were describing as standard, and nothing threatening in that. But really the situation was not so simple. Although I was vague at the time and could not have described my circumstances so aptly, the real situation was this: Babamukuru was God, therefore I had arrived in Heaven. I was in danger of becoming an angel, or at the very least a saint, and forgetting how ordinary humans existed—from minute to minute and from hand to mouth. The absence of dirt was proof of the other-worldly nature of my new home. I knew, had known all my life, that living was dirty and I had been disappointed by the fact. I had often helped my mother to resurface the kitchen floor with dung. I knew, for instance, that rooms where people slept exuded peculiarly human smells just as the goat pen smelt goaty and the cattle kraal bovine. It was common knowledge among the younger girls at school that the older girls menstruated into sundry old rags which they washed and reused and washed again. I knew, too, that the fact of menstruation was a shamefully unclean secret that should not be allowed to contaminate immaculate male ears by indiscreet reference to this type of dirt in their presence. Yet at a glance it was difficult to perceive dirt in Maiguru's house. After a while, as the novelty wore off, you began to see that the antiseptic sterility that my aunt and uncle strove for could not be attained beyond an illusory level because the buses that passed through the mission, according to an almost regular schedule, rolled up a storm of fine red dust which perversely settled in corners and on surfaces of rooms and armchairs and bookshelves. When the dust was obvious it was removed, but enough of it always remained invisibly to creep up your nose and give you hay fever, thus restoring your sense of proportion by reminding you that this was not heaven. Sneezing and wiping my nose on the back of my hand, I became confident that I would not go the same way as my brother.

A shrill, shuddering wail pulled me abruptly out of my thoughts, made my armpits prickle and my mouth turn bitter. It wailed and trembled for ten long seconds, during which images of witches on hyenas' backs, both laughing hellishly, flitted through my mind. This was no time to be frightened, when I needed all my wits about me to take advantage of all the opportunities the mission could offer. So I became annoyed instead, with myself for being caught unaware by everyday mission sounds and with the mission for having such sounds. Deliberately, nonchalantly, clenching my moist palms and in spite of the fact that there was no one but myself to be impressed by this intrepid display of courage, I stood up to see through the window the results of that shuddering wail. Through the jacarandas in my uncle's yard and the blue gums at a distance, the pale-green school buildings glittered in the evening sun and boarding pupils strolled or walked or ran to the largest of these buildings, which I learnt later was the Beit Hall. The boys wore khaki shirts and shorts as usual, the girls were in dark-blue, belted gym-slips over pale-blue blouses.

"It's for them to go to assembly," chuckled Anna from the dining-room. "We'd had a rest from it during the holiday, but now it's begun again. It's frightening, isn't it? The day I first heard it, my whole body dried up. Dry and stiff. Like bark. That sireen! But you get used to it."

"You really are dying to get to school, aren't you?" joked Maiguru from the door opposite the window. "E-e-h! Sisi Tambu," she smiled, advancing to greet me with her right arm bent upwards from the elbow, with her palm facing me and swinging her hand down so that I was forced to slap palms with her by way of greeting, in the way that you do when you greet your age mates or friends. "So you have arrived, Sisi Tambu. That is good. I always think there is something wrong with my house when Babawa Chido's relatives do not want to visit."

Maiguru was too modest. I did my best to reassure her. "Don't even think such things, Maiguru. Everybody loves to come here. They all say you treat them so kindly. If they could, they'd be here every day."

Maiguru smiled ruefully and then recovered her good spirits. "Then it is all right," she said. "But you never know with some people. You see them leave quietly and you think they are satisfied, but what they say afterwards, that is another story."

"Oh, no, Maiguru," I hastened, "I've not heard anyone say anything bad. They are proud of you. They say you work so hard for them." Then I greeted her. It was necessary to sit on the floor to do this. I sat, folding my legs up under my bottom. I clapped my hands. "Nyamashewe, Maiguru. How are you?"

"We are all fit and jolly," Maiguru answered. "But get up, child, and sit comfortably in the seat." Maiguru called Anna to ask her to prepare tea. While we waited she asked me about my mother, the tone of her voice saying much more about the concern she was feeling than her words. I answered as briefly as was polite, because it was not something I liked to talk about. I preferred to keep thoughts of my mother's condition to myself.

Anna returned carrying a tray with the tea things on it. There were pots and jugs and cups and saucers, all flowery and matching, with a teaspoon for the sugar and two more for Maiguru and me to stir our tea with. It was all very novel and refined. At home we boiled the milk up with the water, when we had milk, and then added the tea leaves. Lifting a round spoon-shaped object from the tray, Maiguru poured my tea.

"What has amused you, Sisi Tambu?" she asked, seeing a smile hover over my mouth.

"That little sieve, Maiguru. Is it really just for sifting tea?"

"The tea-strainer?" my aunt replied. "Haven't you seen one before? The tea wouldn't be drinkable without it. It would be all tea-leaves."

So this tea-strainer was another necessity I had managed without up until now. Maiguru seemed to think it was absolutely vital to have one. I would hardly have described it like that. Interesting, yes, but vital? And imagine spending money on a sieve so small it could only be used for sifting tea! When I went home I would see whether tea really was less pleasant to drink without the strainer.

There was food too, lots of it. Lots of biscuits and cakes and jam sandwiches. Maiguru was offering me the food, but it was difficult to decide what to take because everything looked so appetising. We did not often have cake at home. In fact, I remembered having cake only at Christmas time or at Easter. At those times Babamukuru brought a great Zambezi slab home with him and cut it up in front of our eager eyes, all the children waiting for him to distribute it. This he did one piece each at a time so that for days on end, long after the confectionery had lost its freshness, we would be enraptured. We would spend many blissful moments picking off and nibbling, first the white coconut and then the pink icing and last the delicious golden cake itself, nibbling so slowly such little pieces at a time that we could hardly taste them, but could gloat when everyone else had finished that we still had some left. Biscuits were as much of a treat as cake, especially when they were dainty, dessert biscuits with cream in the middle or chocolate on top. Jam was another delicacy that appeared only on festive occasions.

Maiguru must have guessed my thoughts from the expression on my face and the way I hesitated to help myself. Cordially she invited me to eat as much as I liked of anything I liked, even if that meant everything. Not wanting my aunt to think me greedy, I had to be more restrained than usual after that, so I chose one small biscuit that did not even have cream in the middle and bit into it slowly so that I would not be obliged to take anything else. This made Maiguru anxious. My sweet little aunt, who liked to please, interpreted my diffidence as her own shortcoming.

"Did you want Mazoe, Sisi Tambu? Or Fanta? Ginger Ale maybe? It is all there. Just say what you want."

I hastened to reassure her by taking a great gulp of tea. Being used to enamel mugs which warned you when the tea was too hot by burning your lips before you let the liquid reach your mouth, the boiling tea scalded my tongue. I was in agony. My eyes watered and my nose too. Choking and spluttering, I deposited my cup shakily back in its saucer.

"What are you doing to her, Mum? She looks about to burst into tears," asked Nyasha, bouncing into the living-room, all flour and rich baking smells.

"Go and clean yourself up, Nyasha. Say hello to your cousin," instructed Maiguru.

"Hello," my cousin said cheerfully, half-way across the room.

"Nyasha!" Maiguru insisted.

"I have said hello, before you came out," Nyasha called, passing out of the living-room into the depths of the house. "Anyway," she added pointedly, "I'm going to clean myself up."

It really was very sad that Maiguru, who was the embodiment of courtesy and good breeding, should have such a rumbustious daughter. It was so embarrassing, the way Nyasha thought she could say anything to her mother. I did not know where to look.

"They are too Anglicised," explained Maiguru, with a little laugh so that it was difficult to tell whether she was censoring Nyasha for her Anglicised habits or me for my lack of them. "They picked up all these disrespectful ways in England," she continued conversationally, "and it's taking them time to learn how to behave at home again. It's difficult for them because things are so different. Especially this business of relatives. Take you, for example, Sisi Tambu, the way your brother was here and the way you have come yourself. They didn't see these things while they were growing up in England so now they are a bit confused. But it doesn't matter. You mustn't worry about Nyasha's little ways. We keep trying to teach her the right manners, always telling her Nyasha, do this; Nyasha, why didn't you do that. But it's taking time. Her head is full of loose connections that are always sparking. Nyasha! Ha, Nyasha! That child of mine has her own thoughts about everything! Have you finished your tea, Sisi Tambu?" she asked, glancing into my empty cup. "Then come, I will show you where you will sleep."

I followed Maiguru into the hall, which was dark, there being no windows, but not too dark to hide a long row of pegs in the wall from which hung heavy overcoats and lightweight raincoats. These people, I saw, never got wet or cold.

Maiguru stopped in front of a closed door, knocked and entered. I followed her into a room that comfortably contained two three-quarter beds, a wardrobe that must have been too big for one person's clothes and a dresser with a full-length mirror so bright and new that it reflected only the present. Nyasha lounged, propped up against the headboard of her bed, which was the one against the wall, her legs raised and crossed at the knee, apparently deeply engrossed in a novel, although her eyes strayed from time to time to observe herself in the mirror. Maiguru and I stood in the doorway for a long time. I think we were both wondering what was going to happen next.

"What are you reading, Nyasha-washa, my lovey-dove?" Maiguru eventually asked, advancing into the room. Nyasha raised her book so that her mother could see for herself.

Maiguru's lips pursed into a tight, disapproving knot. "Oh dear," she breathed, "that's not very good. Nyasha, I don't want you to read books like that."

"There's nothing wrong with it, Mum," Nyasha reassured her.

"Don't tell me that, Nyasha," Maiguru warned in a

tone that I approved of although I could not follow the language very well. I thought Nyasha ought to be more respectful. "I read those books at postgraduate level," Maiguru continued. "I know they are not suitable books for you to read."

"But it's meant to be good, Mum. You know D. H. Lawrence is meant to be good," objected Nyasha.

"You mustn't read books like that. They are no good for you," Maiguru insisted.

"But, Mum, I get so bored. I've read everything in the house that you say I can and there's not much of a library at school. What's all the fuss about anyway? It's only a *book* and I'm only *reading* it."

Maiguru's face tightened, I thought in annoyance, but she may have been wincing. Ignoring Nyasha (who also began to ignore her mother, diverting her attention sternly to her book so that the concentration furrowed her brow with delicate lines of mental activity) Maiguru turned to me. "Well, Sisi Tambu, this is where you will sleep," she smiled vivaciously, adding unnecessarily, "with Nyasha." She indicated the unoccupied bed.

If I had been apprehensive from the minute we entered my cousin's bedroom, I was thoroughly distressed now that my fate had been made clear. From what I had seen of my cousin, I was intrigued and fascinated with one part of my mind, the adventurous, explorative part. But this was a very small part. Most of me sought order. Most of me was concrete and categorical. These parts disapproved of Nyasha very strongly and were wary of her. Nyasha, I thought, would have too many surprises; she would distract me when all I wanted was to settle down to my studies. There was something about her that was too intangible for me to be comfortable with, so intangible that I could not decide whether it was intangibly good or intangibly bad. There was a certain glamour to the idea of sharing a room with my Anglicised cousin. Nyasha herself was glamorous in an irreverent way that made me feel, if not exactly inadequate at least uneducated in some vital aspect of teenage womanliness. But for all the glamour, the thought persisted that Nyasha would not be good for me. Everything about her spoke of alternatives and possibilities that if considered too deeply would wreak havoc with the neat plan I had laid out for my life. The sense of being alien and inadequate that had departed while I drank tea under Maiguru's maternal surveillance reasserted itself. Needing a scapegoat I blamed Nyasha, who had not been cordial enough to say a single word to me in all the time that I had been standing in her room.

Maiguru was fussing, cooing and clucking and shaking her feathers. "These are your things, Sisi Tambu, your clothes and your washing things," she chirped brightly, pulling a suitcase from beneath the bed that was to be mine, and opening the suitcase to display my new wardrobe. There was the uniform, two dark-blue gym-slips with wide box pleats and four light-blue short-sleeved shirts to wear underneath the gym-slips. There were half a dozen pairs of white ankle-socks and a pair of black side-buckled shoes that turned out to be half a size too small, which was not too small to wear. My aunt showed me too the underwear, the smooth nylon slips and sensible panties. To my great joy there were two smart casual dresses in pastels—pale pink and pale yellow—both brand new with little puffed sleeves and full, gathered skirts set into chicly dropped waists. My heart brimmed over with gratitude and love for my aunt and uncle. All the excitement, uncertainty, anxiety and happiness mixed into such a steamy emotion that I was almost reduced to tears. I tried to say something to my aunt, some appropriate words of thanks, but

Maiguru was still chirruping away. "You see, Sisi Tambu, you see, don't you, what good care your uncle is taking of you? He has fixed everything. Here the toothbrush, here the vaseline and the flannel and a comb. You see, everything! But if something has been forgotten, don't be shy. Tell us at once. Or tell Nyasha. She'll help you get settled. Nyasha, sugar pie!" I held my breath.

"Yes, Mum?" answered the daughter decorously. I breathed again.

"Help Tambudzai get settled, lovey."

"Yes, Mum," Nyasha murmured.

Chapter 5

Nyasha remained stern for some time after Maiguru left us. The creases of concentration furrowed her brow ever more deeply. There was nothing for me to do—my bed had been made, my clothes were neatly packed in my suitcase. I sat on my bed and waited, not daring to speak to Nyasha, whose detachment, when she was not disarming you with the full force of her precocious charm, was very intimidating. Fortunately, it was not in her nature to remain detached for long. She could not resist eyeing me quickly and cautiously when she thought I wasn't looking, and I was able to catch her at it because of course I was doing the same. Our eyes met and Nyasha burst out laughing.

"We shall have to speak to each other sooner or later," she laughed. "And anyway, it's not you I'm cross with."

She was, it seemed, well-disposed towards me. There followed the usual pleasantries about how the situation was at home and my eager questions about school at the mission. What time did lessons start in the morning? What time did they end? Were those buildings I had seen through the living-room window the classrooms? The siren, that was the bell, wasn't it? And what about the teachers, were they harsh or kind?

"I'm glad," said Nyasha when we began to talk seriously, "that we have to share this room. It means we'll be friends. But you curled your lip at us when we came back from England, so I didn't know what was going to happen when you came. I just said to myself, I'll try to be nice, I'll try to be friendly and we'll see what happens."

"But I did not sneer at *you*," I protested, speaking in Shona. Our conversation was laboured and clumsy because when Nyasha spoke seriously her thoughts came in English, whereas with me, the little English I had disappeared when I dropped my vigilance to speak of things that mattered. "You know what happened? I was so disappointed when you wouldn't speak to me, you and Chido. Not a word! You didn't even greet me. Just Nhamo—he was your favourite."

"Actually," confessed Nyasha with unusual diffidence, so that if I had not heard her speak before I would have said she was shy, "actually we were frightened that day. And confused. You know, it's easy to forget things when you're that young. We had forgotten what home was like. I mean really for-gotten—what it looked like, what it smelt like, all the things to do and say and not to do and say. It was all strange and new. Not like anything we were used to. It was a real shock!"

Looking back, I see that that is how our friendship began. In fact it was more than friendship that developed between Nyasha and myself. The conversation that followed was a long, involved conversation, full of guileless openings up and intricate lettings out and lettings in. It was the sort of conversation that young girls have with their best friends, that lovers have under the influence of the novelty and uniqueness of their love, the kind of conversation that cousins have when they realise that they like each other in spite of not wanting to. You could say that my relationship with Nyasha was my first love-affair, the first time that I grew to be fond of someone of whom I did not wholeheartedly approve.

"We shouldn't have gone," Nyasha was saying, looking disheartened. "The parents ought to have packed us off home. They should have, you know. Lots of people did that. Maybe that would have been best. For them at least, because now they're stuck with hybrids for children. And they don't like it. They don't like it at all. It offends them. They think we do it on purpose, so it offends them. And I don't know what to do about it, Tambu, really I don't. I can't help having been there and grown into the me that has been there. But it offends them—I offend them. Really, it's very difficult."

The intimacy that had permeated the room by that stage was heady. It made me reckless in the way that draining the dregs in my father's gourd had done when I was little. It made me tell Nyasha frankly what I thought. "Even if you have been to England, you should respect your mother," I told her. "I would not speak to my mother in the way I have heard you speak to Maiguru."

Nyasha sucked air between her teeth. "Tss! Don't worry about my mother," she answered bitterly. "She doesn't want to be respected. If people did that she'd have nothing to moan about and then what would she do? She spends most of her life complaining."

I was overwhelmed by my temerity in telling Nyasha what I thought, but I was quite sure that she was wrong. The Maiguru I knew was nothing like Nyasha said. My Maiguru was concerned about everybody. She was gentle, conscientious and caring. I felt a strong moral obligation to explain this to Nyasha, who judged her mother so harshly, but it would have taken me a long time to find suitable words for such a complex and delicate matter. Consequently, I was relieved when Anna came and knelt down in the doorway to tell us that supper was nearly ready.

"For heaven's sake, Anna, stand up!" commanded Nyasha irritably. "Every time you come in here I tell you not to kneel down, but you keep on doing it. What's the matter with you?" And then she was ashamed of herself. "Now, honestly, just listen to me. Getting all cross and crotchety! But really, Anna, there's no need to kneel when you speak to me."

Anna continued her message on her knees: "Mami says that if Tambudzai has not washed it is all right for today, but after eating you must show her the bathroom." She departed as inconspicuously as she had arrived.

Nyasha looked me over and pronounced me clean enough to sit at table. She wanted us to go and help with the dishing-out because her parents liked to see her being dutiful, but I needed to use the bathroom, so she showed me where it was, saying she would be in the kitchen. I had not used a panelled toilet before so it was necessary to experiment. I climbed on to the seat and squatted, first facing the cistern and then, more comfortably, facing away from it.

Anna was drawing the golden living-room curtains as I passed through on my way to the kitchen. It was not dark yet, there being an orange glow in the west which had migrated and now occupied the south. I did not mind. East, west, north, south—it was all the same to me as long as the sun did rise at one point and set in the opposite. I was more concerned with how early it was, much too early to be eating the last meal of the day. At that rate I would be hungry by the time I went to bed, and I had nightmares when I slept without a comforting mound of *sadza* warming my stomach.

The food was already on the table when I entered the dining-room, many large dishes in the centre of the table, many plates and glasses and knives and forks at each place. Nyasha sat at her place reading her novel. She put it away on the dresser when Maiguru walked in to take her place at the table, graciously inviting me to sit beside my cousin.

"Shall we say grace?" Maiguru enquired when I was seated. I almost agreed that we should, but seeing

Nyasha bow her head, did the same without comment. Maiguru recited an English prayer which Nyasha joined at the end to say "Amen" and I repeated this after them because I had not known beforehand when the prayer ended.

Babamukuru came in through the back door as we finished saying grace.

"Good evening, Baba," Maiguru greeted him in Shona.

"Good evening, Daddy," Nyasha said in English.

"Good evening, Babamukuru," I said, mixing the two languages because I was not sure which was most appropriate. Babamukuru grunted briefly by way of reply, in a way that told you at once that he had weightier matters on his mind than the goodness of the evening, and you wondered whether you ought to have bothered him with such mundane details in the first place.

"How has the day been?" Maiguru asked in English.

"Have you spent the day well?" Nyasha asked in Shona.

"Have you spent the day well, Babamukuru?" I repeated.

Babamukuru grunted again, at greater length this time, which indicated that the day had been tolerable. He seated himself at the head of the table in the place set with a pile of plates.

"You had already started," he observed to Maiguru. "Did you think I wasn't coming, even after you telephoned to say supper was ready and I said I was coming?"

"No, no, my Daddy-dear," chirped Maiguru, fussing with the dishes. "We were only just about to begin. But now you have come. Help yourself, my Daddy-pie!" With this she removed the lid from the serving-dish nearest Babamukuru and put it away on the sideboard. Then she picked up a plate from the pile in front of Babamukuru and held it for him respectfully with both hands while he spooned food on to his plate. When he had finished with the first dish, Maiguru put her husband's plate down in her own place. She exchanged the dish from which Babamukuru had helped himself for another and then picked up his plate to hold it for him while he helped himself once more. This carried on until Babamukuru had helped himself from the third dish, when it was discovered that Anna had forgotten to make the gravy. Babamukuru said he liked gravy.

"I'll make it," volunteered Nyasha, leaping out of her chair. "I'll be quicker than Anna. Honestly, it won't take a minute."

Maiguru thought the food ought to go into the warmer to keep it warm while Nyasha was making the gravy. This done, Babamukuru, Maiguru and I waited for her to finish.

"Do you see the kind of books your daughter is reading?" Maiguru asked my uncle, taking Nyasha's copy of *Lady Chatterley's Lover* from the dresser and showing it to my uncle.

Babamukuru was distressed, looking sad, then hurt, then ultimately annoyed. "Tss!" he shook his head. "I don't know what's wrong with our daughter. She has no sense of decency, none whatsoever." So saying, he took the book and left the room, returning a minute later without the offending volume.

"You think she shouldn't read it?" Maiguru asked. "I thought so too, but Nyasha is intelligent, and a good girl, and that is only a book, I thought—"

"If I let you, Ma'Chido, you would spoil these children. No daughter of mine is going to read such books."

Then Nyasha came back with the gravy, Anna following with the rest of the meal. Maiguru said that

Babamukuru's old meal was no longer fresh. She said she would eat it herself, that Babamukuru should serve himself another portion of food. Babamukuru thought his wife was making a fuss about nothing, but she insisted, so the ritual dishing out of my uncle's food was performed again. This time Nyasha did not wait for her father to finish. By the time he was on to the third dish, she was helping herself to rice.

"What are you doing, Nyasha?" Babamukuru asked, without looking at her, so that one wondered how he had noticed.

"I thought you had finished with the rice," Nyasha replied, ladling meat and gravy on to her rice.

"What about your mother, here?" Babamukuru asked conversationally. "Do you think she doesn't know what she's doing, waiting on me like this?"

"I don't like cold food," Nyasha pointed out, as willing as her father to engage in dialogue.

"Are you sure you have enough meat, my Daddy-d?" Maiguru interrupted fondly. "Let me give you some more."

"I don't think I need more, thank you, Ma'Chido," declined Babamukuru. But Maiguru took the serving-spoon from between his fingers and spooned several hefty chunks of beef on to his plate. In spite of looking a little nauseous, Babamukuru tucked in manfully; then Maiguru served me and finally herself.

The food looked interesting, which made me suspicious of it since I knew that food was not meant to be interesting but filling. Besides the rice, there was something that might have been potato: I could not be sure since it was smothered in a thick, white, tasteless gravy. Although I gallantly placed small portions of it in my mouth, it refused to go down my throat in large quantities. In fact nothing was going down my throat in large quantities. I discovered that using a knife and fork was not as easy as it looked; most of my supper was landing on the table, on my chest, in my lap—everywhere except in my mouth. In a way this was not a bad thing because the taste of those potatoes made everything else, even the meat, which was properly cooked with plenty of salt and onions and tomatoes, taste funny.

Without breaking the conversation she was having with Babamukuru—which was about whether all the students had turned up for school, whether they had paid their school fees and whether the classes had been filled to capacity yet—Maiguru rang the little silver bell, that sat next to her. The sound brought Anna hurrying to kneel beside her.

"Would you bring us a little *sadza*, Sisi Anna?" Maiguru requested. "And a spoon. I think you forgot to give Sisi Tambu a spoon."

I was very pleased to see the *sadza* when it came, although nobody else seemed to care for it. This was embarrassing. There were many things that were embarrassing about that meal: my place looked as though a small and angry child had been fed there; here I was with a spoon in my hand instead of a fork and now Maiguru was dishing *sadza* on to my plate, *sadza* that nobody else would eat. She was being very kind.

"When we went to England," she was saying, "it was terrible. It took me months to get used to the food. It has no taste, you know, and there was so little of it. I used to be hungry day and night. Sometimes it was so bad I couldn't sleep! So, Sisi Tambu, you put into your stomach whatever will fill it up and give you a good night's rest."

"I don't mind going to bed hungry," said Nyasha.

"When did you ever go to bed hungry? Not in this house!" snapped Maiguru.

"All I wanted to say," Nyasha replied apologetically, "was that when I can't sleep usually what I need is a good read. Really! Sometimes I have to read until one o'clock, but after that I usually drop off."

"Then that's what you should have said," said my aunt.

"Talking about books," Nyasha went on, "I could have sworn I brought that D.H. Lawrence in here. Have you seen it, Mum?"

"I don't see it anywhere."

"But I'm pretty positive I brought it in here," insisted Nyasha, wrinkling her forehead and forgetting to eat in her effort to remember where she had put her book. "Gosh! If I didn't bring it in I'm getting awfully absent-minded." She took a mouthful of food, then pushed her chair back. "It's bugging me. Just let me check in the bedroom."

"Sit down, Nyasha," Maiguru told her. "For God's sake don't carry on about that book. I told you I don't want you reading books like that."

Nyasha froze half-way out of her chair and then stood up and confronted her mother. "You haven't taken it, have you?" she asked, and then answered herself. "Sorry, Mum. I know you wouldn't do anything like that."

"And what if I have?" Maiguru asked.

"But you wouldn't, would you? Not without telling me, would you?" asked Nyasha in consternation. Maiguru looked so unhappy you could not blame Nyasha for thinking her mother had taken her book. "But, Mum! How could you? Without even telling me. That's—that's—I mean, you shouldn't—you've no *right* to—"

"Er, Nyasha," said Babamukuru to his food, "I don't want to hear you talk to your mother like that."

"But, Dad," persisted the daughter incautiously, "I'd expect, really, I'd expect—"

"*I* expect you to do as *I* say. Now sit down and eat your food."

Sulkily Nyasha sat down and took a couple of mouthfuls. "Excuse me," she said. She rose from the table, her food unfinished.

"Now where are you going?" Babamukuru demanded.

"To my bedroom," replied Nyasha.

"What did you say?" cried Babamukuru, his voice cracking in disbelief. "Didn't you hear me tell you I don't want to hear you answer back? Didn't you hear me tell you that just now? Now sit down and eat that food. All of it. I want to see you eat all of it."

"I've had enough," explained Nyasha. "Really, I'm full." Her foot began to tap. Instead of sitting down she walked out of the dining-room.

Babamukuru started after her, which made it necessary for Maiguru to restrain him. "Don't take her seriously, Babawa Chido. She's over-excited because Tambudzai is here," soothed the wife.

"I don't know what's wrong with her," muttered the father, allowing himself to be pacified. "But there's something wrong with her, something very wrong. A good child doesn't behave like that. I tell you, Ma'Chido, sometimes I don't sleep, thinking about the way that daughter of mine has turned out."

"She was asking about her book," smiled my aunt sweetly. "After all, you did take it, and so she was asking."

Perhaps Maiguru thought Babamukuru had calmed down enough to be able to be objective about the matter. Perhaps she was fed up with taking the blame for my uncle's actions. I don't know, nor did I want to find out. Shovelling the last morsel of *sadza* into my mouth, I thanked my aunt for the meal and retreated.

"Will you come with me?" asked Nyasha as I walked into the bedroom.

"Where to?"

"To smoke a cigarette."

"You smoke cigarettes!" I was aghast. Babamukuru was right! His daughter was beyond redemption.

"Yes," said Nyasha, trying to be cool in spite of her seething anger and succeeding in sounding strained. "I need to relax with all the hysteria in this house. You don't have to smoke," she assured me, "but I'd like some company. Really, I would."

I tried to change the subject, hoping that the cigarette she had fished out of her bookbag would disappear, or that at the very least she would put it back in the bookbag and tell me she was carrying them for somebody else. I was terrified that Babamukuru would come in and catch her holding it. It would be too much for him after what had gone on at the table. Either he would kill her or the shock would kill him.

"I want to read a book," I said, even speaking English in my effort to distract her. "I enjoy reading books," I continued, wondering what else could be said to divert her.

"Read whatever you like," Nyasha said, waving generously at the bookshelf. Dropping the cigarette and a box of matches into her bra, she left me alone in the bedroom.

I was not alone for long. Anna came, knocked, entered and knelt. "You are wanted, Sisi Tambu," she said, "in the living-room."

It was strange the way she had begun to call me "Sisi," because she was older than I and so did not need to call me that; nor had she done so when she came home for Nhamo's funeral or when I arrived, a matter of a few hours ago. Not that it was important in itself. After all, Maiguru called me "Sisi," affectionately and companionably, so Anna might have picked it up from her. It only became important when you considered it with all the other strange ways she was adopting, of kneeling down to talk to me and not looking at me as she talked but at a spot on the floor a few inches in front of me. The worst thing was that she hardly talked at all, said no more than the few words necessary to convey her message. You have met Anna as she was before she began to behave like this, and I think you will agree with me that nothing on earth could have changed her so quickly into a quiet, reserved person. The change then had to do with me. It was very sobering to think that my change of address had changed me into a person Anna could not talk to. It was disconcerting too, because I was aware only of the change of address. The self I expected to find on the mission would take some time to appear. Besides, it was not to be such a radical transformation that people would have to behave differently towards me. It was to be an extension and improvement of what I really was. Anna's behaviour made me feel uncomfortably strange and unfamiliar with myself, so I spoke roughly to her.

"Why are you kneeling? Just to talk to me?" I asked, but she had already risen and left without answering.

So, I was wanted in the living-room! I had expected to be called. Anna's behaviour would have worried me more if there had been time to think about it, but this summons was too important to allow time for brooding. Important because Babamukuru and Maiguru would now formally welcome me into their home; formally disinter me, my mind and my body, from the village.

"Sit down, my child," invited Babamukuru cordially as I tiptoed into the living-room. Actually, I walked in normally, placing my whole foot on the floor, but it felt like tiptoeing, so respectful was my gait. "On the seat, my child, on the seat," he added, as I sank humbly to the carpet in the corner next to the doorway through which I had entered.

I stood up, but hesitated, not knowing where to sit. It was a complex problem. Babamukuru was sitting in his armchair, the one that faced the fireplace, while Maiguru sat at one end of the sofa. There was room on the sofa between Maiguru and Babamukuru's chair, as well as an unoccupied armchair beside Babamukuru, but I could not take those seats since it would not do to sit so disrespectfully close to my uncle. There was no alternative but to sit in the only other vacant seat in the room, an armchair across from both Baba and Maiguru which placed the three of us as far away from each other as was possible in that room. Having sat down in that chair I began to wonder whether it would have been more appropriate in this English place to sit closer to my uncle and aunt. I debated seriously, agonisingly, for at least two minutes, whether to change my seat to the sofa or not. This did not help, because I found that the advantages and disadvantages of transferring myself were about equally matched. To resolve the matter I decided that the issue was not really important since my uncle had not commented on where I was sitting. I told myself that I had been making a fuss about nothing, sternly pointed out to myself that I had been doing it all afternoon: the dogs, the bell, Nyasha's cigarette— everything had made me jump. Even Anna's metamorphosis had been unnerving when I should simply have talked normally to her and have put a stop to it. In this rational way I vanquished the alien feelings. I settled more comfortably in my chair.

All this thinking took quite a long time and a great deal of concentration, so I missed the first part of my uncle's speech. By the time my attention was free to focus on him, he had said many things. But Babamukuru liked to address, to expound, to impress points upon people. Fortunately, this meant that I had not been required to say anything.

". . . as you will see for yourself," he was saying when I began to attend, "I do not often find time to sit at home like this in the evening. Most of the time I am at my office, working. There is a lot of work that needs my attention, especially now, at the beginning of the school year," he informed me, while Maiguru made soft, assenting noises at the back of her throat. "Er, be that as it may," continued my uncle, "I felt it necessary, as your father, to take some time off from my work to speak to you as a father should speak to a child."

Babamukuru was always impressive when he made these speeches of his. He was a rigid, imposing perfectionist, steely enough in character to function in the puritanical way that he expected, or rather insisted, that the rest of the world should function. Luckily, or maybe unluckily for him, throughout his life Babamukuru had found himself—as eldest child and son, as an early educated African, as headmaster, as husband and father, as provider to many—in positions that enabled him to organise his immediate world and its contents as he wished. Even when this was not the case, as when he went to the mission as a young boy, the end result of such periods of submission was greater power than before. Thus he had been insulated from the necessity of considering alternatives unless they were his own. Stoically he accepted his divinity. Filled with awe, we accepted it too. We used to marvel at how benevolent that divinity was. Babamukuru was good. We all agreed on this. More significantly still, Babamukuru was right. This was why my heart swelled with gratitude as he impressed upon me the great extent of the sacrifice he had made in leaving his work to fetch me from the homestead that afternoon, impressing upon me particularly that the work he had left to fetch me was the work that paid my school fees and bought the food that I was to eat in his house.

"I do not often leave my office in the afternoon," he concluded, turning to Maiguru, who had been silent for some time, sitting with her arms folded and staring detachedly into invisible distances. "Isn't that so, Mai?"

"It is very true," my aunt replied. "You should try to work as hard as your uncle," she told me. "He works; he never stops. It is even difficult for him to find time to take me to town for the groceries."

"It is as your aunt there says," agreed Babamukuru modestly. "But that is not what we called you here to talk about."

As it turned out, Babamukuru had summoned me to make sure that I knew how lucky I was to have been given this opportunity for mental and eventually, through it, material emancipation. He pointed out that the blessing I had received was not an individual blessing but one that extended to all members of my less fortunate family, who would be able to depend on me in the future as they were now depending on him. Lastly, he explained, at the mission I would not only go to school but learn ways and habits that would make my parents proud of me. I was an intelligent girl but I had also to develop into a good woman, he said, stressing both qualities equally and not seeing any contradiction in this.

"It is necessary," he told me, "because there is nothing that pleases parents more than to see their own children settled in their own families. I know these things are very far away, but it is never too early to begin to plan for your future." Here he digressed to tell me how he had begun to plan for his own future at the age of nine, the story I had heard so often from my grandmother. He concluded by defining for me my immediate tasks: "to be good, to listen to what we, your parents, tell you to do, to study your books diligently and not let your mind be distracted by other things. That is all I have to say to you." Turning to my aunt, he asked her whether there was anything he had left out that ought to have been said. She said there was not. Babamukuru dismissed me and prepared to return to his office.

As I left the room Chido came in, greeted us all pleasantly and explained to his parents that he had been detained at the Bakers' house waiting for Mr. Baker, who was late home, so that they could organise the following day's journey back to school. "I hope Nyasha's made my cake," he ended. Maiguru assured him that Nyasha had. "Good," he said. "Because you never know with Nyasha."

I entered our bedroom vowing earnestly that I would be like Babamukuru: straight as an arrow, as steely and true.

"Switch the light off when you've finished, Tambu," Nyasha told me sleepily. She was in the mood for bedtime talk, telling me that she could not sleep with the light on but had left it on for me so that I would not bump my toe against a bed-leg or some other piece of furniture in the unfamiliar room. I was not impressed with her light-induced insomnia, which I thought was only to be expected in a person as frivolous and shallow as my Anglicised cousin. Nor was I impressed with her consideration for me, steeped as I was in the greater virtue that I believed was mine; a virtue which her behaviour had instigated and which Babamukuru's homily had nourished. I pulled off my dress and jumped into bed in silence.

"What about the light?" Nyasha reminded me.

What about the light? Where was the switch and how did you work it? Should I admit my ignorance to Nyasha, to whom I was feeling so superior, or should I ignore her? It was good to be feeling superior for a change, for the first time since I entered my uncle's house, so I ignored my cousin. Nyasha climbed out of bed, advising me to make an effort to stop being a peasant, which distressed me no end. I knew what the word meant because we had come across it one day in a poem in an English lesson and our teacher had explained that a peasant was a land-fowl which looked something like a guinea fowl. Nyasha must have been very annoyed, I thought, to be so rude and I was on the verge of apologising and confessing my ignorance, but stopped myself by remembering that she was always rude, if not to me then to her parents. I decided she expected too much of people so I kept quiet. I would have liked to have turned to the wall to emphasise my disapproval, but since I could not confess my ignorance about the lights, I had to watch Nyasha closely.

Nyasha was perceptive. I had admired this about her when we talked earlier that evening, but now it annoyed me, made me feel silly.

"This is it," she said, pointing to a black patch in the wall beside the door. "It's down now, which means it's on. It's off when it's up." She switched the light off and on again to demonstrate.

"Switch it off," I told her nastily, "otherwise you won't sleep."

She switched the light off and climbed back into bed. Typically she had the last word: "You haven't put your bedclothes on. You'll have to do it in the dark."

I did not ask what bedclothes were since we were quarrelling. Instead the smug determination that Babamukuru's talk had instilled in me evaporated. I began to feel inferior again. I was a bit masochistic at that age, wallowing in my imagined inadequacy until I was in real danger of feeling sorry for myself. Then I reprimanded myself for this self-indulgence by thinking of my mother, who suffered from being female and poor and uneducated and black so stoically that I was ashamed of my weakness in succumbing so flabbily to the strangeness of my new circumstances. This gave me the fine lash of guilt to whip myself on with. I reaffirmed my vow to use the opportunity my uncle had given me to maximum advantage.

A lot of my reactions were of this complicated kind in those days, requiring a lot of thought to sort them out into organised parts. But the activity and excitement of that day's events had exhausted me: I fell asleep before I could order my thoughts neatly. I think this is why I dreamt of my brother.

He was laughing at me as usual. Dribbling a ball gracefully through maize plants that had sprung up in the football field of our old school, he paused from time to time to pick a fat, juicy cob and stuff it into his mouth. The cobs were full of white gravy. From my desk in my class at the mission, which happened to be at the top of the maize field, I saw him eat and became alarmed that he would make himself ill with the strange mealies. In one graceful leap I bounded to his side to beg him to stop, but he laughed in my face and told me that no one would take me seriously because I was smoking a cigarette. The dream became a nightmare when I realised that my fountain pen was in fact a long smoking cigarette. Nhamo howled with vicious glee, telling me that I would come to a bad end, that I deserved it for deserting my husband, my children, my garden and my chickens. He spoke with such authority that I was ashamed of deserting this family that I did not have. So when my husband appeared at the bottom of the field I was not surprised, only terrified, to see that it was Babamukuru and his two ferocious dogs tracking me down to return me to my spouse. Then I remembered that I was at school and began to explain this to Babamukuru, but Maiguru interrupted to say I should wash first. I was half-way to the bathroom before I realised that I had woken up.

The joy of that bath! Steaming hot water filled the tub to the brim until I was forced reluctantly to turn the taps off so that the water would not overflow when I stepped in. I washed and scrubbed and rubbed, soaping myself three times over, not because I thought I was that dirty but simply because it felt so enjoyably warm and wet and clean. Splash, splash, I went and water slopped out on to the blue lino. Maiguru knocked to find out whether I was all right and I remembered that other people needed to wash. Jumping out, I pulled the plug out and was pleased with myself for having managed my first bath without being taught. Then I looked around and found under the sink some old rags that I used to clean the bath and mop the floor.

Feeling clean and warm and expansive, I ran Nyasha's bath. She thanked me most graciously for this favour, and so we were able to stop quarrelling. All the same, I did not feel up to confessing that I had not known what bedclothes were, but it did not matter. Observing what Nyasha was wearing I found something similar in my suitcase. These, then, were the bedclothes. I made my bed, folding the bedclothes neatly at its foot.

When I was dressed I admired myself in the mirror. I looked better in that uniform than I had ever looked before, even though it was blue (which I now know does not suit my complexion) and had angular four-inch pleats down the front. It was a shock to see that in fact I was pretty, and also difficult to believe, making it necessary for me to scrutinise myself for a long time, from all angles and in many different positions, to verify the suspicion. Nyasha, returning from her bath, caught me at it and did not allow me to be embarrassed. Generously, sincerely, she confirmed my own impressions.

"Not bad," she agreed, standing beside me to

observe my reflection. "Not bad at all. You've got a waist. One of these days you'll have a bust. Pity about the backside," she continued, slapping it playfully as she turned away. "It's rather large. Still, if you can look good in that old gym-dress, you'll look good in anything."

I was flattered by everything she said and did, the examination, the approval, the teasing. Any attention from Nyasha, who did not often attend to things other than the excursions and forays of her unpeaceful mind, was enough to make me tingle with pleasure. I came close to being infatuated with myself. Thinking back to my maize field, I was convinced for a moment that my present propitious circumstances were entirely of my own making.

At breakfast the food would not go down. My throat constricted more tightly with each mouthful I tried to swallow, so impatient was I to be at school, where I was sure I would breeze through the whole syllabus in a single morning. It was nerve-wracking. Watching Nyasha work her way daintily through egg and bacon and tea, having declined the porridge and toast because too much food would make her fat, I saw myself walking into the classroom late and conspicuous on my first day. But the siren did not wail and while Nyasha ate I found time to be impressed by these relatives of mine who ate meat, and not only meat but meat and eggs for breakfast. As for roasting bread before you ate it, as if it had not already been baked, well, yesterday I would have been surprised, but today I was aware that all things were possible.

Maiguru fussed around me, clucking concern over my lack of appetite.

"Eat, my child, eat," she urged. "Otherwise you'll be so famished you won't hear a word the teacher says. What do you like to eat?" she asked. "Shall we find you *rukweza* for your porridge?"

"I'm glad I'm only your daughter," observed Nyasha. "You'd easily kill your nieces with kindness."

"But she'll get hungry!" fluttered my aunt.

"She's probably dieting because I told her her bottom is fat."

"Go on with you, lovey-dove! Sisi Tambu isn't fat. Don't worry about Nyasha's little ways," she advised me unnecessarily, because at that moment I had no intention of worrying about anything except school, especially things that did not make sense.

"Little ways," commented Nyasha. "Little ways. Now, I wonder. Who's got little ways?"

"You'll be late, honey-bunch, if you don't hurry," Maiguru told her, rummaging in her bag for a shilling to give me so that I could buy buns at break-time to carry me through until lunch. A shilling was a lot of money in those days. It could buy a loaf of bread which was enough food for a whole family's breakfast. So much money for buns at break embarrassed me. I wanted to return it, but Nyasha drained her cup, taking a long time over it to hide a smile, and that made it impossible for me to embarrass my aunt by declining her gift. Slipping the coin into my sock, I thanked Maiguru and assured her that I was so full from last night's meal that I would bring the entire amount home with me at lunchtime.

Nyasha finished her breakfast. We set off for school, dressed in identical blue gym-slips, socks and shoes, carrying identical briefcases. To look at us you would have thought we were sisters, which is how I would have arranged matters had I been consulted. I strutted along beside my thoroughbred cousin, imitating her walk and the set of her head so that everyone would see that we were a unit.

Thus began the period of my reincarnation. I liked to think of my transfer to the mission as my reincarnation. With the egotistical faith of fourteen short years, during which my life had progressed very much according to plan, I expected this era to be significantly profound and broadening in terms of adding wisdom to my nature, clarity to my vision, glamour to my person. In short, I expected my sojourn to fulfil all my fourteen-year-old fantasies, and on the whole I was not disappointed. Freed from the constraints of the necessary and the squalid that defined and delimited our activity at home, I invested a lot of robust energy in approximating to my idea of a young woman of the world. I was clean now, not only on special occasions but every day of the week. I was meeting, outside myself, many things that I had thought about ambiguously; things that I had always known existed in other worlds although the knowledge was vague; things that had made my mother wonder whether I was quite myself, or whether I was carrying some other presence in me.

It was good to be validated in this way. Most of it did not come from the lessons they taught at school but from Nyasha's various and extensive library. I read everything from Enid Blyton to the Brontë sisters, and responded to them all. Plunging into these books I knew I was being educated and I was filled with gratitude to the authors for introducing me to places where reason and inclination were not at odds. It was a centripetal time, with me at the centre, everything gravitating towards me. It was a time of sublimation with me as the sublimate.

When I tried to describe to Nyasha a little of what was happening in my world, she laughed and said I was reading too many fairy-tales. She preferred reality. She was going through a historical phase. She read a lot of books that were about real people, real peoples and their sufferings: the condition in South Africa, which she asked Maiguru to compare with our own situation and ended up arguing with her when

Maiguru said we were better off. She read about Arabs on the east coast and the British on the west; about Nazis and Japanese and Hiroshima and Nagasaki. She had nightmares about these things, the atrocities; but she carried on reading all the same, because, she said, you had to know the facts if you were ever going to find the solutions. She was certain the solutions were there. She wanted to know many things: whether the Jews' claim to Palestine was valid, whether monarchy was a just form of government, the nature of life and relations before colonisation, exactly why UDI was declared and what it meant. "So," she advised, concerning my fairy-tales and my reincarnation, "enjoy it while you can. These things don't last." And she helped me to enjoy my heady transition by pointing out which books were worth reading (although I did not always agree with her, because her tastes had grown serious), by straightening my hair and putting ribbons in it at weekends; by filing my nails and sometimes painting them bright purple in spite of Babamukuru's frowns; by cooking with me heavily spiced dishes out of Maiguru's recipe books which Babamukuru and I did not like but which she and Maiguru tucked into with relish.

Not only was I succeeding in my own context, but in other people's as well. I had not been going to school long before I realised that Nyasha did not have many friends. The girls did not like the way she spoke. They were still imitating her behind her back when I went to the mission, which was three years after Babamukuru's return. And if I thought that Nyasha ought to have lost more of her accent in that time than she had allowed herself to, I also thought that her classmates had had long enough to grow used to it. As it turned out, it was not Nyasha's accent they disliked, but Nyasha herself. "She thinks she is white," they used to sneer, and that was as bad as a curse. "She is proud," pronounced others. "She is loose," the most vicious condemned her. "The way she dresses for the Saturday night dances! And the way she was acting with George [or Johnson or Mathias or Chengetai]! It's obvious. It shows for everyone to see." After that there would be a discussion about what Nyasha had or had not actually been doing on the dance-floor and the talk would end with someone voicing the general opinion that she could get away with anything because she was the headmaster's daughter.

I was lucky not to have been endowed with any of these vices. My English soon became fluent from all the reading I was doing and from talking to Nyasha all the time, but I spoke without an accent. I was not the headmaster's daughter but a poor relative whose background was as needy as anybody else's, if not more so. As far as boys were concerned, I was obviously uninterested. No matter how persuasively Nyasha pleaded, she could not often induce me to go to a Record Night at the Beit Hall. Maybe I am being unfair when I hint that Nyasha did not want my company for its own sake, but at the time I was convinced I would be more of an embarrassment to her than an asset since I did not jive in those days, partly because I did not like the western beat they played in the Beit Hall and had never learnt to move gracefully to it, and partly because I had come to the mission for more solemn reasons than dancing. Nevertheless, Nyasha was always urging me to go with her and in the end told me frankly that while Babamukuru could not forbid her going because the dances were a school activity from which it would not be appropriate to debar his daughter, he believed them to be sinful all the same. She wanted to present a united youthful front that took the position that they were not. But I would bury my nose in *The Wind in the Willows* and tell her that I could not dance.

Even the teachers liked me. They were always asking me to keep order when they had to leave the classroom, always citing my diligence as an example to the rest of the class. In spite of this my classmates elected me class monitor at the beginning of the third term. It was surprising, surprising and strange. Nyasha, my teachers, my classmates—I was not used to being so warmly liked. The only thing that was not strange in those days was that I continued to be one of the best students in my class. The standard at the mission was higher than at Rutivi School and we had tests often, but I performed better there than I had done at home because Baba and Maiguru knew that my school work was important and did not disturb me when I was studying. I could not help being pleased with myself and with the way things were turning out, but it was a wholesome pleasure in living that people could respond to positively, so no one took offence. Generally people were pleased with me too.

As my body and mind relaxed and Maiguru tended me solicitously like a mother bird, ever ready to drop tasty morsels into my mouth, I grew quite plump. I began to menstruate. I was very calm about it in the beginning. Conferences with older cousins and younger aunts, and the questions of older aunts and grandmothers had prepared me for the event. So when, during my first vacation home, my mother gave me some old napkins of Rambanai's which had been a congratulatory present from Maiguru, and instructed me to keep the napkins and myself particularly clean at that time of the month, I took them matter-of-factly and waited for them to become a necessary part of my hygiene. The onset of my menses, then, should have been placid, but when it came to washing those rags in Maiguru's white bathroom, to making a mess in the toilet bowl before I flushed it away, the business became nasty and nauseating. I became morose and moody about it.

In the end Nyasha offered me some tampons, and I died of embarrassment because I had thought I was being discreet. Still, Nyasha was concerned for my comfort, so she gave me a box of tampons with the instructions to read. Those instructions, with their curvaceous line-drawings, were intriguing because we had not studied human reproduction at school. Did it really look like that inside? I examined a tampon, from the outside only without removing the wrapper because I did not want to waste one, and considered aloud the consequences of pushing the offensively shaped object into my vagina, but Nyasha laughed at me and teased me. She said I was better off losing my virginity to a tampon, which wouldn't gloat over its achievement, than to a man, who would add mine to his hoard of hymens: "They wear them around their waists, like scalps," she teased. After that it took her a long time to convince me that she had been pulling my leg, but when finally she did and I nervously inserted a tampon with minimum discomfort, I was glad she had introduced me to them. There was a problem though: tampons were expensive. Nyasha reassured me again. Although Maiguru knew that tampons were offensive, that nice girls did not use them, she would be pleased enough to know that we were not pregnant to be persuaded to provide. She chuckled. "No, really," she conceded. "Mum's quite sensible underneath all the feathers." That cousin of mine! Shocking and funny; disrespectful and irrepressible. I was no longer wary now that I knew who she was. I thought she was wise too, although I was not sure why. I admired her abundance of spirit even though I could not see where it was directed: Nyasha had everything, should have been placid and content. My cousin was perplexing. She was not something you could dissect with reason.

Nyasha thought she was very reasonable. "You

have to keep moving," she said. "Getting involved in this and that, finding out one thing and another. Moving, all the time. Otherwise you get trapped. Look at poor Mum. Can you imagine anything worse? If it weren't for Chido she'd go stark raving crazy!" I could imagine many things worse than being Maiguru, did not have to imagine them because I had seen them. I told Nyasha so, and she agreed with me but said it was all relative and that it all boiled down to the same thing, although she was not terribly clear what that thing was. She gave me one of her sidelong looks that said a lot but told me nothing, and we left it at that. All the same, I could not help wondering what my cousin had seen that I had not.

This was the way Nyasha was, persistently seeing and drawing attention to things you would rather not talk about; shredding to bits with her sharp wit the things she thought we could do without, even if everybody else thought they were important. People like me thought she was odd and rather superior in intangible ways. Peripheral adults like her teachers thought she was a genius and encouraged this aspect of her. But her mother and father were worried about her development. I did not think that her probing of this and that and everything was good for her either. I thought it was not safe, but when I thought it over seriously and methodically I remembered some of the inconsistencies I had forgotten in the first flush of excitement of life on the mission.

There was, for example, Anna, who had been someone to talk to, to spend time with, to relax with when I arrived in January, but who now was merely boring. It hadn't been strange as it happened. In fact it had all followed neatly, step by step, a natural progression. The result was that I had stopped thinking of Anna as a friend and companion in spite of having preferred, on that first day, the thought of sharing a bed with her in the tired-looking sheds that were the servants' quarters than sharing a bedroom with Nyasha. Thinking these thoughts I almost felt sorry for Anna. But then I remembered that she had anticipated me.

Maiguru, always smiling, always happy, was another puzzle. True, she had good reason to be content. She was Babamukuru's wife. She lived in a comfortable home and was a teacher. Unlike her daughter, she was grateful for all these blessings, but I thought even the saints in heaven must grow disgruntled sometimes and let the lesser angels know. I thought Maiguru deserved to be beatified. She was occasionally upset but never angry. She might be disappointed at times but she was never discouraged. I was concerned that she did not have many people to talk to, but I supposed it was the consequence of her being so educated since none of the other married women at the mission with whom she might have been friendly had degrees, not even a Bachelor of Arts, let alone a Master of Philosophy like my aunt did.

I was astonished the day I found out how highly educated my aunt was. It was on a Sunday. We went to church as we usually did. All of us went to church on Sunday, even Nyasha, and Anna too on the days that she managed to finish the washing-up on time, which depended on whether she was feeling devout or whether she wanted to sit by herself for an hour or two with no one to question her. Nyasha went because she was at a devout stage of development: she liked having causes and the Christian cause, which was conformist but could clandestinely be translated into a progressive ideology, was ideal for her. In addition she enjoyed the singing. She had been a committed member of the school choir until they omitted to take her on a trip because it would not have done for the headmaster's daughter to see the choirmasters enjoying themselves.

What actually happened on Sunday was that at a quarter to nine Nyasha and I set off, wearing our blue gym-slips, to our Bible lessons. Sunday School for me was conducted in the classroom in the Central Primary School, each grade of the central school being taught by a prefect from the secondary school. These prefects wore black skirts and white blouses on Sundays if they were female, long black trousers with white shirts if they were not. They were very smart and beautiful people; we dreamt of becoming one of them. When a male prefect was dashing enough to wear a tie, our blood pressures soared although we were healthy little adolescent girls, and I suppose the female prefects who dared to wear stockings instead of socks, perhaps even seamed ones, had the same effect on the boys in our class.

In Sunday School we learnt about Charity and Love and Sin, which the prefects said were all different things, but then, if they were different, I wondered, how did you explain the Prodigal Son, or Mary Magdalene? The hymns were less confusing. They were about respecting our parents to increase our days and rolling our burdens away. That pragmatic and uninspired approach to life was something I understood well. Then, at a quarter to ten, the siren sounded from the secondary school, signifying the end of our Bible period. We lined up in front of our classrooms in two lines, a khaki line of boys against the wall, the girls' blue beside them. We filed quickly but quietly across the green through corridors of stern prefects who kept order and took their duties seriously. The senior classes followed on behind the junior classes so that by ten o'clock the whole school was assembled outside the church. Sometimes we were inspected as we stood outside the church for missing buttons, dirty collars and socks, indecently long and coloured fingernails or lipstick, and sometimes we were not; but we always began to file into church at a quarter past. The service began at half past. From the minute the siren sounded at a quarter to ten until the service ended between half past twelve and one o'clock we kept silence. After the service we filed out again and the boarding pupils hurried to their boarding houses to be in time for lunch.

When the boarders had gone I would meet up with Nyasha. We would stand outside the church greeting friends, exchanging gossip and, if it was during the school holidays so we did not have to wear school uniform, eyeing and coveting each other's dresses.

Nyasha liked to avoid her parents and their friends at these times because they were bound to say something offensive, like complaining that her gym-slip was too short or grumbling that in three years she had still not learnt the correct way of greeting her elders. Their comments made her self-conscious, quite in contrast to the desired improving effect. So Nyasha avoided them, or when this was impossible, grunted a greeting with a sad lack of technique and escaped as quickly as possible. Her behaviour embarrassed Babamukuru, so he too preferred that she should keep her distance.

I, on the other hand, wanted to stand outside the church with my aunt and uncle. I wanted to be known to be of their kind because I thought the atmosphere of the homestead clung to me and made me look different. But after a few weeks of waiting with them while they discussed with the pastor the state of subscriptions and the decline in collection takings, I grew bored and preferred to be with Nyasha and my friends. The test came on the days when Babamukuru, feeling particularly benevolent, drove Maiguru to church in the old Rover, and, if we presented ourselves at the right time, drove us all home again afterwards. Nyasha thought we should be consistent and avoid them even when they were driving. But I still loved my car-rides and argued pragmatically that we avoided them when it suited us but, since a car-ride suited us, we should not avoid them on such occasions. Nyasha conceded the logic but not the premise of this argument, pointing out that she for one preferred to walk, but she indulged me all the same and we had our car-rides.

On one such occasion Nyasha and I stood waiting for Baba and Maiguru while they talked to my headmaster. The headmaster, seeing us standing there, naturally began to talk about us. This made Nyasha indignant, because she did not like being referred to in the third person in her presence: she said it made her feel like an object. I did not mind, because he was being very complimentary.

"Sure, Mr. Sigauke," he beamed at Babamukuru, "you must be very happy with your daughters. Nyasha was always coming first in the Central Primary School and I hear she is keeping it up there in the secondary. She wants to bring us a Master's Degree, just like her mother. And Tambudzai, that one takes after her uncle. She works so hard, all the time."

All three of them were pleasantly impressed by this speech and with themselves. The headmaster was pleased because Babamukuru assured him that our prowess was the result of his diligence as headmaster of the primary school; Baba and Maiguru were pleased because our ability reflected their own and indicated that they had strong genes. They smiled and laughingly disclaimed, and insisted and congratulated each other on these achievements over and over again.

The process was mellowing. "Nyasha," called Babamukuru, "aren't you going to greet your old headmaster who used to teach you? He did a good job, he did a good job," he repeated smiling. Nyasha approached warily; I followed. The smile faded from Babamukuru's face. "What's the matter, you? Don't you hear the nice things Mr. Satombo is saying?"

We did not have a comfortable ride home that afternoon because Babamukuru made it very clear to Nyasha, at angry length, that she should not expect to ride in his car if she could not be polite to his colleagues. "What will people say of me when my daughter behaves like that?" he demanded. Nyasha remained silent. The bad feeling sat down with us at the dinner table. Nyasha had forgotten it, or was ignoring it. She had been impressed by the fervour of the sermon but questioned Maiguru on a technical point: it was all very well to render unto Caesar what was his, but who was to say what was Caesar's? Caesar. Then everything would be his! As always, I was impressed by her mental agility, but Babamukuru was irritated by it.

"Er, Nyasha," he said, "there are some matters I want to discuss with your mother. Don't you know it's not good for a child to be talking all the time?" I was disappointed, because I had been wanting to ask Maiguru whether she really had obtained a Master's Degree, but after that I did not dare. Nyasha did not say another word, nor did she eat much, excusing herself soon afterwards. I was afraid that my uncle would insist that she finish her food, but besides pointed glances at her half-full plate, neither Baba nor Maiguru commented.

"Is it true, Maiguru?" I asked later that afternoon when I went to the verandah to read and found my aunt marking her books there. "Do you really have a Master's Degree?"

Maiguru was flattered. "Didn't you know?" she smiled at me over the top of her glasses. How could I have known? No one had ever mentioned it to me.

"But Maiguru," I answered immediately, emboldened by the thought of my aunt obtaining a Master's Degree, "did you ever say?"

"Did you ever ask?" she countered, and continued, "yes, we both studied, your uncle and I, in South Africa for our Bachelor's Degrees and in England for our Master's."

"I thought you went to look after Babamukuru," I said. "That's all people ever say."

Maiguru snorted. "And what do you expect? Why should a woman go all that way and put up with all those problems if not to look after her husband?"

Maiguru was more serious than she had ever been before. Her seriousness changed her from a sweet, soft dove to something more like a wasp. "That's what they like to think I did," she continued sourly. The lower half of her face, and only the lower half, because it did not quite reach the eyes, set itself into sullen lines of discontent. She bent over her books to hide them, and to prove that she was not unhappy at all she made a chuckling sound. I think she thought gaily but sounded pained. "Whatever they thought," she said, "much good did it do them! I still studied for that degree and got it in spite of all of them—your uncle, your grandparents and the rest of your family. Can you tell me now that they aren't pleased that I did, even if they don't admit it? No! Your uncle wouldn't be able to do half the things he does if I didn't work as well!"

"You must earn a lot of money," I breathed in awe. My aunt laughed and said she never received her salary. I was aghast.

"What happens to your money?" I asked. "The money that you earn. Does the Government take it?" For I was beginning to understand that our Government was not a good one.

"You could say that," my aunt laughed, forcing herself to be merry again but not succeeding. She gave up, took off her glasses and leaned back in her seat, staring wistfully through the verandah's arches to the mountains and beyond. "What it is," she sighed, "to have to choose between self and security. When I was in England I glimpsed for a little while the things I could have been, the things I could have done if—if—if things were—different—But there was Babawa Chido and the children and the family. And does anyone realise, does anyone appreciate, what sacrifices were made? As for me, no one even thinks about the things I gave up." She collected herself. "But that's how it goes, Sisi Tambu! And when you have a good man and lovely children, it makes it all worth while."

Personally, I thought it was a great shame that Maiguru had been deprived of the opportunity to make the most of herself, even if she had accepted that deprivation. I was all for people being given opportunities.

I did not tell Nyasha about this conversation because I guessed she had heard it herself many times and would say irritatingly, "I told you so." Besides, the things Maiguru had talked of were reasonable; they did not mean she was always complaining. I felt sorry for Maiguru because she could not use the money she earned for her own purposes and had been prevented by marriage from doing the things she wanted to do. But it was not so simple, because she had been married by my Babamukuru, which defined her situation as good. If it was necessary to efface yourself, as Maiguru did so well that you couldn't be sure that she didn't enjoy it, if it was necessary to efface yourself in order to preserve his sense of identity and value, then, I was sure, Maiguru had taken the correct decisions.

My uncle's identity was elusive. At first I was disappointed when I came to the mission. I had thought it would be like the good old days, the days before England, with Babamukuru throwing us into the air and catching us and giving us sweets, metaphorically speaking, but I hardly ever saw him, because he was so busy. We hardly ever laughed when Babamukuru was within earshot, because, Maiguru said, his nerves were bad. His nerves were bad because he was so busy. For the same reason we did not talk much when he was around either.

Nyasha's exuberant nature suffered under these chilly conditions and even Maiguru sometimes observed, "I do waste a lot of time cooking. You know, cooking food that isn't eaten." "Then stop cooking," Nyasha would snap. Or else Maiguru would apologise at table for not having bought us cream to go with our jelly. "I tried to find some," she would flutter, "but we got there so late everything was gone. As usual!" Nyasha would not compromise. She told Maiguru to learn how to drive. "And where do you think I would get the car from?" her mother retorted. "Do you think I can afford to buy one?"

Chapter 6

Another thing that was different about the mission was that there were many white people there. The Whites on the mission were a special kind of white person, special in the way that my grandmother had explained to me, for they were holy. They had come not to take but to give. They were about God's business here in darkest Africa. They had given up the comforts and security of their own homes to come and lighten our darkness. It was a big sacrifice that the missionaries made. It was a sacrifice that made us grateful to them, a sacrifice that made them superior not only to us but to those other Whites as well who were here for adventure and to help themselves to our emeralds. The missionaries' self-denial and brotherly love did not go unrewarded. We treated them like minor deities. With the self-satisfied dignity that came naturally to white people in those days, they accepted this improving disguise.

Today there are fewer white people on the mission. They are called expatriates, not missionaries, and can be seen living in unpainted brick houses. But they are deified in the same way as the missionaries were because they are white so that their coming is still an honour. I am told that whether you are called an expatriate or a missionary depends on how and by whom you were recruited. Although the distinction was told to me by a reliable source, it does not stick in my mind since I have not observed it myself in my dealings with these people. I often ask myself why they come, giving up the comforts and security of their more advanced homes. Which brings us back to matters of brotherly love, contribution and lightening of diverse darknesses.

At the time though—and you must remember that I was very young then, very young and correct in my desire to admire and defer to all the superior people I found at the mission—at that time I liked the missionaries. In particular I liked the young ones. They had smooth, healthy, sun-brown skin. This took away most if not all of the repulsion towards white people that had started with the papery-skinned Doris and her sallow, brown-spotted husband. I used to feel very guilty about feeling that way. I used to feel guilty and unnatural for not being able to love the Whites as I ought. So it was good to see the healthy young missionaries and discover that some Whites were as beautiful as we were. After that it did not take long for me to learn that they were in fact more beautiful and then I was able to love them.

Because there were so many Whites on the mission I had a lot to do with them, but their behaviour remained difficult to understand. What I noticed, very early on, was that some of the missionaries were definitely strange, strange in the way that Nyasha and Chido were strange when they came back from England. These missionaries, the strange ones, liked to speak Shona much more than they liked to speak English. And when you, wanting to practise your English, spoke to them in English, they always answered in Shona. It was disappointing, and confusing too for people like me who were bilingual, since we had developed a kind of reflex which made us speak English when we spoke to white skins and reserved our own language for talking to each other. Most of these missionaries' children, the children of the strange ones, did not speak English at all until they learnt it at school, just as we did and in the same classroom as we did, because their parents sent them to school at the mission with the rest of us. I often wondered how they would manage when they went back home and had to stop behaving like Africans.

Not all the missionaries were like this though. The other sort, and this was the majority, were somewhat more normal. They spoke English more freely and sent their children to the Government school in town, where they would be among their own kind. This arrangement must have been less painful for the children, but more so for their parents since these Government schools represented everything that the missionaries were praying against. We used to have debates about it: which was the better missionary—one who sent his child to a Government school or one who sent his child to the mission school?

There was a missionary child of the former, strange sort at our secondary school. Her name was Nyaradzo, which is a beautiful name and, to me, poetic: it has a soothing sound. Nyaradzo was my age, my age and Nyasha's. She and Nyasha were great friends, and if Nyasha did not have many friends, she did at least have this one very good friend. I was allowed to make the duo a trio on the grounds, I suppose, that my normality would not upset the balance.

Nyaradzo had two brothers. One, whose name was Brian, was a year older than Nyaradzo. The other brother, called Andrew, was three years older. I did not see much of these boys, because they went to secondary school, and though they had done their primary schooling on the mission, their parents had sent them to Salisbury for secondary school. You could tell from what Nyaradzo said that it was a very special kind of school that her brothers went to, much like our mission school, where both black and white children could attend if they wished. But on the other hand very different, because there were few black children and many white. It was strange to think of a white people's school which black people could attend if they wanted to, and surprising, therefore, that there were so few black people there. Nyaradzo explained this by telling us that the fees were very high, so high that black children who wanted to go there could only do so if their fathers could afford to send them, or even if they did not want to but their fathers could afford it anyway. Although, to tell the truth, I never met a single black child who did not want to attend one of those schools. Except, of course, Nyasha. Nyasha and I used to discuss it. We agreed that there would be more "life" at one of those schools than there was at the mission, and "life" in the adolescent way we used the word was something beneficial. By life we meant books and games and people and cultural activities, as well as a more abstract atmosphere of vitality that meant that things, exciting, interesting, useful things, were about to happen. In spite of our talks we knew that we would never attend a multiracial school because Babamukuru was already battling to keep Chido at his school, where the fees were so high. Nyasha said that this was a blessing in disguise since, once we got there, the "life" we talked of would overtake us and we would have to fight with the consequences. She was not very explicit about these consequences beyond assuring me that they would follow, and I did not push her because, in spite of the warning, I would still have liked to go to a multiracial school, and I liked the feeling of ambition and aspiration that went with this desire.

Chido went into Standard Six in the year that Babamukuru returned from England. This meant that he was going to secondary school the following year. Babamukuru had intended him to stay on at the mission to counteract the unAfrican exposure he had been subjected to in England, but Mr. Baker, as Nyaradzo's father is called, arranged for Chido to take the entrance examination to his son's school. So determined was this good missionary that Chido should have the best in life that he personally drove my cousin to Salisbury, where the examination was taking place. Not surprisingly, since Whites were indulgent towards promising young black boys in those days, provided that the promise was a peaceful promise, a grateful promise to accept whatever was handed out to them and not to expect more, Chido was offered a place at the school and a scholarship to go with it. Nyasha was sure that Mr. Baker had had a hand in that scholarship. To ease his conscience, she said. "A word with the headmasters" she told me when Nyaradzo was not present. "You know how it is, *bwana* to *bwana*: 'The boy needs the cash, old man!'; 'He's a good boy, what. Pity to waste him. We'll see what we can do.' So Chido gets his scholarship and Mr. Baker feels better about sending his sons there in the first place. Really! The things they get up to to pull the wool over our eyes. Really!" Nyasha's analysis made sense because Babamukuru did not approve of European habits, easy options or unnecessary expenditure. Without the scholarship Chido certainly would not have gone to that school and Mr. Baker would have had his sons' superior education nibbling away at his conscience. The upshot of all this was that Chido did go to this boarding school and by the time I went to the mission he had adapted remarkably well to private-school life. He had acquired the usual courteous, self-indulgent, private-school habits and was firm friends with the Baker boys. As a result I did not see much of him or of the Baker boys, except for a day or two at the beginning or the end of the holidays, because their school ran according to a calendar that was different from the one we used at the mission.

Since Nyasha was in Form Two in that year, my first year at the mission, she was writing her first set of public examinations. Actually, they were her second set, because she had sat her Standard Six examinations, but Nyasha, who had benefited from a head-start programme for gifted children in England, pooh-poohed those Standard Six examinations. Characteristically underrating herself in a way that made her sound big-headed if you did not know her, she said anyone with a normal amount of common sense could pass Standard Six examinations even if they only went to class for one week. The Form Two examinations were different, she said. They required real competence and would determine whether she went to Form Three or was screened out of the school system.

At any rate, that was the theory. But Nyasha, as the headmaster's daughter, did not really have to worry about being screened out of school. She could afford to fail as long as she didn't do it too badly. Even with the vicious competition for the strategically small number of Form Three places the Government gave us, the headmaster would have been able to find a place somewhere for his daughter. And if she did fail dismally, he would probably have been able to use his influence to allow her to repeat the exam. The authorities thought Babamukuru was a good African. And it was generally believed that good Africans bred good African children who also thought about nothing except serving their communities. So Nyasha really didn't have to worry.

Nyasha found a lot to be amused about in that situation. Practising such nepotistic ways of getting advantages would mean that Babamukuru would no longer qualify as good, and though he valued, if not his children, then at least their education, he valued being honourable even more. Maliciously, Nyasha threatened to fail her exams to observe the conflict or, as she put it, to see what her father would do. But everybody except Nyasha knew that fail was one thing she could not do. She was working much harder than I had ever seen her work before, up long before her usual time, so that when breakfast was ready she had been studying in a concentrated state for an hour or more. At night it was the same: by eight o'clock she was curled up in bed with her books, but the light rarely went out before one. Everybody agreed that she was overdoing it. She was looking drawn and had lost so much of her appetite that it showed all over her body in the way the bones crept to the surface, but she did not seem to notice.

Maiguru asked me to talk to her daughter because Nyasha was stubborn and did not take kindly to her mother's concern. "Those loose connections!" smiled Maiguru fondly, rolling her eyes and gesturing so effectively with her hands that it was very easy to see what went on inside Nyasha's head.

When I did mention her overworking to her, Nyasha confessed that she was nervous. "As if there's everything to learn and I'll never know it all. So I have to keep reading and memorising, reading and memorising all the time. To make sure I get it all in." She gave me one of her looks. "I know it's not so desperate, but I keep thinking it is. I can't help it. If I stop for a minute, I get so worried." So I made it a point to talk to her as often as she would let me, to keep her mind off her exams. I know I have said everybody was worried about Nyasha's exam nerves, but in fact it was not everybody. Babamukuru was very impressed by his daughter's industry. "There's hope for her yet," he observed contentedly. "When she makes up her mind to be serious she works very well, yes, very well indeed."

Nyasha did pass, of course, in the first division and with the highest aggregate in the whole school, but we did not know this until the end of the Christmas holidays. I looked forward to that particular holiday more than I usually looked forward to the holidays. Although it was good to go home and be with my mother and look after her for a little while, I always hated leaving the mission and all my friends and Nyasha. But this was the Christmas vacation. Babamukuru and family were coming home and Babamukuru had generously agreed to allow me to stay on at the mission until we all went home for Christmas.

There were lots of good outcomes from this. Not only would I stay at the mission longer and be accompanied by my relatives when I did go home, so that there would be no sad partings, but I would also get the chance to see more of Chido than I had seen until then. Chido was big, athletic and handsome. He knew how to tease you so deliciously that you giggled and felt yourself prickling and blushing, and loved every moment of it. I looked forward to being teased by my cousin and to teasing him back in the tinselly way the other girls did. If only my tongue would not tangle itself up in knots!

Nyasha had finished her exams by the time Mr. Baker brought his sons and Chido home. Her appetite had returned to normal and she was sleeping peacefully for five or six hours a night instead of the three or four hours of fitful rest she had been getting during the exams. She was laughing at herself too, for having made such a fuss, and excusing herself on the basis that it was the first time she had had to do something that mattered; the first time that she had had to do something that had serious consequences. Adding up imaginary marks for each part of each question in each paper, she admitted that she might just have scraped through. It was funny how Nyasha's mood affected the way the rest of us felt. The house had been dismal during that exam period, but we were all feeling much brighter by the time Chido came home.

The weekend of Chido's return was the last week-end of our school term. To celebrate, the student powers organised a "raving" Christmas party at the Beit Hall. The three of us went, Nyasha, Chido and myself, with Nyasha bright-eyed and sparkling for days beforehand because she loved to "rave" and did not often get the chance. On the actual night she was sulking a little because by the time she had finished dressing herself up and making up and was standing impatiently outside the back door waiting for us to come out, Babamukuru did not recognise her. He thought she was someone who had come to look for a place at the school. He could not understand why, if this was the case, she insisted on being his daughter. When finally he was convinced, he disapproved. He wanted to know where his daughter thought she was going dressed up in such an ungodly manner and told her that, whatever she thought, she was in fact going nowhere. Then Maiguru appeared and innocently asked Babamukuru whether he was proud of his fine-looking daughter. "I bought her that dress for working so hard at her exams," Maiguru beamed and contrived to remain beaming while her husband half-heartedly accused her of compromising his daughter's decency. Chido and I did not think it was serious because Nyasha was looking very attractive, and that, we told her, was what Babamukuru was objecting to. We laughed about it and teased her: "It's your fault. What do you expect if you insist on dressing up like that?" "Be careful when you get to the Beit Hall, otherwise the boys will eat you alive." You could see her wondering whether to brood or be gracious. In the end she was gracious and joined in the laughter, which made Chido turn serious and tell her that Babamukuru was right—she should make the most of the little decency she had. Poor Chido! I do believe he felt obliged to carry on the tradition in the normal, unanalytic male fashion, because when we refused to be subdued and laughed at him instead, he reverted to his usual lovable self.

All this gaiety took us down the drive, up the road where the pale *bauhinias* on the verge glimmered like ghosts in the moonlight and on a less merry occasion would have been frightening, all the way to the Beit Hall, where the crash of electric guitars and percussion reproduced on the old music system with very little fidelity made it pointless for us to talk any more. We hurried in to the lights, the music, the people and the dancing.

I have said that I did not often go to those dances. I preferred the debates and film shows, where I could concentrate quietly on what was going on; the dances, with the noise and the moving, mingling, boiling crowds, were taxing. I was not like Nyasha, who could forget where she was so entirely that she could do whatever she fancied and as a result usually did it well. I was always aware of my surroundings. When the surroundings were new and unfamiliar, the awareness was painful and made me behave very strangely. At times like that I wanted so badly to disappear that for practical purposes I ceased to exist. People who caught me in such a state and were unlucky enough to have to talk to me could not get more out of me than an ingratiating grin or a string of banalities that would not pass even as very small small-talk. These conversations were a tough experience both for myself and whoever I was talking to. I do not know how I came to be like that. If you remember, when I was at home before I came to the mission, I could assert myself and tell people what was on my mind. So I suppose that in spite of my success and settling down well, my going to the mission was such a drastic change that it unnerved me. Whatever the case, I had grown very tentative. The dance was going to be an ordeal.

For the first ten minutes I was sure I was going to have an awful time. The sound, when we entered, blasted my whole body from my hair to my toenails. It must have been something to do with the dominant frequencies of that particular song, because it felt like several hundred volts frolicking through my nerve-endings. Distantly, I was aware of Nyaradzo and brothers, all flowing hair, grinning teeth in nebulous faces, and outstretched hands, bearing down on us. When I recovered, I was alone. Andy, having appropriated Nyasha, was jerking his shoulders and stamping his feet in enthusiastic counterpoint to her undulating movements. Nyaradzo and Chido were swaying in a rhythmic and sedate manner, while Brian, who had sensed that I was a non-starter, was doing his own thing beside them. Spotting Jocelyn and Maidei on the other side of the hall, I reeled over to them, weaving my way through the beat-conscious bodies and only narrowly avoiding losing an eye as one athletic and energetic dancer snatched the rhythm out of the air. I was sweating by the time I reached them, because everybody else was warmly moist from their exertions and the whole hall had grown hot and humid. But I was glad that I had found my friends. They were as surprised as I was to find me at this sort of gathering and insulated me from its more orgiastic, sinister aspects. Dancing discreetly in a group, we laughed and pointed out heterosexual couples who had recklessly moved too close together. Within the security of the group I could listen to the music and found that it was definitely contagious. My feet began to slide and glide and tap of their own accord. The rest of my body followed suit. To my surprise I discovered I could dance quite well. I had to show off. Flitting over to Nyasha and Andy I demonstrated a few intricate steps and boogeyed on to Nyaradzo, Chido and Brian.

After that I danced with hundreds of people. Three young men came up to me and told me they fancied me, but I could see from the way they talked that they really fancied themselves. I was content. My social bit came off very well and I enjoyed myself immensely, but by ten o'clock I was so exhausted I was only too glad to leave when Chido called. Nyasha, as usual, wanted to begin again and go on dancing all night. Reluctantly she dragged herself away, with Andy walking her home, or rather dancing her there, because the pair of them capered and cavorted and yodelled all the way down the road. Then, at the top of our drive, Andy remembered that there was this new dance that he just had to teach Nyasha, and Nyasha felt she wouldn't sleep if she didn't learn it at once. We waited a while, Chido and I, for them to finish giggling and prancing and getting it wrong and having to start all over again. Andy said we ought to learn it too, but Chido was getting impatient. "Na-a-ah! Break it up," he said.

"I've nearly got it," called Nyasha, but found she had got it wrong and had to start the sequence again.

"We might as well go in," I suggested, because my feet were aching from the unfamiliar exercise.

"Can't," objected Chido. "The sitting-room lights are on. Dad's still awake."

"Then let's walk down slowly," I persisted, anxious to be in bed.

At the bottom of the drive we got bored with waiting and peeped through the sitting-room curtains to see whether Babamukuru was there, just as he drew them apart a couple of inches and peeped out. Of course we ducked and scuttled away, swallowing great giggles and congratulating ourselves on being so lucky. Of course Babamukuru saw us and scraped the back door open and demanded, "What are you children doing?" in stentorian tones that brooked no disobedience. "Come on, come inside at once," he commanded. Sheepishly we entered, willing Nyasha to follow immediately because Babamukuru was not angry yet, our hearts sinking as we heard her whoop from the top of the drive.

"You children are up to no good," observed my uncle cordially, beginning to close the door. "Out so late at night! Ts! That's not the way decent children behave. Now, where is Nyasha?" he asked, noticing her absence.

"She's coming," replied Chido briefly. "Good-night, Dad," he said, hoping to escape to his bedroom, but Babamukuru was not having that.

"Er, Chido! Do you mean to tell me that you have just left your sister out there to do what she wants?"

"No, Dad," Chido answered disarmingly. "She's at the top of the drive. She's talking to Nyaradzo. She won't be long."

Babamukuru walked out of the house without another word. We fled to our bedrooms. From the bedroom I heard my uncle come back into the sitting-room and settle down to his papers. Ten minutes later Nyasha walked in, followed soon after by Babamukuru, who was so agitated that he did not knock but walked straight in, so that I was glad I was under the covers in my pyjamas instead of still undressing. Nyasha stuffed the pantie-hose she had just removed down the foot of the bed and straightened her dress, which was so short it did not need much straightening. They looked at each other.

"Er, Nyasha," began Babamukuru, "can you tell me why you are back so late?" He examined her as though she was an obstinate budget which ought to balance but wouldn't.

"I'm sorry, Daddy," Nyasha said. "I was talking to friends."

"Do Chido and your cousin there not have friends

to talk to?" he enquired logically. "What sort of friends are these that you are out all night talking to them? Good friends would know it is late and time to go home."

Nyasha was silent.

"Answer me, girl," Babamukuru insisted. "Don't you hear me speaking to you? Don't the others have friends?"

"They have friends," Nyasha muttered, sulking.

"Then why are you the only one to stay out so late?" Babamukuru asked, and answered himself triumphantly. "You are lying. You were not talking with friends. You were talking to that Baker boy. I saw you with my own eyes. I saw you! What were you doing?"

Nyasha did not cave in completely, which was unwise of her. "I was only talking. And dancing," she explained. "He was teaching me a new dance."

Babamukuru was shocked. "What! What is this you are saying, this nonsense you dare to put in my ears! Tambudzai. Leave the room. I want to settle this matter with her."

"I wasn't doing anything wrong!" insisted Nyasha.

The atmosphere in that room was growing hostile, the communication tangential. Voices were rising and threatening to break. Scrambling out of bed I knew I had to do something, because you could see that they were out for each other's blood. I woke up Maiguru, did not have to explain much because we could hear them accusing each other and retaliating, condemning bitterly and stubbornly resisting, all the way down the passage. Maiguru climbed out of bed, and put on her dressing-gown and slippers, muttering all the while about her nerves and how the inmates of her house would be the death of her. We hurried to the bedroom, meeting Chido looking annoyed and uncertain in the passage.

"The little fool," he whispered. "Why does she always have to stand up to him?"

"No decent girl would stay out alone, with a boy, at that time of the night," Babamukuru was insisting in a quavering tenor. "But *you* did it. I *saw* you. Do you think I am lying, that these eyes of mine lie?"

Nyasha, unfortunately, was still unrepentant. "What do you want me to say?" she asked. "You want me to admit I'm guilty, don't you. All right then. I *was* doing it, whatever you're talking about. There. I've confessed."

"Do not talk to me like that, child," warned Babamukuru. "You must respect me. I am your father. And in that capacity I am telling you, I-am-telling-you, that I do not like the way you are always walking about with these—er—these young men. Today this one, tomorrow that one. What's the matter with you, girl? Why can't you behave like a young woman from a decent home? What will people say when they see Sigauke's daughter carrying on like that?"

I like to think Nyasha really believed that the confrontation had taken a conciliatory turn. She smiled that the number of her male acquaintances was the one thing that should put her father at ease.

"You know me," she told him, but of course she was mistaken. "You've taught me how I should behave. I don't worry about what people think so there's no need for you to." She did not know her father either, because anyone who did would have retreated at that stage.

"Don't push me too far," Babamukuru pleaded. Mustering up his courage, Chido tried to help. "They were only talking for a few minutes, Dad," he said, and was ordered to be silent.

"You, Chido, keep quiet," Babamukuru snapped. "You let your sister behave like a whore without saying anything. Keep quiet."

"Babawa Chido," began Maiguru, but was silenced immediately.

Nyasha grew uncharacteristically calm at times like this. "Now why," she enquired of no particular person, "should I worry about what people say when my own father calls me a whore?" She looked at him with murder in her eyes.

"Nyasha, be quiet," Chido advised.

"Chido, I have told you to keep out of this," reminded Babamukuru, gathering himself within himself so that his whole weight was behind the blow he dealt Nyasha's face. "Never," he hissed. "Never," he repeated, striking her other cheek with the back of his hand, "speak to me like that."

Nyasha fell on to the bed, her miniscule skirt riding up her bottom. Babamukuru stood over her, distending his nostrils to take in enough air.

"Today I am going to teach you a lesson," he told her. "How can you go about disgracing me? Me! Like that! No, you cannot do it. I am respected at this mission. I cannot have a daughter who behaves like a whore."

Nyasha was capable of pointing out that by his own definition that was exactly what he had, but she did not. "Don't hit me, Daddy," she said backing away from him. "I wasn't doing anything wrong. Don't hit me."

"Yuwi, yuwi, yuwi!" Maiguru moaned. "Babawa Chido, do you want to kill me with your anger? She is only a child, Babawa Chido, a child."

"You must learn to be obedient," Babamukuru told Nyasha and struck her again.

"I told you not to hit me," said Nyasha, punching him in the eye.

Babamukuru bellowed and snorted that if Nyasha was going to behave like a man, then by his mother who was at rest in her grave he would fight her like one. They went down on to the floor, Babamukuru alternately punching Nyasha's head and banging it against the floor, screaming or trying to scream but only squeaking, because his throat had seized up with fury, that he would kill her with his bare hands; Nyasha, screaming and wriggling and doing what damage she could. Maiguru and Chido could not stay out of it any longer. They had to hold him.

"No, Babawa Chido, *kani*," pleaded Maiguru. "If you must kill somebody, kill me. But my daughter, no, leave her alone. Please, I beg you, leave her alone."

Babamukuru insisted he would kill Nyasha and then hang himself. "She has dared," he said, sweat pouring off him, his chest heaving with the grossness of the thought, "to raise her fist against me. She has dared to challenge me. Me! Her father. I am telling you," and he began to struggle again, "today she will not live. We cannot have two men in this house. Not even Chido, you hear that Nyasha? Not even your brother there dares to challenge my authority. Do you hear what I am saying, do you hear? Your salvation lies in going away from my house. Forever. Otherwise," he spat in her face because, still securely held, he could not strike her, "otherwise I-will-kill-you." He spat again. Nyasha rose from the floor, walked out of the room. "She walks! She just walks away. She is proud. That is her problem. She is proud. Pthu! Sis! She is not my daughter."

"Yes, Baba, we have heard," soothed Maiguru. Chido said nothing but made sure that he held on to his father.

"Nyasha," I said as she walked past me, but she did not answer. I followed her to the servants' quarters, where we sat, she smoking a cigarette held between shaking fingers and I feeling bad for her and thinking how dreadfully familiar that scene had been, with Babamukuru condemning Nyasha to whoredom, making her a victim of her femaleness, just as I had felt victimised at home in the days when Nhamo went to school and I grew my maize. The victimisation, I saw, was universal. It didn't depend on poverty, on lack of education or on tradition. It didn't depend on any of the things I had thought it depended on. Men took it everywhere with them. Even heroes like Babamukuru did it. And that was the problem. You had to admit that Nyasha had no tact. You had to admit she was altogether too volatile and strong-willed. You couldn't ignore the fact that she had no respect for Babamukuru when she ought to have had lots of it. But what I didn't like was the way all the conflicts came back to this question of femaleness. Femaleness as opposed and inferior to maleness.

If I had been more independent in my thinking then, I would have thought the matter through to a conclusion. But in those days it was easy for me to leave tangled thoughts knotted, their loose ends hanging. I didn't want to explore the treacherous mazes that such thoughts led into. I didn't want to reach the end of those mazes, because there, I knew, I would find myself and I was afraid I would not recognise myself after having taken so many confusing directions. I was beginning to suspect that I was not the person I was expected to be, and took it as evidence that somewhere I had taken a wrong turning. So to put myself back on the right path I took refuge in the image of the grateful poor female relative. That made everything a lot easier. It mapped clearly the ways I could or could not go, and by keeping within those boundaries I was able to avoid the mazes of self-confrontation. At least that was how I had been when I first came to the mission. But having grown to love Nyasha—Nyasha who thrived on inconsistencies and liked to chart them so that she could turn her attention to the next set of problems in the hope of finding fundamental solutions—I was having to revise my thinking. Whereas in the years since I went back to school I had grown content to let events pass me by as long as they did not interfere too deeply with my plans, the way Nyasha responded to challenges reminded me of the intensity and determination with which I had lived my early years. I became embarrassed with my acquired insipidity, but I did not allow myself to agonise over it, nor did I insist on any immediate conclusions. I felt secure at the mission under Babamukuru's shadow and I could not understand why Nyasha found it so threatening. Comfortable in the envelope of Maiguru's concern, growing in the presence of Nyasha's stimulating company, I thought there was time to see what would happen, to decide what needed to be done. I thought I was wise to be preserving my energy, unlike my cousin, who was burning herself out. I put it to her: couldn't she wait to make the points she thought needed to be made? But she thought that if she waited she would forget what those points were.

"It happens," she assured me. "You get so comfortable and used to the way things are. Look at me now. I was comfortable in England but now I'm a whore with dirty habits."

"But, Nyasha," I began.

"I know," she interrupted. "It's not England any more and I ought to adjust. But when you've seen different things you want to be sure you're adjusting to the right thing. You can't go on all the time being whatever's necessary. You've got to have some conviction, and I'm convinced I don't want to be anyone's underdog. It's not right for anyone to be that. But once you get used to it, well, it just seems natural and you just carry on. And that's the end of you. You're trapped. They control everything you do."

I sighed and wished she would put out her cigarette,

because there had been enough trouble for one evening. It was all very unpleasant but there was nothing I could do. I was glad when Chido joined me.

"Come back to the house," he said.

Nyasha wanted to finish her cigarette, but Chido was nervous and naturally disapproved of the habit. He took the cigarette from her and ground it out.

"Nyasha," keened Maiguru from the back door. "Chido, Chido, have you found her?"

"She's coming, Mum," Chido called back, helping Nyasha to her feet. "Don't upset her any more," he told her. "She doesn't need it."

"What about me?" Nyasha asked plaintively. "Does anyone care what I need?"

Of course, we thought she was sulking.

"You are the daughter," Chido informed her. "There are some things you must never do."

Maiguru's relief showed all over her face when Nyasha walked into the house. Instinctively her arms stretched out to her daughter, but the daughter walked by in a stony denial. Maiguru's arms sagged.

"Good-night, Nyasha," she said.

For a week Nyasha withdrew into herself and Babamukuru withdrew out of the house. He did not even come home for meals, but he did not lose much weight so I knew Maiguru was coaxing him to eat when we were in bed or at other times when we were not watching. How they suffered, the pair of them. In spite of disciplining the daughter with an hour-long sermon and fourteen lashes, because she was fourteen years old, in the sitting-room while Maiguru looked on, Babamukuru was still hurt. But I was more concerned about Nyasha, because Babamukuru had Maiguru to look after him and the solace of knowing that Nyasha was wrong. The general feeling was that Nyasha was sulking because she had not been able to have her own way. But I was closer to her than anybody else and so I sensed the conflict that she was going through of self versus surrender and the content of sin. Although I did not understand her anguish, because the distinction between right and wrong, what was and what was not sinful, was still very clear to me in those days and followed very closely the guidelines set out for us at Sunday School, I worried about the effect the situation was having on my cousin. Not only had she stopped talking to us, but she was growing vague and detaching herself from us. She was retreating into some private world that we could not reach. Sometimes, when I talked to her, quite apart from preferring not to answer, she simply did not hear me. Once, when I passed my hand in front of her eyes, she did not see me either and I had to shout very loudly to bring her back.

Maiguru saw that the situation was serious but did not know what to do. "Do you know," she told me as we sat at the lunch table alone together, because Nyasha had stopped eating again and Chido usually had lunch with the Bakers. "Do you know," she said, close to tears and embarrassing me horribly, because I would not have known what to do if my aunt had succumbed to her sorrow, "your uncle was waiting up for you before he let the dogs out. You know how vicious they are. So he didn't let them out. I said to him, let Chido do it when they get back, and he said he would rather do it himself to make sure it was done. That's how he is. He never sleeps until you come back from your functions and he's always covering it up with one reason or another. But I know him. And now he's hurt and Nyasha is hurt, and really, my child, God only knows where these things will end. To tell you the truth, it frightens me, because you don't play lightly with such tempestuous feelings—you have to handle them gently—but those two, they are always tearing each other to pieces."

I told Nyasha what Maiguru had said as we lay in bed in the dark that night. I talked on and on about many things, talking into the darkness, not knowing whether she was listening or not. I talked about how I had come to be two years too old for my class, about my father and Nhamo and my maize field. Then I told her what Maiguru had said.

She understood. "I know," she said. "It's the same everywhere. But he has no right to treat me like that, as though I am water to be poured wherever he wants. I know I should trust and obey and all that, but really he hasn't the right." She sobbed up great lumps of pain. I understood that she was grieving for whatever she had lost when she struck her father so I left her for a while, then climbed into her bed, where we cuddled up to each other and fell asleep.

Maiguru was not very pleased the next morning when she found us in bed together, but she could not mind that Nyasha was beginning to feel better and so nothing was said. I knew that Nyasha was all right because she said to me, with an attempt at her usual grin and typical exaggeration, "Thanks, Tambu. You saved my life."

Her periods came the next day, which was nine days early.

"I wish I had done it," she said, brandishing a tampon at me, "but the only thing that will ever get up there at this rate is this! Honestly, even on my wedding day they'll be satisfied only if I promise not to enjoy it." I agreed with her. We didn't know what we were talking about but we were impressed with ourselves for being so advanced. We giggled hysterically, but my merriment didn't last long. Now that Nyasha was all right I felt sorry for my uncle, who would not be able to shed the tears that would wash away his grief. I remained impressed with Nyasha's resilience, though. What I admired most about her was her capacity to forgive herself. I was quite sure that had I been the one to strike my father I would have done as Babamukuru threatened and hanged myself.

Chapter 7

We went home for Christmas on 23 December, my uncle and aunt and Nyasha and myself. Chido wriggled his way out of it because he had been invited to some shooting in the Zambezi Valley by one of his schoolfriends whose parents had a ranch there. The friend actually lived in Umtali, which made it easier since he could pick up Chido and the Baker boys on Boxing Day on his way to the Zambezi. Babamukuru was disappointed that Chido preferred to go to Chirundu rather than to the homestead. He even offered to drive his son from home to the mission on Boxing Day. But Chido did not know the exact time that his friend would come to fetch him and so this was not possible: he could not go home at all. You couldn't blame him really for not wanting to go home, because he was too old now—we all were, and too civilised too—to be amused by eating *matamba* and *nhengeni*, and by trips to Nyamarira. And Chido would have had no company at home, to make it doubly depressing. So he stayed with the Baker boys over Christmas, and they, as usual, were delighted to have him. Nyaradzo, I expect, was as delighted as any of them, because she thought my cousin was cool and debonair and exciting.

Nyasha didn't want to go home that Christmas either, and this made me apprehensive, because it was likely that there would be another of our bloody family scenes. Maiguru tried to talk to her but even she was petulant too at that time. "Just because Chido isn't going, is that why you think you can stay?" she asked her daughter nastily, and wouldn't believe Nyasha, who pouted and said that Chido had nothing to do with it. "But what's so special about us?" she asked. "Babamunini hasn't been home for ages. Neither has Tete. So why do we have to keep the home-fires burning?"

"Now you are talking nonsense," Maiguru told her. Her voice was sharper than necessary and, looking back on those days now that I am more able to perceive implications, I think this was because she did not want to go either. "Babamunini was home in the year that we returned, and that's only three years ago. As for Tete, try to think straight, Nyasha. How can Tete come to her father's home when she is somebody's wife?"

I thought Nyasha was simply being provocative. Having been so quiet since that awful fight, I thought she was bored and needed some excitement, because really, she could not very well have lived in that house all alone for two weeks. She would have been frightened to death by the end of the first day, I thought. But Nyasha laughed and asked me whether I had ever heard the expression "safe as houses." "Especially mission houses," she added sarcastically, which was strange because she ought to have been pleased about that. When she talked like that, though, I could see her managing very well on her own, getting up when she pleased, eating her meals as and how she fancied, reading or knitting or gardening or visiting Nyaradzo as the mood took her.

Naturally, though, Babamukuru would not hear of it. "No daughter of mine," he decreed, "will stay in a house all alone. Such things have never been done." Nyasha was quick to point out that she would not be alone, since Sylvester would officially be at work in the garden except on Christmas Day and Boxing Day. This upset my uncle and aunt very much and even I had to remember that Nyasha had no tact to stop myself being annoyed with her.

We were all preparing for battle, Babamukuru with threats and recrimination, Maiguru with pleading and cajolery, I with attempts to show her what she would be missing if she did not come home, which was difficult since there was not much on the homestead to entice Nyasha from the mission. But to everyone's surprise, Nyasha did not insist. Having made her inclination known, she gave in quite graciously and we were, by our erstwhile standards, a cheerful little group that drove off to the homestead that December afternoon in 1969.

Baba and Maiguru sat in front, Nyasha, Anna and myself behind, among the provisions. The back of the car and the boot were packed with food and necessities—a side of an ox chopped into limbs to make it fit, pounds of mealie-meal, dozens of loaves of bread and buns, much margarine, sugar and tea. There were packets of powdered milk, bottles of cooking oil and orange juice and peanut butter, tins of jam, cans of paraffin, soap and detergent. In fact, there was everything we needed for the two weeks' stay and more besides, because Babamukuru always provided not only the Christmas meal but Christmas itself for as many of the clan that gathered for as long as they gathered. We did not have Father Christmas but we had Babamukuru.

Maiguru was grumbling that a side of an ox was too much meat, and I thought she must have disagreed with Babamukuru about some serious matter, because it was unusual for her to grumble. But it was just as unusual to think of her disagreeing with Babamukuru and so I decided that Babamukuru's masculine ignorance of such wifely tasks had really caused him to buy too much meat.

"Ma'Chido," he asked, not bothering to hide his irritation. "If I, as head of the family, don't provide food, who will provide? Do you want Jeremiah to go into the kraal and kill an ox when you know I have forbidden him to slaughter those animals?"

"A whole ox would be too much," Maiguru pointed out logically. "Even a side is too much. But what I object to is the way everybody expects me to spend all my time cooking for them. When you provide so much food, then I end up slaving for everybody," she continued obstinately and tried to atone for her obstinacy by sounding tired and weak.

"That's nothing to worry about," Babamukuru dismissed her kindly. "Here are all these girls to help you! You'll manage. Nyasha! Tambudzai! Do you see that river, girls? That's where I used to water the cattle as a herdboy on Mandigumbura's farm. Mandigumbura! His real name was Montgomery, but we called him Mandigumbura. And he really used to do that. Ha! The man was cruel, but it was good training. He was a good farmer. By the time I went to the mission I already knew how to work hard. I was a responsible boy because of the training I got from Mandigumbura! Mandigumbura! Ha-a-a!" Babamukuru chuckled, remembering his boyhood, and began to hum a song, a hymn, one of his old favourites. It was a good sign, to hear him hum like that in his easy bass, because I had not heard him hum since the fight with Nyasha, not even at night in their bedroom, where he and Maiguru used to say their bedtime prayers if Babamukuru had not been home in time to pray with us before we went to bed. Unaccountably, unusually, Babamukuru was happy. Free of tension and in the best of spirits, he looked younger and more lovable than he ever did at the mission.

As we drove on to the homestead I repeated the comparisons I had made on that first day that I went to the mission, but this time in reverse. What I saw made it hard to understand Babamukuru. As far as I could see, the only affection anyone could have for that compound had to come out of loyalty. I could not imagine anyone actually wanting to go there, unless, like me, they were going to see their mother. This time the homestead looked worse than usual. And the most disheartening thing was that it did not have to look like that. The thatched roof of the kitchen was falling out in so many places that it would be difficult to find a dry spot inside when it rained. Great holes gaped in the crumbling mud-brick walls of the *tsapi*, and the *hozi* was no more than a reminder of shelter, so that I wondered where Takesure was sleeping. When I went to the pit latrine that was once a good one and built under Babamukuru's supervision and with his finances downwind from the huts, I gagged. The latrine had been dug deep at its construction with holes neither too wide nor too narrow. In the early days, when my mother had insisted I wash it down daily when there was water to spare, it had never smelt and its pink plaster walls had remained a healthy pink. But now faeces and urine contaminated every surface, so that it was impossible to find a place to put your feet and you were tempted not to bother to weave your way to the holes. Glistening pale maggots burrowed fatly into the faeces; the walls had turned yellow. Large bottle-blue flies with nauseous orange heads buzzed irritatingly around my anus as I squatted.

"Why don't you clean the toilet any more?" I reproached my mother, annoyed with her for always reminding me, in the way that she was so thoroughly beaten and without self-respect, that escape was a burning necessity.

She shrugged and gave me sound advice: "Clean it yourself if you want it clean."

I did clean the latrine, with Nyasha's help. Not that I asked her to—I was too embarrassed to do that—but she agreed with me that the latrine had to be cleaned, so that was what we did. But it was never really healthily clean after that, so Nyasha and I went back into the bushes as we had done before the latrine was built. I thought about it for a little while and then decided that there was no need to feel bad about boycotting our toilet, because the day after we arrived Babamukuru put on an old pair of khaki trousers and made my father and Takesure help him fix a roof on the *hozi* although he did not sleep there.

The conversation I had with my mother about the toilet happened four or five days after we arrived. On the day we arrived, when the car rolled to a stop under the shade of the mango trees, we were greeted by depressing silence. When people did come to welcome us it was only Netsai and Rambanai, more naked than dressed in their tattered frocks, their legs and their arms and even their hair and faces grey with *shena*. Dirty and dusty, they embraced us, wrapping their arms around Babamukuru first and then Maiguru, Nyasha, myself and lastly Anna: "You have come, Babamukuru. You have come, Maiguru. You have come, Sisi Nyasha," and so on until we had all been ritually embraced.

"Yes, yes, we have arrived. At last," smiled Babamukuru and asked my sisters where everybody had gone. "Where is your father? Is Mainini not here?"

He found the boot key on his keyring. We stood to attention by the boot ready to pounce on the packages and carry them to the house as soon as the boot was open, because Babamukuru did not like to waste time.

My mother, Netsai told us, was lying down because she was not feeling strong these days. But Netsai did not know where my father was. He had left the homestead late in the morning with Takesure. Perhaps they had gone to the fields, but she did not think so, because they had not asked for food to be taken to them and in any case they had just finished cultivating the day before. "So, I think he's gone visiting, with Takesure," she ended up.

Babamukuru was shocked. "What did you say?" he asked in disbelief. "Did I hear you say Takesure! Jeremiah has gone with Takesure! When I told Takesure to leave my home and take the girl with him. You say Takesure is still here?"

"Yes, we are still here, Mwaramu," called Lucia, casually emerging from the *hozi*. "Takesure and Jeremiah have gone to the shops. They said they were thirsty."

Babamukuru preferred to talk to Netsai. "Is the house open?" he asked her, and when she told him it was, because my mother was resting there, he told her to go and make sure that the doors were wide open, because we had a lot to carry. All puffed up with the responsibility Babamukuru had given her, Netsai ran off.

"Even if you do ignore me," Lucia continued, "it doesn't mean I'm not here. And anyway, Mwaramu, maybe you can tell me plainly: where do you want me to go? We both know I can't go home. Their sending me here in the first place, it was because there was no food, and no work either at that place, isn't it? It's true, you know it. So where do you want me to go? As for going with Takesure, ha-a-a! I know it's the way you joke, Babamukuru. What would I go to do at Takesure's home?"

I wished Lucia would be quiet. Her case was a serious one and it did not help to be rude to Babamukuru. Lucia was my mother's sister, several years younger than my mother and a wild woman in spite of—or maybe because of—her beauty. She was dark like my mother, but unlike my mother her complexion always had a light shining from underneath the skin, so she could afford to scoff at the skin-lightening creams that other girls used. "Fanta and Coca-Cola!" she laughed. "Aiwa! Not me. I prefer to be the same colour all over." As a result, her skin was not deteriorating and breaking; it remained glowing and healthy.

My mother's family was very poor, poorer even than my own. At the time that my father took my mother, there were no cattle at all in my grandfather's kraal. Because of this, some people had believed it was a blessing that the first two of my maternal grandparents' children were girls. "Otherwise," they reasoned optimistically, "if he had had sons, how would those sons have taken wives? See now, the daughters will bring cattle, the cattle will enable the old man to work his fields, the family will prosper, and when the sons are of an age to marry, by then they will have accumulated their *roora*." The wise and the cynical disagreed. "Who knows?" they dissented. "If there had been sons earlier, they would have helped the old man on the land. The family would have been better off than they are now. Besides," they added significantly, "a man can't be sure about daughters!"

Thus the debate continued in my mother's village, way up in the north-west of the country, until my father, visiting a distant relative, saw my mother, impregnated her and was obliged to take her home with him. It was unfortunate that it happened this way because, under these circumstances, my grandfather could not claim a very high bride-price for his daughters and so my mother's marriage did not improve her family's condition very much. That was when my grandfather's daughters gained a reputation for being loose women. "At least the elder one did the respectable thing and went with her man," the villagers said. And then they clapped their hands in horror and shook their heads. "But look at that Lucia!

Ha! There is nothing of a woman there. She sleeps with anybody and everybody, but she hasn't borne a single child yet. She's been bewitched. More likely she's a witch herself." Thus poor Lucia was indicted for both her barrenness and her witchery; and so, when after nineteen years my mother sent word that she had lost her first surviving child and was going through a difficult pregnancy, my grandparents were only too happy to pack my aunt Lucia off to look after her sister.

At the same time, Uncle Takesure, a distant cousin of Babamukuru's, came down from Gandanzara to help on the land. I am not sure who propositioned whom, but in a very short time after Takesure's coming Lucia was carrying his baby. Naturally, people said she had done it on purpose in order to snare a husband. But Lucia knew that Takesure had two wives at his home whom he did not like and that this was why, in spite of a strong aversion to labour, he had been so ready to come and help my father when Babamukuru suggested the arrangement. Until a very late stage Babamukuru continued to believe, in his uncomplicated way, that Takesure had come to help out on the homestead so that with the money my uncle paid him he would be able to finish off the payments on his second wife. The problem was only with the second one because her family kept reminding Takesure of the outstanding amounts, whereas his first wife's family had allowed their reimbursement to lapse. But Babamukuru was mistaken. The truth of the matter was that Takesure wanted to get away. He did not like being a husband and Lucia knew that he neither wanted, nor could afford, nor was able to be one three times over. Takesure did not want to work either, but very correctly did not believe that my father would make him do that and so he agreed to come to the homestead, where he thought, I suppose, that burdens were relatively light.

Lucia, who had grown shrewd in her years of dealing with men, denied that the foetus was Takesure's. She accredited it instead to my father, although this could not have been true. My father, doing his best not to offend Babamukuru, had sensibly not allowed himself to enjoy Lucia's voluptuousness until after she had fallen pregnant. From this feat of self-control Lucia had deduced that my father had marginally more stamina than Takesure and for this reason would make a better father. For his part, my father was quite taken with the idea of having Lucia as a second wife. Although she had been brought up in abject poverty, she had not, like my mother, been married to it at fifteen. Her spirit, unfettered in this respect, had experimented with living and drawn its own conclusions. Consequently, she was a much bolder woman than my mother; and my father, who no longer felt threatened by a woman's boldness since he had proved his mettle by dispiriting my mother, was excited by the thought of possessing a woman like Lucia, like possessing a thunderstorm to make it crackle and thunder and lightning at your command.

Lucia had managed somehow to keep herself plump in spite of her tribulations. Maybe, some said, because of them, since her afflictions consisted mostly of dalliances with men who did not want to settle down with her but who were often very rich. And Lucia was strong. She could cultivate a whole acre single-handed without rest. Altogether she was a much more inviting prospect than my mother if you did not scrutinise her past too closely. And, of course, my mother always insisted that the rumours about her sister were no more than that. Anyway, Lucia had been living her life hundreds of miles away and so we knew very little about her at the time. My father found her desirable and argued besides that the child might be a boy, which would be good since at the moment he only had daughters.

He pointed out that my mother and Lucia, being sisters, would get on comfortably together and reminded Babamukuru that as Lucia was a good worker, it would be useful to have her permanently about the home.

Not even for such advantages, though, would Babamukuru consider keeping a bigamist in his family. He was surprised that my father did not know that such things were sinful and would bring the wrath of God down on the entire family. "Such things do not happen in my home," he decreed. "Takesure must leave and take his woman with him." My father was much more afraid of Babamukuru's wrath, which he had experienced, than of the wrath of God, which he had not, so reluctantly he had promised to make sure that Takesure went and took Lucia with him.

But here Lucia was, embracing Maiguru passionately, telling her how pleased she was to see her again and wondering how long it had been since they had last met. "It was in March, no April, when you brought Tambudzai home." And she gushed on and on about how quickly the time had flown, how pleased my mother would be to see Maiguru, and reproached my aunt for not having visited more often. Maiguru, smiling broadly if somewhat mechanically, expertly extricated herself from Lucia's embrace without seeming to do so since she retained hold of Lucia's arm and shook it, all the while assuring Lucia that she was just as pleased to see them as Lucia and my mother were to see her. Lucia threw her arm companionably around Maiguru's shoulders.

"Maiguruka," she began, propelling my aunt housewards while the rest of us unloaded the boot, which Babamukuru had recovered himself sufficiently to be able to unlock. "Maiguru, it's Providence that you came! I am going mad, truly, as you see me here! Mad enough to take off my clothes. If only you knew what I am having to put up with, with these men. You know these men are mad, isn't it, Maiguru!"

"Er—Lucia," intoned Babamukuru in his most peremptory voice, which was usually only heard in the Beit Hall at assembly when he was admonishing the boys not to smoke or drink or spend the night in the girls' hostel, or when he was speaking to Nyasha. "Er—Lucia," Babamukuru repeated.

Although Lucia had made up her mind that Babamukuru was irrelevant when she began to talk to Maiguru, not even she could ignore the authority of that voice. She stopped and turned around. "Lucia," intoned Babamukuru for the third time, but not superfluously, "is that what you do where you come from, not greeting people and walking away when there are many things to be carried to the house?" Lucia opened her mouth, but Maiguru was quicker.

"Oh, my Daddy-dear," she laughed. "When women get talking! We'd only have remembered the food when we began to cook!" She disengaged herself from Lucia for the second time and moved rapidly, gratefully to the car.

"Don't worry yourself, Maiguru," said Lucia. "Takesure and Jeremiah will carry all that when they get back." But Maiguru chirped that she wanted to see her provisions all safely stored away, and continued to lift boxes out of the boot. Lucia knew she had been rebuffed and took it graciously.

"If you say so, Maiguru," she conceded, throwing a fifteen-pound bag of mealie-meal on to her head and grasping another in her fist. All of us except Babamukuru and including Rambanai, who carried a loaf of bread, staggered to the house weighed down with provisions. "Whew," groaned Rambanai, one hand on her hip, wiping her forehead with the other, "whew. I'm tired." Grateful to her for giving us a reason, we laughed the uneasiness away. "You are tired," I teased, swinging her on to my hip. "Why, what have you been doing? Hey? To make you so tired, hey? What have you been doing?"

"Welcome, welcome," my mother called ailingly from the adjoining room to remind us she was there. "So you've finally managed to climb the steps," she remarked drily as I entered the dim, musty sickroom. "I've been listening to you laughing and talking for a long time and wondering when you would remember that somebody gave birth to you."

I defended myself. "We were carrying the provisions inside," I told her, setting Rambanai down much to her very vocal disgust, and kneeling beside the disintegrating *koya* mattress on which my mother lay to embrace her.

"Netsai says you have not been well for some time. What pains are you having?" I asked, taking care to observe the formalities so as not to disappoint her further. I was surprised at how difficult it was to be correct with my mother when I managed so becomingly, so naturally, with Baba and Maiguru. My mind drifted away from my mother and her suffering, which she said took the form of unlocalised aches all over her body and which she thought was a bad omen for the child she was carrying. I wondered: if I grew more used to my uncle, would I stop deferring to him, as Nyasha had, and I banished the thought from my mind because it was so dreadful.

"Go-go-go, Mainini," called Maiguru from the living-room. "May we come in? Babamukuru is here to see how you are."

"Come in, come in, Maiguru," my mother responded, with more strength in her voice than you would have expected from an invalid. She raised herself to lean against the wall so that people would not find her reclining. "So you have finally arrived," she welcomed my aunt and uncle as they embraced. They were formal this time, merely placing their hands on each other's shoulders. "We were thinking that this year our Christmas would be lonely," she continued disingenuously, because really she meant hungry, or at the very best unappetising.

"Why should you think such things, Mainini?" Babamukuru reassured her warmly, looking around for somewhere to sit and finally perching himself on the edge of the bed he had bought for my father in June, and of course not thinking of the unscrupulous twists that my mother's mind took. "Not come home for Christmas, Mainini! Ha-a! That could never happen."

"How would we have known?" my mother continued unkindly, hiding the bite in her voice under a laugh. "We expect the mission to be more entertaining than this little homestead of ours. Don't you think so, Maiguru?" she said, turning her insincerity on my aunt, who had seated herself on the bare floor, her legs stretched out in front of her and crossed at the ankle. "Maiguru!" My mother was shocked. "Must you sit on the floor? Yet there are chairs? Tambu, go fetch a chair for Maiguru."

"No, Mainini, I am quite comfortable," protested Maiguru politely, whereupon my mother insisted that Maiguru at least accept a mat, but I had already fetched the chair. We all gazed at that chair upon which Maiguru steadfastly refused to sit and wondered what to do with it. My mother suggested that Babamukuru would be more comfortable on the chair, but he claimed that the bed was ideal for sitting on. My mother was very distressed that neither my uncle nor my aunt, in fact nobody, would sit on that chair, that wooden dining-chair which was really a kitchen chair and had only one rung missing from its back. In the end Nyasha, whether she intended to be rude or not, got up off the floor, where she had been sitting beside her mother.

"Well, I'll be more comfortable here even if no one else will," she announced, planting herself in the chair. I thought Nyasha was behaving very badly, in a much less civilised way than she was capable of. My mother was delighted with Nyasha's bad manners.

"Is that what you do?" she pounced maliciously. "You sit in chairs but you can't be bothered to say hello to me!"

"Nyasha, go and greet Mainini," ordered Babamukuru.

"Nyasha, go and greet Mainini," ordered Maiguru simultaneously.

Nyasha jumped out of the chair to embrace my mother, who relished her victory and consolidated it by exclaiming what a big girl Nyasha had grown into.

"The breasts are already quite large," she declared, pinching one and causing Maiguru to wince with embarrassment. "When do we expect our *mukwambo*," my mother teased her niece.

Babamukuru was valiant. Overcoming his inbred aversion to such biological detail, he took my mother's question seriously. "Our Nyasha," he sighed in real distress. "Is she the type to bring us a son-in-law? No, she is not the type. And even if she did, it would be a question of feeding the cattle—the man would soon be wanting them back."

"Now, Babamukuru," sparkled my mother, "she is your daughter, isn't she? What could prevent her from finding a good husband?"

Nyasha didn't like being discussed in the third person, nor did she like the sort of talk going on, because she thought that the question of her husband was a personal one which she would look into when she felt moved to. Her foot began to tap and I stopped breathing. It was at times like this that Nyasha was liable to say the first thing that came into her head, and those things were usually disastrous.

Lucia too was bored with this meandering talk. "Nyamashewe, Mwaramu," she interrupted, beginning the formal greetings. Technically she shouldn't have begun the greetings. Being of such low status, she ought to have waited for her superiors to start enquiring about each other's health before she opened her mouth. But these days people were not too strict about such things, and being Lucia and being notorious she could get away with this behaviour. The greetings and the enquiries about which aches and pains people were suffering from reminded me of my mother's condition. I examined her closely, but she was not looking ill at all. In fact, she was looking much stronger than she had been when I last saw her. I hoped she was not suffering from some wasting disease which progressed imperceptibly in the early stages only to ravage quickly and finally at the end.

"Nyamashewe, Mainini, Nyamashewe, Mainini Lucia," Nyasha intoned awkwardly, her cupped hands making just the right sound as she clapped.

Babamukuru looked at his daughter, raised his eyebrows and stretched his lips in agreeable surprise, then remembered what he was doing and set his features back into their usual stern contours.

"Yes," said my mother, flattered by this little attention from her Anglicised niece, "our daughter is really growing up. I tell you, Babamukuru, whatever you say, you will have a fine son-in-law one of these days."

Tete Gladys and Babamunini Thomas and their families did come to spend Christmas at home that year after all. We did not know they had changed their minds so their arrival was quite unexpected and upset the sleeping arrangements no end. Nyasha, Netsai, Rambanai and myself were affected quite badly. On our first night, the night before the rest of the family arrived, we were allowed to sleep in the living-room in the house, which was an exciting adventure. Entering into the spirit of things, forgetting that we were moulding ourselves into young women of the world, we pushed the chairs back against the wall and spread our blankets under the table, making ourselves a comfortable little hut in which we giggled and whispered until late into the night. But when Uncle Thomas and Tete Gladys came, the living-room was given over to Uncle Thomas and his wife. Tete and her husband moved into Takesure and Lucia's *hozi*. They would have been more comfortable in the house but this was not possible. Because of her patriarchal status, my Tete could not sleep in such a public place as the living-room when more private rooms were available. My parents insisted, as a matter of form, that Tete take over their room in the house. Equally formally, Tete declined. Christmas was going to be comfortable and well catered for after all. Everybody could afford to be polite and generous.

So Babamunini took over the living-room and all the unmarried women, including Lucia, slept in the kitchen. There were at least eight of us sleeping there for the whole two weeks that our reunion lasted. I was comfortable enough because I had slept in the kitchen all my life, but Nyasha could not fall asleep until the last people had stopped talking. And, she said, it was just as well that she had grown used to smoke from cigarettes, otherwise the smoke in the kitchen would have made her uncomfortable. It was true. The kitchen was smoky, because we cooked on the open hearth in the centre of the room. The hearth was a depression in the floor surrounded by a tripartite tripod of iron on which the pots were balanced; a depression surrounded also by large, smooth stones which were for balancing as well and enabled us to cook more than three pots at one time. Cooking on this hearth was a tricky business if you were not used to it, because it was easy to tip the pots over if you hadn't balanced them properly; or, if you were careless, to let the heat from one part of the hearth influence the cooking of a pot on the other side. Although the high conical thatched roof was designed to let the smoke rise and seep out through the thatch, there was no chimney. Nor was there a window apart from a small rectangular hole, maybe eight inches by five, half-way up the wall and opposite the door. It alarms me to think of all that carbon monoxide hanging about in the air to asphyxiate people, and all the inflammatory products of combustion that we breathed in that had already by that time made my father permanently asthmatic and bronchitic. Although we didn't think so at the time, the unattached young men had a better deal. My mwaramu, Tete's husband, had started a small transport business in that year and had come home in his half-ton truck. The boys slept in the back of it in the clean December night.

During that holiday I realised that some things were not as they should have been in our family, though I call it a holiday when actually it was not. There were four families at home then, five if you count Takesure and Lucia, which made ten adults. Tete had brought four of her youngest children—two toddlers and a girl and boy of seven and nine—as well as a girl to help with the chores. Babamunini Thomas had two boys aged about five and seven, a daughter aged eight, as well as a cousin of his wife's who was about sixteen and lived in my uncle's household to help with the housework. Counting Nyasha, Anna, Netsai, Rambanai and myself, there were twenty-four people altogether on the homestead, which was twenty-four stomachs to fill three times a day Twenty-four bodies for which water had to be fetched from Nyamarira daily. Twenty-four people's laundry to wash as often as possible, and Tete's youngest was still in napkins. Now, this kind of work was women's work, and of the thirteen women there, my mother and Lucia were incapacitated a little, but nevertheless to some extent, by pregnancy. Tete, having patriarchal status, was not expected to do much and four of us were only ten years old or younger. So Maiguru, Nyasha, the three helping girls and myself were on our feet all day.

The mornings began early with heating water for the adults to wash. We did not have enough enamel basins—we needed ten and had only two, which meant that only two people could wash at a time, so the whole business took literally hours. Breakfast could not be eaten until people had washed the sleep away, and so by the time the fires had been lit, the water heated and the adults cleaned, it was usually past ten o'clock. Then we began the breakfast—hunks of bread cut thick, spread with margarine and taken with tea poured out of a huge enamel kettle, yellow with green around the rim, in which the milk and the water were boiled up together. Bread and margarine! I would have preferred egg and bacon! We brewed the tea in the kitchen because once Maiguru had her Dover Stove alight, which was the first thing she saw to after she was up and washed, Anna and my aunts' girls set about cutting up the meat and boiling it for the afternoon meal.

While the adults ate their breakfast, we gathered the children together to feed them. Sometimes we managed to snatch a bite while the children were eating. But more often, what with making sure that no one went hungry in the house, our breakfast had to wait until everyone else had finished and we had set Netsai and her little cousins to washing up, in the enamel basins by the *dara*. Then we swept the yard, cleaned the women's toilet and the house. After that it was time to go to Nyamarira because Babamukuru's water-tank, which he unlocked when he came home, could not be expected to cater for twenty-four people.

We took it in turns to go to Nyamarira, either Nyasha, Anna and myself or the other two girls, and this was not such a chore, because the outward journey with our empty drums was pleasant. There were several homesteads on the way, each well supplied with fruit trees of one kind or another and we were on friendly terms with, or related more or less closely to, the families who lived on the homesteads. So although we had mangoes—the orange, curved kind that are very sweet and juicy—and *hute* as well at home, we enjoyed the peaches and guavas and mulberries we were offered on our way to the river. Although the tasks themselves were tiring, the laundry and the drawing and carrying of water, we did not feel it too heavily, because we could bathe and sun ourselves on the rocks while we waited for the clothes to dry. And when we felt dangerous we raised false alarms for the sensual fun of it, shouting that a lascivious male was leering at us from the ridge, and we would scuttle shrieking to our clothes to cover ourselves.

Sometimes we returned in time for the afternoon meal, eaten between two and three o'clock, and sometimes we did not. But whatever time we returned it was in time to cook the next meal or wash the previous meal's dishes. Maiguru worked harder than anybody else, because as the senior wife and owner of the best cooking facilities as well as provider of the food to cook, she was expected to oversee all the culinary operations. It was ceaseless work and unwise to delegate, because she had to make sure that the food lasted until the end of the vacation. With thirteen extra people to feed—and the lot of us devouring seven loaves of bread and half a pound of margarine each morning, to say nothing of sugar, because (with the notable exception of Nyasha, who believed that angles were more attractive than curves) we liked our tea syrupy—with such appetites to appease, Maiguru had to be strict about sharing out the food, and this made my mother irritable. Maiguru, she said, reporting the matter to Tete, wanted to reserve the food for her own family. Milk was not such a problem because two cows were in milk and the boys took their duty of milking them seriously, so we always had a can of it, warm and frothy and unpasteurised, to put into the tea. There was plenty of meat too, because of the side Babamukuru had bought, but preserving it was a nightmare. Babamukuru had bought a paraffin refrigerator for his wife, but it was not nearly big enough to contain all that meat, and with temperatures ranging between seventy-eight and eighty-five degrees in the shade, the unrefrigerated meat soon began to smell, distantly after the first couple of days and then more and more insistently. This brought the flies in and caused my aunt and me all sorts of anguish: we imagined them buzzing upwind on the putrid aroma, from the latrine straight to the kitchen to engage in their bacterium-infested festivities.

The meat turned green, but we could not waste it. When it was cooked in that state it smelt so powerfully it knocked all the appetite out of you, which was really a good thing, because it was tasting so terrible by that time that it would have been worse to look forward to eating it and then not be able to. We begged Maiguru to let us start on the refrigerated meat, but she was very steadfast in her refusal: she would not let us touch it. She was being very careful with that meat, the fresh meat, because on the third or fourth day after we arrived Tete delicately spat a mouthful of greenish meat into her hand, wrapped it up in her handkerchief and, turning green herself, suggested that Maiguru be more responsible in future. "It surprises me," said Tete, "that Mukoma can swallow such food." This threw my aunt, who was a good woman and a good wife and took pride in this identity, into a dreadful panic. She took to cooking, twice a day, a special pot of refrigerated meat for the patriarchy to eat as they planned and constructed the family's future.

An issue of immediate concern was the case of Takesure and Lucia. One evening, just after the breaking of the new year of 1970, Babamukuru summoned a kind of family *dare* which consisted of the patriarchy—the three brothers, who were Babamukuru, my father and Babamunini Thomas, and their sister—and the male accused.

"I do not wish to go over the facts of this case," began Babamukuru weightily when the *dare* was assembled in the house, the patriarchy sitting around the dining-table sternly examining Takesure, who shrank into a corner of the sofa, petrifying him with the threat of imminent justice as they turned in their straight-backed chairs to transfix him with the full impact of their authority. "I do not wish to do that," explained Babamukuru, "to go over the facts, because it will just take up time without getting us any further than we are now since we have heard everything before and have agreed on what happened. What happened is this: Lucia was asked to come here by her sister, our Mainini—who, as you know, is carrying a baby—to help her while she was in this condition, in poor health. On the other side, Jeremiah here approached me, asking me to find him someone to help him on the land, because since—since—the passing of the one who went—we all know the grief I talk of—since that time there has been too much work here for Jeremiah to do alone, since that time there has been a shortage of labour. I must say that I was very pleased when Jeremiah came to me with that request, because it showed me that he was becoming responsible about developing the home. So I was very happy to approach our uncle Benjamin, who told me that our cousin Takesure was looking for work so that he would be able to finish paying his wife's *roora*. This was good luck for all of us, and that was why you saw Takesure coming here to work with Jeremiah. There was no trouble. We talked the matter over nicely, agreed about certain things, and that is how Takesure came, when everything was happy and peaceful here at our home. For my part, I assured *Sekuru* Benjamin that I would keep an eye on—er—er—on Takesure." Here Babamukuru dropped his narrative style and addressed Takesure directly. "Takesure, you know that in all matters concerning Jeremiah and our home here you were to approach me as the head of the house, but you did not. The first time you did what you did with Lucia, you kept quiet. Then, when we found out what had happened, you were told—I told you personally after you had ignored Jeremiah here, whom I had sent to tell you—I told you personally that you must go back, back to your home, but you did not do it. Why have you disobeyed my orders?"

"I would have gone, Mukoma," muttered Takesure, "but Lucia refused. She refused to leave her sister."

"And why did you not inform me of Lucia's stubbornness?" demanded Babamukuru. Takesure hung his head.

Now we, the women and children, were in the kitchen when the *dare* began. We all knew what was going on and my mother and *maininis* threatened to become quite violent in their opposition to the system.

"Have you ever seen it happen?" demanded my

mother, whose health had been greatly restored by the arrival of Tete and Babamunini Thomas and his wife. "Have you ever seen it happen," she waxed ferociously and eloquently, "that a hearing is conducted in the absence of the accused? Aren't they saying that my young sister impregnated herself on purpose? Isn't that what Takesure will tell them and they will believe it? Ehe! They are accusing Lucia. She should be there to defend herself."

"It's true!" agreed Mainini Patience, who, having been married for only eight years, still had enough identity left not to feel disloyal to Babamunini Thomas for agreeing with my mother. "We all know that hearings are not private affairs," she went on. "But this family we have been married into! I don't know what frightens them about coming out in the open, but everything they do is hushed up and covered. Hidden. Even from us, as though we were children. Do they think we will curse them? Putting a curse on the Sigaukes? Aren't our children Sigauke?" The mutterings and malcontent carried on, my mother and aunts fanning each other's tempers until Lucia, who enjoyed battle and liked to be ferocious at it, was seething with anger.

"It is all right for you," she boiled. "They are not telling lies about you. It's not your names they are spoiling. I am the one they are talking about. I am the one they are judging up there. Isn't it, Maiguru?" she asked, to draw Maiguru into the fierce, sisterly solidarity they had established there in the kitchen. "What do you say, Maiguru? Isn't it they want to spoil my name? So what do we do, Maiguru? We are looking to you to give us a plan."

It was embarrassing the way Lucia wouldn't give up on Maiguru. Maiguru, who thought that Lucia ought to suffer the consequences of her fecund appetites, perhaps felt sorry for her too, but preferred all the same not to become involved in matters of the flesh or the earth, although she did not like this preference to be too obvious since it meant she was setting herself above the rest of us. Now, with Lucia insisting that Maiguru take sides, come out in the open, we were in a very delicate situation.

What was needed in that kitchen was a combination of Maiguru's detachment and Lucia's direction. Everybody needed to broaden out a little, to stop and consider the alternatives, but the matter was too intimate. It stung too saltily, too sharply and agonisingly the sensitive images that the women had of themselves, images that were really no more than reflections. But the women had been taught to recognise these reflections as self and it was frightening now to even begin to think that, the very facts which set them apart as a group, as women, as a certain kind of person, were only myths; frightening to acknowledge that generations of threat and assault and neglect had battered these myths into the extreme, dividing reality they faced, of the Maigurus or the Lucias. So instead of a broadening from both positions, instead of an encompassing expansion and a growth, the fear made it necessary to tighten up. Each retreated more resolutely into their roles, pretending while they did that actually they were advancing, had in fact initiated an offensive, when really, for each one of them, it was a last solitary, hopeless defence of the security of their illusions.

Maiguru grew very distant. "This matter is not my concern," she shrugged, carelessly turning down the corners of her mouth. "Am I of their totem? I am not. I was taken. Let them sort out their own problems, and as for those who want to get involved, well, that's up to them. I don't want to intrude into the affairs of my husband's family. I shall just keep quiet and go to bed."

Maiguru's words released a flurry of offended rustlings and mutterings from my mother and my aunts, but as she continued, the protests subsided into stunned disbelief. By the time she had finished speaking the kitchen was still. Then my mother gave a long, bitter laugh.

"He-e-e!" she cackled, clapping her hands. "Aiwa! Girls, would you say this one is a *muroora* like the rest of us? She speaks as though she were born into our husbands' family, she regards herself as highly as they do. You have heard her, girls, haven't you? Doesn't it make you wonder why she came here tonight? Tell us, Maiguru, what were you thinking to do in the kitchen with us this evening when you know the matters that are arising?"

"But, Mainini," replied Maiguru evenly, "why do you ask? You know very well that you called me here. I am waiting for you to tell me why. As for this matter arising, you all know—I have told you many times—I was not born into my husband's family, therefore it is not my concern. Takesure is not my relative. What he does with Lucia is no business of mine—she is not my relative either. If they make problems for themselves, well, they will just have to see what they can do. But what they do does not concern me."

Lucia must have been cut to the heart by Maiguru's rejection, but she did not let it show. "And you are quite right, Maiguru," she agreed staunchly, "quite right. If those people up there understood that I am not their relative either, they would not speak my name so freely and tell lies on top of it."

"Well," said Maiguru, preparing to leave to avoid being drawn deeper into the discussion, "as I said, I shall go to bed. Good-night, Mainini Ma'Shingayi, Mainini Patience, Mainini Lucia. We shall see each other in the morning."

"Good-night, Maiguru, we'll see each other in the

morning," replied Lucia, but she was the only one who answered.

"She is proud," denounced my mother when Maiguru had gone. She turned to me. "See what a proud woman your Maiguru is," she sneered. "Proud and unfeeling. Do you think she cares about you? Never! You are no relative of hers. It's my blood that's in you. Not hers."

"But, Mother," I protested mildly, wanting to stop the conversation because Nyasha was with us. "But Mother, Maiguru was only speaking plainly, telling us what she thinks."

"And why does she think differently from the rest of us? She thinks she is different. She thinks she's perfect so she can do what she likes. First she kills my son—"

"Mother!" I gasped and turned to Nyasha before I could stop myself, and wished I hadn't, because I did not want Nyasha to see the shame in my eyes. Nor did I want to see the pain and confusion in hers.

"Sisi!" remonstrated Lucia, "contain yourself! Why do you want to hurt yourself by saying such painful things? Especially when you know they are not true!"

But my mother was in a bad way and there was no holding her. The things that were coming out had been germinating and taking root in her mind for a long time.

"Ha! You!" mocked my mother, raving at her sister. "You think you can tell me to contain myself, you! He-he-e-e! Now this is something to make a woman laugh! When Lucia, just tell me, when, did you ever contain yourself? Do you even know what it means you who were in the blankets with my husband the moment you arrived? And with Takesure. You were probably there, the three of you together, Jeremiah having his ride, enjoying himself, and then Takesure, and so it carried on. So don't tell me about containing myself. You know nothing about it." We thought she had finished, but she was only pausing to breathe. "And anyway," she continued, "in what way am I not restraining myself? I am only saying what I think, just like she did. She did tell us, didn't she, what she thinks, and did anyone say anything? No. Why not? Because Maiguru is educated. That's why you all kept quiet. Because she's rich and comes here and flashes her money around, so you listen to her as though you want to eat the words that come out of her mouth. But me, I'm not educated, am I? I'm just poor and ignorant, so you want me to keep quiet, you say I mustn't talk. Ehe! I am poor and ignorant, that's me, but I have a mouth and it will keep on talking, it won't keep quiet. Today I have said it and I am saying it again: she is a witch, a witch. Have you heard me properly? She-is-a-witch. She steals other women's children because she could only produce two of her own, and you can't call those two people. They're a disgrace to decent parents, except that Maiguru is not decent, because first she killed my son and now she has taken Tambudzai away from me. Oh, yes, Tambudzai. Do you think I haven't seen the way you follow her around," she spat at me fiercely, "doing all her dirty work for her, anything she says? You think your mother is so stupid she won't see Maiguru has turned you against me with her money and her white ways? You think I am dirt now, me, your mother. Just the other day you told me that my toilet is dirty. 'It disgusts me,' that's what you said. If it is meat you want that I cannot provide for you, if you are so greedy you would betray your own mother for meat, then go to your Maiguru. She will give you meat. I will survive on vegetables as we all used to do. And we have survived, so what more do you want? You have your life. Go to your Maiguru and eat sausage." And she sat there with her arms tightly folded across her chest, her mouth thrust out in a defiant pout, defying us to change her mind.

"Aiwa-wo, Sisi," soothed Lucia, taking no notice of all this resoluteness. "How can you talk such nonsense? As soon as the child is born and you have settled down, you will laugh at yourself. But now be calm. Otherwise you will do yourself damage. It is over, isn't it?"

"Hm!" grunted my mother. "Over! When I see Nhamo in front of me, then, only then, will it be over."

"You know, Mainini Lucia," mused Mainini Patience, "I think there is some truth in what Maiguru Ma'Shingayi has said."

"And how would you know?" snapped Lucia, whose patience was limited and had to be reserved for her sister. "Which one of your children has died?" Mainini Patience was effectively silenced. "Come, Sisi," Lucia cajoled, turning once more to my mother, "we do not deny you your grief, but let the anger be over. Come, let us go and hear what they are saying about us at the house."

But my mother was still resolute. "No," she said. "I am no longer interested."

"But you will be interested," Lucia persisted, "when the story is out. You will wish you had heard it for yourself."

"Lucia, Lucia," sighed my mother. "Do you think I am a child? After all these years and all these things, do you think I am still a child to be distracted by the nonsense in the house? Nonsense I have lived with and seen every day for nineteen years? No, I cannot be distracted, but the matter is serious and it concerns you. So let us go to the house."

She rose heavily to her feet, balancing herself on her hands and knees before making the effort. The two sisters left the kitchen, my mother steadying herself against the door-frame because with her pregnancy her centre of gravity shifted unpredictably into precarious positions. Mainini Patience followed them because there was nothing else to do.

I wanted to go too, to hear the proceedings, but I was afraid that my eagerness would appear disloyal to Nyasha. I was sure she would prescribe a boycott, but when I looked round to put my case to her I could not find her. When had she left? How much had she heard? The last time I looked at her her face was impassive in the paraffin lamp-light and I had seen that she did not understand and was badly hurt by the things my mother was saying. But it was a relief that she had slipped away; I would not have to explain away my own mother in order to keep my cousin. And again, this was a mistake, a misjudgment on my part, because when we did talk about it, as we eventually did talk about most things, Nyasha closed her face and said it did not matter; that my mother had shown us her suffering just as Maiguru was always showing hers. When I questioned her about this, asked her aggressively to tell me how Maiguru could possibly be suffering when she lived in the best of all possible circumstances, in the best of all possible worlds, Nyasha was reticent. Some things could not be explained, she muttered. Such things could only be seen. But this happened later, much later, when we were back at the mission. At that particular time, on that particular evening, I was worried that my mother would succumb to her misery before I was able to do anything about it. So I went to the house to take my mind off the matter and to find out what was going on.

Maiguru reached the house just as Takesure was explaining that Lucia had refused to leave her sister.

"Yes," he was saying, "it's Lucia's fault. Ehe! That's what she did, that Lucia of yours. She refused, absolutely refused, to leave. She knew she had taken this pregnancy of hers, but she just refused to leave."

"May I pass?" asked Maiguru at the door, curtseying and bringing her hands together in a respectful, soundless clap.

"Ma'Chido," reprimanded Babamukuru sternly, "we are listening to a very important case here. Sit down and listen with us."

"Could it be that important?" demurred Maiguru, passing through the room with a deferential stoop of her back. "We did not know anything about it."

"Ma'Chido," Babamukuru insisted, his voice breaking ever so slightly, "I have invited you to sit down and listen to this case."

"Very well, Baba," acquiesced Maiguru, subsiding to the floor and folding her legs up under her.

"I am sure it is not necessary," adjudged Tete, the female patriarch. "Maiguru works very hard all day. Maybe it is best for her to sleep."

"If she is tired, why doesn't she say so?" Babamukuru enquired irritably of Tete, and to Maiguru he graciously gave permission to leave. Maiguru accepted the permission and passed on to the bedroom. The men looked after her.

"Shame," sympathised Babamunini Thomas. "She is so tired, too tired even to sit and listen. But it is true. Maiguru works hard. Ya, she really works hard to keep things comfortable here." And Babamukuru was pleased enough to let the matter pass.

The rest of us stood whispering outside, listening to these goings on and peering in at the window when the talking was intense and we thought no one would notice.

"Finish what you were telling us, Takesure," ordered Babamukuru.

"Yes," continued Takesure, darting pleading glances at my father, who remained patriarchally impervious and stern. "Yes," Takesure quivered, "this is what I was saying. She just refused to go with me. Ehe! I told her, Mukoma said we must go, and she laughed! She just laughed and said she could go with Mukoma if Mukoma asked because he is her mwaramu, but she would not go with me. Ehe! That is what she said, Mukoma, I swear by my grandmother who died in 1959! That is what she said."

"I see," said Babamukuru magnanimously, while Lucia in the shadowy moonlight choked on chuckles that would not be suppressed. "What you say is not surprising," went on Babamukuru. "It is understandable, because it is well known that she is an immodest woman. But why did you not report the matter?"

"I was afraid, Mukoma, truly afraid," Takesure quavered. "You know what is said of her, that she walks in the night?" This allegation was Takesure's undoing. Babamukuru cleared his throat and fixed his cousin with an uncompromising eye. Takesure had lost his advantage but he blustered on. "She threatened terrible things. And we know what she is like. She would do them. Ehe! She would do them. She's probably the one bewitching Mukoma Jeremiah's children, so that he will marry her. She wants Jeremiah, not me!"

It was no use telling Lucia not to go into the house, so we did not even try. We just watched her as she strode in there, her right eye glittering as it caught the yellow paraffin flame, glittering dangerously at Takesure, who wisely shrank back into his corner of the sofa. "Fool!" snorted Lucia, looming over him, arms akimbo. "Fool!" And she whirled to face Babamukuru, so that now her left eye glittered. "Look at him, Babamukuru! Look at him trying to hide because now I am here." Takesure looked braver when he had only Lucia's back to contend with, but his reprieve was brief. "If you have an issue with me,"

Lucia advised him, "stand up and let us sort it out plainly." In two strides she was beside him and, securing an ear between each finger and thumb, she dragged him to his feet.

"Let me go, let me go," he moaned. I always maintain that I saw smiles slide over the patriarchy's faces, but it might have been my imagination because I was laughing myself. We were all laughing outside. The next thing that I remember clearly was my father starting out of his chair and Lucia warning him to stay in it if he preferred Takesure with ears. Then Babamukuru, who was wise, told my father to sit down and let Lucia speak.

And Lucia spoke. "Tell me, Babamukuru," she asked companionably, her hands at waist height so that Takesure was bent double. "Tell me, Babamukuru, would you say this is a man? Can it be a man that talks such nonsense? A man should talk sense, isn't it? So what can this be?" and she tweaked its ears to find out what it would say. "Let me tell you, Babamukuru," she continued earnestly. "Maiguru asleep in her bedroom there is the only one with a sensible head on her shoulders. She knows better than to poke into what does not concern her."

"Er, Lucia," commanded Babamukuru, deploying his peremptory tone which had worked so well at the beginning of the vacation. "Er, Lucia, contain yourself. Do not do anything of which you will be ashamed."

"And of what should I be ashamed?" she retorted. "I just want this Takesure," and she shook his head to make the point, "I just want this Takesure to stop talking nonsense about me. Takesure, have you ever seen me riding a hyena's back? Have you ever seen me, hey? Answer me." Viciously she tweaked, enjoying herself.

"No," moaned Takesure. "I have never."

"Then what is this nonsense you are saying? Ha!

You make me sick, the lot of you." She flung Takesure back on to the sofa, where he sat rubbing his ears. "I shall leave this home of yours, Babamukuru, and I shall take my sister with me," she told my uncle. "But before that, Babamukuru, I want to tell you why I refused to go. It was because this man, this Jeremiah, yes, you Jeremiah, who married my sister, he has a roving eye and a lazy hand. Whatever he sees, he must have; but he doesn't want to work for it, isn't it, Jeremiah? And why do I bother to tell you? You know it, all of you; you know it. So could I go and leave my sister alone with this man who has given her nothing but misery since the age of fifteen? Of course not. It was not possible. As for Takesure, I don't know what he thinks he can give me. Whatever he can do for me, I can do better for myself. So, Babamukuru, don't worry. I'm going. Right now. There's nothing to keep me. But I'm taking my sister with me."

They wanted to talk to her. They wanted her to sit down and be calm and discuss the matter rationally, but Lucia had had enough and came back out to join us. The patriarchy put its heads together and conferred in low voices because now they knew we were listening. I imagined all sorts of dire consequences.

"Lucia," I whispered, "if you go and take Mother, I'll have to leave the mission. I'll have to come back to look after Baba and the children."

Lucia laughed. "Don't worry yourself," she reassured me. "This is a storm. It will pass."

In the house Babamukuru was deeply perplexed and annoyed with my father for stirring up this trouble.

"Jeremiah," he scolded, "see what problems your irresponsibility has landed us with. Now what is to be done? You are giving us a headache trying to sort out your affairs. And this one is serious. We need a sound solution."

"Ehe!" agreed Takesure, still smarting it seemed, from the look on his face. "We need a good strategy to outsmart that woman. She is vicious and unnatural. She is uncontrollable."

"Tete, what do you say? You should know how best to handle a woman. What do we do in a case like this?" asked Babamunini Thomas deferentially, but Tete declined the honour.

"Aiwa, Thomas," said Tete. "There is only so much that I can do and this business is beyond me. Maybe the pregnancy is Takesure's this time, but Jeremiah should never have done anything with her that could not be done openly. The solution is for Jeremiah to behave sensibly, but he has never been very good at it."

"Maybe some medicine," suggested Takesure, "to fix Mukoma Jeremiah. Ehe! To fix him. So that he cannot be influenced by that woman."

My father approved wholeheartedly and had ideas of his own. "He's right, indeed. Yes, he's right. But it needs more than just medicine for me. The problems are everywhere in the family. Mukoma is always saying that that Nyasha is impossible these days, and sometimes Maiguru too. And you are saying too that the money matters are not so good these days, aren't you, Mukoma? When was it? Just the day before yesterday you were saying you wished you had the money to buy a tractor. But before all these troubles began there was money for these things. Do not misunderstand me, Mukoma, I am not saying you are tight-fisted. I am only saying we have problems these days. I-i-h! We have problems. Even Tete with two pregnant daughters who have no husbands and the eldest son beating his wife so badly—she was in hospital last time, wasn't she, Tete? And then Thomas worrying about his youngest, who is a bit of an idiot. Hi-i-i. These are serious misfortunes. They do not come alone. They are coming from somewhere. It's obvious. They are being sent. And they must be made to go back where they came from, right back! It is a matter for a good medium. A good medium to do the ceremony properly with everything—beer, a sacrificial ox, everything. We must call the clan and get rid of this evil—"

"Jeremiah," interrupted Babamukuru in an incredulous tenor, "am I hearing you correctly? Do I hear you say you want to bring alcohol and—er—and witchdoctors here—into my home! Tonight, Jeremiah," he said sadly, "you are disappointing me. Everytime you speak, senseless things come out of your mouth. Surely, my young brother, you know that what you are saying is impossible. I do not allow such things to happen here."

"But, Mukoma—" began Tete.

"That is enough," Babamukuru interrupted. "What Jeremiah is saying cannot be done. I will not discuss it. But I have one thing I want to tell you." Everybody settled attentively in their chairs. "Do not think I have not been considering these things," Babamukuru said. "Do not think I have not seen the things that Jeremiah has described. Oh, yes, I have seen them. For a long time now these misfortunes have been on my mind. We cannot deny that these problems are with us. But rather than say they are the result of an evil spirit that someone has sent among us, I have been thinking they are the result of something that we are doing that we should not be doing, or the result of something that we are not doing that we should be doing. That is how we are judged, and blessed accordingly. So I have been thinking about what these things could be for a long time. And then, after much thought, I remembered that our mother, our mother always insisted that Jeremiah must have a church wedding. Yes, Jeremiah, even now, so many years after our mother passed away, you are still living in sin. You have not been married in church before God. This is a serious matter, so I have been saving a little, a very little bit of money for a wedding for you and Mainini. I wanted you to know that these are the things that I have been thinking about, but we will discuss the details some other time since now it is very late."

As soon as I had the chance, which was the next morning while we prepared breakfast, I told Nyasha in detail, as much detail as I have included here, about what had happened at the house—the arguments, the debates, the conclusions. She was pleased with Lucia, which surprised me, because when Lucia was around Nyasha reserved herself, said little. She was amused by my father's solutions and the idea of a wedding. She was curious too about the proposed cleansing ceremonies, confessed that her ignorance of these things embarrassed her and asked me about all sorts of fine details, details that I was not very sure of since we did not often perform the rituals any more. And I was quite proud of this fact, because the more I saw of worlds beyond the homestead the more I was convinced that the further we left the old ways behind the closer we came to progress. I was surprised that Nyasha took so much interest in the things our grandparents and great-grandparents had done. We had quite a debate about it, but I was sure that I was right, because Babamukuru himself had opted for a wedding rather than the cleansing ceremonies. When I confronted Nyasha with this evidence of the nature of progress, she became quite annoyed and delivered a lecture on the dangers of assuming that Christian ways were progressive ways. "It's bad enough," she said severely, "when a country gets colonised, but when the people do as well! That's the end, really, that's the end." It was the end of the debate too. Nyasha said she had had more exposure than me and so had had reason to think about these things, but now that I was being exposed to the issues, I ought to think them out for myself. Not at all clear as to what I had to think about, I dutifully promised to do so and we carried the breakfast to the house where Tete sat in the living-room while Maiguru laid the table.

"Ah, Maiguru," Tete was saying. "I tell you, that woman only missed killing me by a very narrow margin. I nearly died of laughter. That Lucia! Aiwa! That Lucia is mad. And Mukoma's face! Truly you'd have thought Lucia had walked in naked!" Tete wiped the merriment from her eyes. "Ma'Chido! If you'd been there, you'd have had a good laugh!"

"I heard, Tete, I heard," chuckled Maiguru. "But they asked for it. They shouldn't meddle with women like Lucia!" They puckered their faces up and dissolved into helpless giggles.

"And now shall we have a cleansing or a wedding?" Tete asked, her fat face quivering and shaking her head. "Tell us, Maiguru, which is the better cure for Jeremiah's self-indulgence? Those men, aiwa! Those men!"

Chapter 8

I did not think my uncle's plans for my parents were something to laugh about. To me the question of that wedding was a serious one, so serious that even my body reacted in a very alarming way. Whenever I thought about it, whenever images of my mother immaculate in virginal white satin or (horror of horrors) myself as the sweet, simpering maid fluttered through my mind, I suffered a horrible crawling over my skin, my chest contracted to a breathless tension and even my bowels threatened to let me know their opinion. This also began to happen whenever I thought of Babamukuru and put me in a difficult situation. Naturally I was angry with him for having devised this plot which made such a joke of my parents, my home and myself. And just as naturally I could not be angry with him since surely it was sinful to be angry with Babamukuru. Babamukuru who was my benefactor, my father for all practical purposes and who was also good, deserving of all love, respect and obedience. So I banished the anger. Thoughts of the wedding were not allowed to linger in my mind since they had such serious, sinful consequences. To distract myself I set my mind on other things: on trips to Nyamarira on the days that it did not rain; on daydreams about being back at school, which was not too long to wait any more; on joining Nyasha in her latest craze of making clay pots. We used to make clay pots in the days before Babamukuru went to England, when we were young and not very good at it so that the pots were always lopsided and rough. But these days our pottery was smaller and daintier and finished with delicate designs that we scratched into the wet clay with a fine twig, dipping the twig into water with every stroke to make sure that the strokes were smooth. We let the pots dry and then we baked them in Maiguru's Dover Stove. They used to crack all the time when we were little, but we were much more professional now and most of them held together, which pleased Nyasha no end since she took her hobby seriously. She said she would paint the pots and glaze them when she returned to the mission, and use them to hold buttons and jewellery and pens.

As far as I was concerned, people only made clay pots when they were very young and playing at being grown up, or when they were grown up because they had to have pots for storing water and *mahewu* and the like. But we used two- and five-gallon drums for water these days and I had never seen anybody make a proper *hari* although we had several in the house. So those pots were definitely Nyasha's craze, not mine, and while she was very concerned about making sure that they did not crack, while she was meticulous in scratching her designs, they did not matter much one way or the other to me, serving only to pass the time.

I hoped that this pastime would keep the anger, the guilty anger at bay, but it was not so simple. The trouble was that I was not moulding clay pots or going to Nyamarira or thinking about school all the time. Sometimes I was alone with not much to do except keep the *sadza* from burning, or feeling warm and drowsy and soft just before I fell asleep. At these times I would forget that there were things I was not supposed to be thinking of, and the thoughts would creep back in such hazy disguises that they did not startle me into pushing them away but could linger and chip away at my defences, leaving me anxious and sleepless without knowing exactly why.

Gradually I was forced to admit to myself that I did not like the idea of my parents performing a wedding.

But I could not understand why I objected so strongly to the idea of a marriage, the idea of my parents no longer living in sin. When I put it like that, I knew there was definitely something wrong with me because I had grown to understand, very categorically, that sin was something to be avoided. Sin had become a powerful concept for me during my year at the mission, where we went to Sunday School and to church every Sunday without fail and were taught every time that sin absolutely had to be avoided.

It had to be avoided because it was deadly. I could see it. It was definitely black, we were taught. It had well-defined edges, and it was square rather than round so that you knew where it ended. It worked like a predatory vacuum, drawing the incautious into itself and never letting them out. And now Babamukuru was saying that this was where my parents were, which meant myself and my sisters too. I could not associate myself or mine with sin so I smothered my misgivings in literal interpretations of the things we were taught in Sunday School. I convinced myself that sin was what people who had lived long ago, in B.C. and early A.D., had done to each other. Yet Babamukuru was sure enough that my parents were sinning to want to provide a wedding for them, a wedding that would cost a lot of money. It was a complex problem, too complex for me to think my way out of, so I pushed it once more to the back of my mind. I hoped it would go away and leave me to enjoy the remainder of the vacation with Nyasha. Since there wasn't much of it left.

Tete was the first to leave. This caused another rearrangement of sleeping-quarters, with the boys moving into the *hozi*. Babamunini went the day after Tete and Babamukuru the day after that. Nyasha went too on that day, leaving me depressed and unhappy because I would not see her again until term began in three weeks time, and that was a terribly long time for me to think of spending without her. Nyasha was something unique and necessary for me. I did not like to spend too long without talking to her about the things that worried me because she would, I knew, pluck out the heart of the problem with her multi-directional mind and present it to me in ways that made sense, but not only that, in ways that implied also that problems existed not to be worried over but to extend us in our search for solutions. And there were many things that worried me in those days. Deep in the less accessible areas of my mind, although outwardly I would have hotly denied it, I was ashamed of what to me was a pervasive and enervating vagueness. Consciously I thought my direction was clear: I was being educated. When I had been educated, I would find a job and settle down to it, carrying on, in the time that was available before I was married into a new home, Babamukuru's great work of developing the family. Issues were well defined for me at that time: these were the goals and this was how we would reach them. Babamukuru was my touchstone who showed me that this was true. So I should have been content to go to school and achieve my good grades. I should have been content with preparing myself for the life I have described. But Nyasha's energy, at times stormy and turbulent, at times confidently serene, but always reaching, reaching a little further than I had even thought of reaching, was beginning to indicate that there were other directions to be taken, other struggles to engage in besides the consuming desire to emancipate myself and my family. Nyasha gave me the impression of moving, always moving and striving towards some state that she had seen and accepted a long time ago. Apprehensive as I was, vague as I was about the nature of her destination, I wanted to go with her. I did not want to be left behind. And being so young, time measured in hours and half hours, was important, so I did not want to spend three whole weeks away from my cousin.

Knowing I would be at a loss without her, I was tempted to ask Babamukuru whether I could go with them to the mission, but in the end I decided not to because I knew he would refuse and be justified in doing so. There was much work to be done in the fields, in the garden, in the home. And, of course, I could not leave my mother, who was not well.

We all gathered in the yard, my father, my mother, Takesure, Lucia, my little sisters and myself, to wave them off, with everybody laughing and talking, saying my uncle must be sure to come back soon, bringing Maiguru, Nyasha and Chido as well with him. And then my relatives were in the car, rolling out of the yard and out of sight. A sigh escaped from us and we all felt oddly relieved.

"Whew! It was good to have Mukoma here, it was good," observed my father, "but it puts a weight on your shoulders, a great weight on your shoulders!"

"It's true," nodded Takesure, leering lasciviously at Lucia. "Dhiya! There's nothing to be afraid of any more. Won't you come back to the *hozi* tonight?"

"Maybe if you cut my hands off," retorted Lucia. "Then you might be useful."

"But you have the hands and you are still here. So you are waiting, aren't you? Just waiting to come back into the *hozi*."

Lucia was careful not to be provoked. "You know why I'm waiting? For my sister, isn't it? As soon as my sister makes up her mind what she wants, you won't see me here any more."

My father and Takesure found this amusing. They had a good laugh at Lucia's expense.

"Now what is this I am hearing!" gurgled Takesure.

"The woman thinks she can go away. Just like that. Now, Lucia, where do you say you will go? Aren't you waiting for me to take you to my home?"

Those men! They never realised that Lucia was a serious person. Her laughter, like her temper, was hearty and quick but never superficial. And she thought a lot, did Lucia; although she laughed at herself, thinking was a slow painful process for her because her mind had not been trained by schooling to do it quickly. In the days after the *dare* she had thought a lot about whether to leave, but she knew that her actions had consequences and was not frightened by the fact. So she waited for my mother to make up her mind whether she would go as well or not. Since for most of her life my mother's mind, belonging first to her father and then to her husband, had not been hers to make up, she was finding it difficult to come to a decision.

"Lucia," she sighed, "why do you keep bothering me with this question? Does it matter what I want? Since when has it mattered what I want? So why should it start mattering now? Do you think I wanted to be impregnated by that old dog? Do you think I wanted to travel all this way across this country of our forefathers only to live in dirt and poverty? Do you really think I wanted the child for whom I made the journey to die only five years after it left the womb? Or my son to be taken from me? So what difference does it make whether I have a wedding or whether I go? It is all the same. What I have endured for nineteen years I can endure for another nineteen, and nineteen more if need be. Now leave me! Leave me to rest."

So Lucia stayed on to look after her sister, and because her body had appetites of which she was not ashamed, she moved back in with Takesure. She did not make excuses for herself.

"A woman has to live with something," she

shrugged matter-of-factly. "Even if it is only a cockroach. And cockroaches are better. They are easy to chase away, isn't it?"

But I was disappointed in her, disappointed, disapproving and afraid too that she would start sleeping with my father again and increase our portion of sin so much that it would take much more than a wedding to exorcise it. I urged her to do something, something constructive, believing she could. I was sure Lucia could manage things that other women could not, but she would not let me harass her.

"Don't worry about things that don't concern you," she advised gently. "When the time comes when it is more convenient for me to go than to stay, then I shall go, isn't it? Either with Sisi or without her—whichever is best. Don't ask me when or where. At this moment I don't know."

And so life at home settled back into the normal back-breaking routine—up at daybreak, to the river, to the fields, to bed, endlessly, monotonously, excruciatingly, except when it rained, which was even worse. When it rained we huddled in the kitchen, praying with each thunderclap that we would be spared the next stroke of lightning. One day, when it had been lightning and thundering, Takesure came back from *magrosa* with his hair singed off down the middle. Lucia enjoyed the spectacle enormously. "If only it had taken your head right off," she laughed, "perhaps another would have grown and it could not have been worse than the one you have now!" Then I asked Takesure to help me mend the thatch over the kitchen and he refused, so Lucia helped me although she slept in the *hozi* like Takesure and, as a result of her pregnancy, was not as agile as she would have liked to have been.

When Babamukuru came to fetch me he noticed

that the roof was in much better condition. "That's a good job you've done, Jeremiah," he observed. "When the rains are over you can get Takesure to thatch it again. That's what he's here to do."

"Ha! Ya, Mukoma," agreed my father. "There was a job there! You should have seen us! Up there with strips of bark and the fertiliser bags, and tying the plastic over the holes. Ha! There was a big job there, a big job."

Lucia and I could not hide our smiles.

"See, Jeremiah," praised Babamukuru, pleased with my father's labour, "even your daughter is pleased when you have done a good job."

The return to the mission was peaceful. Life carried on there as though there had been no interruption. Maiguru fussed over me, Anna was unobtrusive. Even Nyasha returned to her normal irrepressible self, which was a relief to me but taxed Babamukuru's nerves badly. He preferred peace and quiet, but when he tried to make Nyasha peaceful and quiet they aways ended up in a rough and noisy quarrel. Nyasha did not mind these rows because, she said, they cleared the air and allowed her and her father to understand each other better, since without the confrontation and the hurling at each other of deep-felt grievances, they would never communicate at all. The evidence of the healing effect of these fights, she believed, was that Babamukuru did not beat her any more. But I could see that my uncle was growing more and more disappointed with his daughter. In fact, it became very embarrassing for me, because I had grown much quieter and more self-effacing than was usual, even for me. Beside Nyasha I was a paragon of feminine decorum, principally because I hardly ever talked unless spoken to, and then only to answer with the utmost respect whatever question had been asked.

Above all, I did not question things. It did not matter to me why things should be done this way rather than that way. I simply accepted that this was so. I did not think that my reading was more important than washing the dishes, and I understood that panties should not be hung to dry in the bathroom where everybody could see them. I did not discuss Anna's leave conditions with Maiguru. I was not concerned that freedom fighters were referred to as terrorists, did not demand proof of God's existence nor did I think that the missionaries, along with all the other Whites in Rhodesia, ought to have stayed at home. As a result of all these things that I did not think or do, Babamukuru thought I was the sort of young woman a daughter ought to be and lost no opportunity to impress this point of view upon Nyasha. Far from being upset by these comparisons, she would agree that, apart from being a little spineless (which she thought could be corrected), yes, I was an exemplary young lady. Perhaps she would have reacted differently if she had known her father better. She did not realise how deeply he felt the misfortune of having a daughter like Nyasha. Not considering herself a misfortune, she could not have known how disillusioned her father was. She took seriously the reasons that Maiguru gave for Babamukuru's bad humour—he was busy, he had responsibilities—and on this basis made allowances for him so that she did not judge him too harshly and remained herself in spite of her father's wishes.

Then, in early March, my mother had her baby. She came to the mission hospital to lie in and delivered without complication a healthy seven-pound boy. Lucia wanted to be with her sister during the lying-in because my mother had not been well for most of her pregnancy and Lucia was not sure that the actual birth would be easy. But Maiguru, preferring not to have

Lucia underfoot, promised to take care of my mother herself. It might have been coincidence that the baby was born at a quarter past nine on a Saturday morning and that Lucia stepped off the twelve o'clock bus to arrive at Babamukuru's waving a palm frond and singing "*Makorokoto, makorokoto.*" It might have been coincidence—I do not know. I do know that even if Babamukuru had telephoned the Council Houses as soon as the baby was born, the message would not have reached home and Lucia could not have been at the bus-stop in time to catch the twelve o'clock bus.

Anyway, Lucia came and she was only the first of the entire village. By evening Babamukuru's house was full of aunts and cousins and cousins of aunts and grandmothers who, having visited the hospital, passed through Babamukuru's house to congratulate him as well. Babamukuru escaped to his office but the relatives remained, singing their entire repertory of post-partum congratulations; dancing, drinking tea, which Maiguru brewed by the gallon, and lamenting the fact that there were no buses running to take them back to where they wanted to go. Or if the buses were there, the fares, they sighed, were not. They thought they would have to put up at the mission overnight, but when Babamukuru returned, just before supper, he drove them home in several carloads. Only Lucia remained to keep my mother company during the last few days of her lying-in. Lucia, much bigger now than she had been in December, made full use of that time. Having received little solidarity from my aunt during the Christmas vacation, she focused her efforts on my uncle.

"Do you know, Babamukuru?" she began dispiritedly, being careful to call him by the more dignified title of Babamukuru. "Do you know, Babamukuru, that Takesure is not a good man?"

Babamukuru, who liked to sort out discrepancies as they occurred, could not believe that Takesure had continued to make a nuisance of himself even after the January conference. He urged Lucia to tell him what Takesure was up to, but Lucia only sighed disconsolately and left Babamukuru wondering. "There are things worrying us at home, Babamukuru, but I cannot say what. Maybe it is the way we are living. The way we live on the homestead does not make it easy to do useful things." And she would say no more.

The next day at lunchtime she began again. Ignoring Babamukuru's silence and not giving Maiguru the chance to take up precious time with questions about the baby, Lucia continued her appeal.

"I did not come to your home to bring grief, Babamukuru," she told him seriously. "I have told you already, Babamukuru, why I came—to look after my sister, isn't it? But I see that I have brought problems instead. If going back to my father's house were possible, I would go, but what would I eat when I got there? And anyway, my sister needs me to keep an eye on her. Those who said relatives are hands were not lying, Babamukuru, and my sister needs hands in these difficult times of hers. But I can see that my living at your home has not helped her as I hoped." She paused and applied herself to her food for a while. "Do you know what I was thinking, Babamukuru?" she continued, concentrating on her plate in an effort to remain calm. "I was thinking that if I could find work, any little job in this area, if I could find a little job here in Mutasa's kraal, there would be no more of these problems. The problem of my living at home would be solved, and my sister would have her hands."

Babamukuru said nothing, only chewed and chewed on his last piece of meat and when a piece of it stuck between his teeth asked Nyasha to find him a toothpick. He spent a long time removing the offending particle. "Now, Lucia," he said at last, when Lucia's face, bent over her plate, showed that she had lost hope. "Now, Lucia, these are good words you speak, but what kind of job could you do?"

"Ah, Babamukuru!" smiled Lucia undaunted. "You are joking, isn't it? Don't you see how strong my body is? I can't do things that need education, but anything else! Anything else I can do."

Babamukuru had nothing more to say. To fill the silence Maiguru asked about my mother and the baby. Lucia assured her that they were both happy and healthy. She expected my mother to be released the next day and they would go home together as soon as possible.

The next day Babamukuru fetched my mother from the hospital. Although Lucia was impatient to return home and Maiguru did not press them to stay, Babamukuru had other plans. Lucia wanted to catch an early afternoon bus, but Babamukuru said he would see when he would be able to drive them there. "Don't you see two cars in my garage?" he asked. "Why should you go by bus?" He went to his office and Maiguru went to teach. When Maiguru returned at four o'clock, my mother and Lucia were still relaxing in the living-room. Maiguru instructed Anna to cook more meat for the evening meal. Suppertime came but Babamukuru did not.

"Maiguru," my mother asked, suckling my little brother, "do you think we will go home tonight?"

"How should I know what you and your Babamukuru have planned?" laughed Maiguru. "We shall see when he comes."

Babamukuru did not come until we had all gone to bed. He did not take my mother home that day, or the next, or the next.

"Mainini has been wondering when they will go home," Maiguru probed on the fourth day.

"Oh yes! I said I would take them," remembered my uncle.

At lunchtime the day after he came home looking very pleased with himself. Something very wonderful indeed must have happened for us to be able to see it, because Babamukuru's face did not usually reflect his moods. So we waited and hoped he would share the occasion with us.

"Have you packed, Mainini?" he asked my mother when we were half-way into the meal. "I think I can take you home this afternoon."

"But what about the shopping?" objected Maiguru. "Will there be time to do both?"

"We'll see to that later," Babamukuru dismissed my aunt, and he told my mother to get ready since he wanted to leave straight after lunch. But when Lucia rose too, Babamukuru stopped her.

"Lucia," he said indifferently, "er—if you are going to help Mainini, that is all right. But you yourself will not be going. I have found something for you to do. Not much. A little job. At the girls' hostel. You will help to cook the food there at the hostel. I will take you there today."

"Purururu!" ululated Lucia loud and long, although I do not know how she managed it with such a broad grin on her face. "Purururu!" she shrilled, her hand to her mouth. "Did you hear that, Sisi, did you hear that, Sisi?" she crowed at my mother with a little jump to emphasise each word. "Babamukuru has found me a job. He has found me a job!" She knelt in front of Babamukuru, energetically clapping her hands. "Thank you, Samusha, thank you, Chihwa. You have done a great deed. Truly, we could not survive without you. Those foreign places, those places you went, did not make you forget us. No!

They enabled you to come back and perform miracles!"

My mother came hurrying with her own shrill ululations. "That is why they say education is life," she cried. "Aren't we all benefiting from Babamukuru's education?" and she knelt worshipping beside Lucia. Then it was Maiguru's turn to take her place on the floor. "Thank you, Baba, thank you for finding Mainini Lucia a job."

It was an intoxicating occasion. My first instinct was to join the adoring women—my mouth had already pursed itself for a loud ululation.

"Don't you dare," Nyasha hissed, kicking me under the table. I unpursed my mouth, but the urge to extol Babamukuru's magnanimity was implacable.

"Thank you, Babamukuru," I said as calmly as I could so as not to disappoint Nyasha, "for finding Lucia a job."

I was mesmerised by the sleight of hand that had lifted Lucia out of her misery, and even more seductive was the power that this sleight of hand represented. With the crescendos of praise, Babamukuru grew modest and egalitarian.

"Stand up, stand up. Do not thank me. Lucia is the one who will be doing the work!" he exclaimed.

So Lucia never went back to the homestead to live, although she did go with my mother that afternoon to collect her spare dress and her few other possessions. In the excitement, my mother left behind at the mission a lime-green bonnet and a bright pink bootee which she had received at my brother's birth.

I was so impressed with Babamukuru I could not stop admiring him. That evening as we prepared for bed I simply had to tell Nyasha for the umpteenth time how wonderful Babamukuru was; how good and kind it was of him to be so concerned about Lucia and how, because of all this, he deserved all our love and loyalty and respect. But she told me I had misjudged the situation. It was the obligation of all decent people in positions like Babamukuru's to do such things.

Nyasha had a way of looking at things that made it difficult for her to be impressed by Babamukuru. Her way was based on history. It all sounded rather wild to me then, and it was difficult for me to make the long leaps that Nyasha's mind made between Babamukuru and Lucia and events past, present and future. All the same, I tried hard to understand, because Nyasha was very persuasive and also because I liked to think. I liked to exercise my mind. The things Nyasha said always gave me a lot to think about. This is how I began, very tentatively, to consider the consequences of our past, but I could not go as far as Nyasha. I simply was not ready to accept that Babamukuru was a historical artefact; or that advantage and disadvantage were predetermined, so that Lucia could not really hope to achieve much as a result of Babamukuru's generosity; and that the benefit would only really be a long-term one if people like Babamukuru kept on fulfilling their social obligation; and people like Lucia would pull themselves together.

It all seemed rather far-fetched, having nothing to do with the fact that Lucia now had a job whereas before she had not and that this was all due to Babamukuru's kindness. Not liking to see Baba-mukuru's moral excellence diminished in this way by Nyasha's perspicacity, I turned mulish.

"We know he's doing his duty," I said obstinately, "but we still have to thank him."

"Thank him, yes," agreed Nyasha patiently, "but not make him into a hero. And what about poor Lucia! She's been grovelling ever since she arrived to get Daddy to help her out. That sort of thing shouldn't be necessary. Really it shouldn't."

Eventually we took the debate to Lucia, who was growing more and more placid in her new, happier circumstances.

"But you, Nyasha, are you mad!" she exclaimed. "Babamukuru wanted to be asked, so I asked. And now we both have what we wanted, isn't it?"

Contentedly folding her arms over her six-month pregnancy, she told us that she was going to school to Grade One classes in the evenings. She was so proud. She had not been to school before. She showed us her books, declared that she could already feel her mind beginning to think more efficiently. So Lucia stirred the great drums of *sadza* at the girls' hostel and went to her Grade One classes in the evenings, while my mother on the homestead waited without enthusiasm for her wedding.

The wedding was scheduled for the last week of September. Babamukuru had wanted it to take place sooner. He was anxious that his brother be cleansed of sin as soon as possible, but there was too much to be done. The dilapidated huts had to be restored and the house had to be extended to accommodate the wedding guests. The old latrines were blocked up and hygienically white-washed ones put up in their place.

While these preparations were going on at home, the wedding garments were being sewn in town. I was to be bridesmaid and so was Lucia. Nyasha had politely declined the honour on the grounds that she would be busy organising things. So there were only the two of us as bridesmaids, Lucia and I, with my little sisters as flower-girls and dreadfully excited about the prospect. Nyasha's attitude was disappointing, though: I needed her moral support, since my doubts about the wedding had not resolved themselves. But I did not say anything and the preparations went ahead.

One Saturday morning early in August, Babamukuru fetched my mother and sisters from home, stopping on his way back to pick up Lucia, who by this time had acquired the status of mother. They came down to Babamukuru's house and we all squeezed into the Rover to drive to a tiny dressmaker's shop in Sakubva Township. The shop was very small, no more than a booth, so dark and dingy that you wondered how the dressmaker could see to sew and how she managed to keep the clothes clean, the patterns together. There was dust in every corner, and layers of greasy grime on every surface except the table she used for cutting. Bits of material and pattern-paper were strewn everywhere, having overflowed from a large wooden box which was meant to contain the scraps. There was only one pattern-book, but the dressmaker assured us that we had only to describe what we wanted and she would produce an exact replica. Nyasha was all for sitting down with pencil and paper to sketch some stylish outfits, but Babamukuru, feeling out of place in this feminine place, did not have the time and urged us to choose something out of the book. We paged through the section marked "Bridal and Evening," discussing—that is Lucia, Nyasha and I discussed because my mother was not interested—the relative attractiveness of straight and flared gowns, three-quarter sleeves or full, short maids' gowns versus long. When we had made up our minds Babamukuru was discomforted to learn that we had to buy the material ourselves, that very many yards as well as different kinds were required, and that the expenditure for the material and the making-up was going to be heavy. Maiguru was called in to help. Babamukuru wanted my aunt to lend my mother her wedding-gown; but this could not be done because,

Maiguru pointed out, my mother, in spite of being thin, was much bigger than she was. Then Babamukuru asked Maiguru to have her wedding-gown altered so that it would fit my mother, and Maiguru stopped talking to us for a week. In the end they compromised. Maiguru would lend my mother her veil and supervised the purchase and sewing of the garments. Maiguru consented readily enough, but you could see she was not appeased.

"He didn't make half as much fuss when we got married," she confided to her daughter. "I had one bridesmaid and tea. No dinner. Of course I didn't mind—it was all right then. But you wait and see what happens at your wedding. I bet he won't be so concerned then either."

Fortunately, Nyasha was not thinking of marriage at the time so the threat did not alarm her.

"Don't worry, Mum," she soothed. "I'll help you with the shopping."

In the end Nyasha did not help Maiguru with the shopping. She practically took over. Babamukuru, concerned that time was slipping by without the clothes being ready, made Maiguru promise to see to the purchase of cloth several times, but she always forgot. Finally, in desperation, he took Maiguru to town specifically for the purpose of buying it, but before it could be bought, Maiguru remembered several important accounts that had to be paid and this took up the whole afternoon. And, of course, there were the groceries. Maiguru returned well stocked for the week but minus the cloth. On the pretext of choosing material for her own dress, Nyasha took Maiguru and me in hand. The material was bought in a single afternoon—peach georgette for the bridesmaids and pale amber for the flower-girls, as well as yards of white satin and lace for the bride. We bought a lot of material and took it to the dressmaker, where Nyasha decided that the old patterns we had chosen weren't right for the cloth we had bought and thoroughly enjoyed herself, instructing the dressmaker most artistically which sleeves to put on which bodice to put on which skirt in order to create the desired garment. We fetched the dresses a week before the wedding and they were beautiful. I tried one on. It fitted me perfectly. Nyasha told me I looked gorgeous in it. "Go-o-o-orgeous!" she said, so that I knew exactly what she meant. Nyasha was delighted, with the dresses, with the effect I created when I put mine on, with the whole idea of the wedding. She thought it was quaint.

"You'll look so sweet," she teased, "all flowery and flowing for your mother's wedding. Really!" she chuckled, "I can't wait. I won't see anything so sweet again in a long time."

Sweet. Sweet enough to bring a smile and a chuckle. That was what Nyasha thought about my parents' wedding and it hurt. It hurt even though I knew she was being kind to call it sweet when the truth was much worse than that, when in fact the whole performance was ridiculous. The whole business reduced my parents to the level of the stars of a comic show, the entertainers. I did not want to see them brought down like that and I certainly did not want to be part of it. So I could not approve of the wedding. This I acknowledged with half of my mind, but in the other half the black square of sin reappeared and grew to an alarming size. I could not ignore it. With the preparations in full swing and people talking about nothing else but the wedding, there was no way of pretending that it was not going to happen. I had to think about it, about the fact that I did not want to go to that wedding. A wedding that made a mockery of the people I belonged to and placed doubt on my legitimate existence in this world. I knew I had to come to a decision, take some sort of action, but I was not like Nyasha: I couldn't simply go up to Babamukuru and tell him what I thought. So I pretended to myself that the wedding was a wonderful plan, just what my parents needed. I told myself that my parents had been deprived of the pomp and ceremony of a wedding in their youth and that now Babamukuru's generosity was making it up to them. It was necessary to exaggerate quite wildly to try to convince myself. I even insisted, very strictly, that my parents were eagerly looking forward to the occasion, but it was no use. I simply did not believe these lies. My father always enjoyed a bit of play-acting, a chance to make a show, so he would be all right. He would have a marvellous time playing the part of the groom and would carry it off too, but my mother's case was entirely different. She had tiredly told me that it did not matter one way or the other, and even Lucia was uncharacteristically unpassionate about it. "It is happening," she said, "so we make it good. Otherwise people will laugh. They won't fail. So we make it good, isn't it?"

Lucia's was a sensible attitude, one I tried to adopt. But the advantages and disadvantages of white lace and vows and veils at this late stage battled about in my head so furiously that I could not sleep for nights on end. Yet I said nothing, not even to Nyasha, who would have told me to make up my mind and stick to my principles, and would have called me feeble when I confessed I could not. There was no way out. The dresses were made, the shoes and stockings, real stockings to make our high-heeled peach sandals look even more elegant, all these things were ready and waiting. My role in the comedy had been confirmed and rehearsed, but I still did not want to take part. It was all right for the others, I grumbled to myself; they were not my parents' daughter. I watched Nyasha, who remained amused, and Maiguru, who had gone back to being solicitous, bustling about with her share of the preparations so that the wedding would be a success and, she said, her Daddy-sweet would not be disappointed. I watched the day draw nearer and still I said nothing.

"Er, Tambudzai," Babamukuru said to me at supper on the Thursday before the wedding, "I shall take you home tomorrow, in the afternoon, with Lucia, so that you can help with the preparations over there."

"Do not take me at all. I don't want to be in your stupid wedding," I wanted to shout. Instead I said quietly and politely, "Very well, Babamukuru. That will make things much easier for everybody."

There was definitely something wrong with me, otherwise I would have had something to say for myself. I knew I had not taken a stand on many issues since coming to the mission, but all along I had been thinking that it was because there had been no reason to, that when the time came I would be able to do it.

Coming to the mission, continuing my education and doing well at it, these had been the things that mattered. And since these things had been progressing according to plan for nearly two years, I had thought that ambiguities no longer existed. I had thought that issues would continue to be clearly delimited, with Babamukuru, who was as nearly divine as any human being could hope to be, imposing the limits. Through him, because of him, black would remain definitely sombre and white permanently clear, even in spite of Nyasha, whose strange disposition hinted at shades and textures within the same colour. My vagueness and my reverence for my uncle, what he was, what he had achieved, what he represented and therefore what he wanted, had stunted the growth of my faculty of criticism, sapped the energy that in childhood I had used to define my own position. It had happened insidiously, the many favourable comparisons with Nyasha doing a lot of the damage. It was such a bed of confusion. I would not have been here with Babamukuru if I had not been able to stand up to my own father, yet now I was unable to tell my uncle that his wedding was a farce. And still I could not accept responsibility for my weakness, hoping instead to disguise it by suffering. I let guilt, so many razor-sharp edges of it, slice away at me. My mother had been right: I was unnatural; I would not listen to my own parents, but I would listen to Babamukuru even when he told me to laugh at my parents. There was something unnatural about me.

When school broke up on Friday afternoon, the afternoon that I was to go home to prepare for the wedding, I ran away. I went to the hostel with my friends, and stayed there for the rest of the day and most of the evening. Jocelyn and Maidei were pleased to have me with them for such a long time. Maidei was particularly happy about it. She made no bones about telling me that spending so much time with Nyasha was turning me into a snob. In the end, though, I had to go home. Supper was over by the time I got back to my uncle's house. The door was locked but happily the dogs were not loose, which was good because I would not be savaged and also because it meant my uncle was still at the office. Nyasha was fast asleep. I had to go round the back and knock on our bedroom window to get her to open up for me. The whole process made such a racket, with me tripping over logs and having to bang on the window for a good five minutes to wake Nyasha up, that Maiguru came out of her bedroom to see what was happening.

"Tambudzai!" she scolded anxiously, intercepting us in the passage. "Where have you been? Your uncle is very angry with you."

I could feel myself shrinking. It seemed that I was only a very small spot on the floor when eventually I found enough voice to answer.

"There was homework, Maiguru. An exercise I didn't finish in class," I lied thinly.

"But you should have said," fluttered my aunt. "Now see what has happened. Babamukuru is annoyed."

Nyasha was in a sensitive mood and so she kept quiet. She didn't say a word until I had undressed and turned off the light and climbed into bed, and then all she said was good-night. I felt slightly better. I did not want to have to explain.

The next morning, the morning of the wedding, I found I could not get out of bed. I tried several times but my muscles simply refused to obey the half-hearted commands I was issuing to them. Nyasha was worried. She thought I was ill, but I knew better. I knew I could not get out of bed because I did not want to. But, of course, I could not tell her this. It was easier to lie there on my back, apparently paralysed and staring at the ceiling.

Nyasha talked to me. She tried hard to coax me out of bed, but I was slipping further and further away from her, until in the end I appeared to have slipped out of my body and was standing somewhere near the foot of the bed, watching her efforts to persuade me to get up and myself ignoring her. I observed with interest and wondered what would happen next. It was quite exciting. Maiguru came in and mentioned Babamukuru. That was a bit of a shock and I nearly did get up, but in the end decided to stay at the foot of the bed and watch more of this extraordinary drama. The next thing that happened was that Babamukuru walked into the room, without knocking and looking dangerously annoyed. The body on the bed didn't even twitch. Meanwhile the mobile, alert me, the one at the foot of the bed, smiled smugly, thinking that I had gone somewhere where he could not reach me, and I congratulated myself for being so clever.

"Is she ill?" asked Babamukuru.

"I think so," frowned Maiguru, putting a hand on my forehead and peering closely into my face. Nyasha sat by my head, gently calling my name. Babamukuru, though, had no time for such subtleties.

"Mai," he instructed Maiguru, "get that girl up and washed. Right away." He said I was ungrateful, that I did not respect him. "She is growing into a bad child. I am spoiling her here. She knows she is in my house not because of herself but because of my kindness and generosity. She must get up. Right away."

Babamukuru was always very categorical when he made these kinds of statements. Nyasha had suffered many more of them than I had, but it was what I needed. It was something concrete that I could pin down and react to. The scene became much less focused. I heard them talking from a great distance that rapidly diminished as I slipped back into my body. I found I could speak again and speak I did, although my heart was racing and my voice when it came was high and thin.

"I'm sorry, Babamukuru," I said, "but I do not want to go to the wedding."

Of course, that was entirely the wrong thing to do, calculated, it seemed, to trigger my uncle's volcanic temper. I tried to explain why I could not go, but it was useless.

"You have been having too much of the good life," my uncle raged, his voice rising on each syllable and breaking on the top note. "I do everything I can for you, but you disobey me. You are not a good girl. You must be up and dressed, ready in half an hour. Ma'Chido, come. Let us have breakfast."

He turned on his heel. Maiguru moved aside to let

him pass, hung back for a moment as though to speak, then thought better of it and followed her husband out of the room.

Babamukuru could not leave me alone. "Tambudzai," he returned to warn me, "I am telling you! If you do not go to the wedding, you are saying you no longer want to live here. I am the head of this house. Anyone who defies my authority is an evil thing in this house, bent on destroying what I have made."

He threatened all sorts of things, to stop buying me clothes, to stop my school fees, to send me home, but it did not matter any more. Babamukuru did not know how I had suffered over the question of that wedding. He did not know how my mind had raced and spun and ended up splitting into two disconnected entities that had long, frightening arguments with each other, very vocally, there in my head, about what ought to be done, the one half maniacally insisting on going, the other half equally maniacally refusing to consider it. I knew I was not evil to have endured all that terror in order to be sure of my decision, so when Nyasha asked whether I would go, I was able to tell her calmly, "No." But I accepted that I had forfeited my right to Babamukuru's charity. Taking my suitcase from the top of the cupboard, I began to pack my things. Then I remembered that they were not my things and I put them back in their places. After that there was nothing else to do, so I stood in the middle of the room.

Nyasha was watching me. "You should have told us earlier if it was so important," she said. "Really, Tambu, you should. Shall I be bridesmaid? Will it be better if all you have to do is sit there?"

I did not answer. As far as I was concerned, she belonged to Babamukuru and his beliefs, whereas I did not. Yes, Nyasha, I thought bitterly, we can change bridesmaids' dresses because it's all a joke. And now the joke's over. You told me it wouldn't last.

"He won't send you home," Nyasha soothed. "Goodness, no! Just imagine what people would say."

It was very difficult. When she talked like that I felt an urge to jump to Babamukuru's defence. Maiguru called her. She left the bedroom and a few minutes later I heard the car start.

They told me the wedding was a spectacular success. The whole village turned out to see Babamukuru's brother get married. Expecting worthy entertainment, they were not disappointed. Everybody was impressed by the elegance of the occasion. By all accounts the bride, in her white veil and high-heeled shoes, was as happy as anybody, waited upon hand and foot for once in her life by a robust maid in delicate peach and united at the altar with my waiting father, who cut a dashing figure in his brand-new suit and shoes. My father cutting a dashing figure! Now that was an idea that made me smile. And Babamukuru had killed an ox, to say nothing of the odd goat and sheep, so there was plenty of meat for everybody. Besides, Lucia divulged, with so many people around it was impossible to prevent a few gourds of beer from finding their way down a few throats, which increased the merriment to riotous proportions. To crown it all, Babamukuru had endeared himself to everybody except Maiguru and probably Nyasha by announcing during the presentation of gifts that he was giving the house to his brother as a wedding present and that, in order that my mother not be inconvenienced in her new home when he visited with Maiguru, he would build a bigger and better house for his wife. When I saw the photographs I was sure that I should have gone. But I had not seen them before I had made my decision and the decision at least was mine.

The day after the wedding, on Sunday, in the evening, Babamukuru called me to the sitting-room. He sat with Maiguru, he in the armchair that faced the fireplace, she on the sofa. I sat in the seat I had occupied that first time I had been in conference with Babamukuru on the day I first came to the mission. But this time my feelings were entirely different. I was dreading what was to follow.

Babamukuru talked to me calmly, authoritatively and at length, told me how disappointed he was that I had grown so rebellious when he was doing so much for me, when he had been holding me up for nearly two years as an example of filial virtue for his wayward daughter to follow. Babamukuru said I had to be punished for my disobedience and that although he did not like to beat me, because I was of an age to be treated maturely, my behaviour showed that I was not yet mature and a beating might speed the process. I received fifteen lashes, having turned fifteen in April. Because of the seriousness of my crime, Anna was given two weeks' leave and I took over her duties.

I went about these chores grimly, with a deep and grateful masochistic delight: to me that punishment was the price of my newly acquired identity. Nyasha was not impressed when I let her into this secret. "And what would happen," she demanded, "if nobody punished you? I suppose you would punish yourself. Really, Tambu, I believe you would." She was terribly angry about the severity of my punishment and was all for asking Babamukuru whether he intended to educate me or kill me. She insisted she would help me in spite of the fact that help had been forbidden, and she would have done it too. She would have been up at four o'clock to help me clean the living-room and prepare breakfast. Or else she would have cooked the afternoon meal while I did the cleaning, so that all we had to do at lunch-time was prepare the *sadza* besides reheating the rest. She would have helped me face the dishes when we came back from school in the afternoon, cook the evening meal and clean the bedrooms in-between. She would have done all this for me if I had let her, but I was so frightened of Babamukuru now and my own daring in having defied him once that I begged her not to, and when she saw how upset I was, she agreed not to help. As it turned out, I was not overwhelmed with chores. On the second day of my punishment, when the previous day's disorder had made it clear that life would be uncomfortable under the new system, I woke to find Sylvester cleaning the living-room. He set the table for me too, and when I came back from school the breakfast dishes were clean, the meal ready, the table freshly laid. I did not know what was going on. I was terrified that Babamukuru would find out and make Sylvester stop. Then I thought that perhaps Maiguru had told him to and so it was legitimate. But I didn't dare open my mouth in case I said the wrong thing. Sylvester too kept his thoughts to himself, so I never found out what was happening. Of course, Babamukuru caught on, or perhaps he had planned it. Whatever the case, he did not comment and I was relieved to have the help.

On the first Saturday of the first week of my punishment, Nyasha decided that if Sylvester could help me on a day-to-day basis, she could at least help with big things like the laundry. Anna did the laundry on Tuesdays, Thursdays and Saturdays. Going to school I could only find the time on a Saturday, so it accumulated over the week and there was a lot of it to do by Saturday. In spite of the amount, I explained to Nyasha that it was my punishment and that she would be punished too if she made it hers.

"I'm sorry to deprive you of the pleasure," she retorted, "but I'll do the laundry anyway."

While we were at it, still battling with the whites, which consisted chiefly of my uncle's shirts and underwear and so had to be done thoroughly, Lucia came to visit, carrying little Farai, who was eight weeks old but looked much older because he was so big.

"Whose shirts, now?" she teased. "Not Mwaramu's. Anna washes those. So there are boyfriends about. Tell me their names."

"No boyfriends," Nyasha replied in lugubrious tones. "We are being punished." She put such a doleful look on to her face that the punishment became so funny we collapsed into giggles.

"And quite right too," Lucia approved, "with the mischief you get up to. Look at you. Laughing! I know you two. You're impossible!" Then she became serious and wanted to know why we were being punished, so I explained that in fact the punishment was mine and Nyasha was only helping. I told her too what had brought it about, finding it funny now that the matter had resolved itself, but Lucia did not like what I had to say.

"*Babawanguwe!*" she exclaimed when I had finished. "But there are still mad people in the world, isn't it?"

This sort of talk made me uncomfortable because Babamukuru was taking on ogre-like proportions in my unconscious mind. Vaguely I thought he might suddenly appear and do something dreadful, like take away Lucia's job if he heard her talk like that.

Nyasha had no such qualms. "Exactly," she scoffed. "As if children were meant to be at their parents' wedding!" Looking at it this way it was impossible to be frightened. We grew quite weak with laughter, but Lucia pursed her lips and went to the living-room. She was abrupt with Maiguru when Maiguru went to greet her.

"Is Babamukuru here, Maiguru?" she asked after

no more than a vestigial handshake and a word or two enquiring about Maiguru's health. Maiguru recognised the signs and trod warily.

"What is wrong, Mainini? I see you are upset."

"Don't worry yourself, Maiguru. The matter concerns Babamukuru."

"Are you sure, Mainini?"

"I am sure, Maiguru."

"You can talk to no one but Babawa Chido?"

"No one but Babamukuru."

Lucia's attitude offended Maiguru, who would not normally have left a visitor alone, but this time she went away until Babamukuru returned. When eventually Babamukuru came, Lucia was blunt with him. She told him quite openly that I should not be punished so severely. "Did you ask her what was on her mind?" she demanded. "Did you ask my sister whether she wished her daughter was present? Even the wedding. Did you ask my sister if she wanted that wedding? I do not see that the child did you so much wrong by preferring not to be there."

Something had happened, either to Lucia or to Babamukuru, that allowed him to be patient with her.

"I see, Lucia," he explained, "that you think Tambudzai is being punished because she did me wrong. It is not that, Lucia, but children must be obedient. If they are not, then they must be taught. So that they develop good habits. You know this is very important, especially in the case of girls. My wife here would not have disobeyed me in the way that Tambudzai did."

"Well, Babamukuru," said Lucia, preparing to leave, "maybe when you marry a woman, she is obliged to obey you. But some of us aren't married, so we don't know how to do it. That is why I have been able to tell you frankly what is in my heart. It is better that way so that tomorrow I don't go behind your back and say the first thing that comes into my head."

Babamukuru applauded Lucia in her absence. "That one," he chuckled to Maiguru, "she is like a man herself."

"I think she is right," ventured Maiguru. "Perhaps Tambudzai has been punished enough."

Babamukuru chuckled again. "Ma'Chido! Don't tell me you paid attention to Lucia. You know she says the first thing that comes into her head. As for Tambudzai, we will spoil her if we let her carry on in the way she has begun to behave. She must be disciplined. She must finish her punishment."

"Do you forget, Baba," Maiguru persisted, "that her brother died in this house? What will her parents think when she tells them how she was punished. Truly, this punishment is too much for the child."

"Now, what is the matter, Mai? There is no need to bring up all that. Tambudzai is my brother's daughter, I am her father. I have the right to discipline her. It is my duty."

Maiguru said a lot of things then. "Yes, she is your brother's child," she said. "But when it comes to taking my money so that you can feed her and her father and your whole family and waste it on ridiculous weddings, that's when they are my relatives too. Let me tell you, Babawa Chido, I am tired of my house being a hotel for your family. I am tired of being a housekeeper for them. I am tired of being nothing in a home I am working myself sick to support. And now even that Lucia can walk in here and tell me that the things she discusses with you, here in my home, are none of my business. I am sick of it, Babawa Chido. Let me tell you, I have had enough!"

We could hear them quarrelling. Nyasha, who had picked up a dish full of clothes to take to the line, stopped to listen, forgot what she was doing, tipped the clean clothes back into the dirty water and had to pretend that they needed another rinse. She was shaken. So was I. We had not heard Babamukuru and Maiguru quarrel before.

"Ma'Chido," Babamukuru was saying pacifically, "these are not good words."

"No, they are not," Maiguru retorted recklessly, "but if they are not good things to be said, then neither are they good things to happen. But they are happening here in my home."

"No, Ma'Chido," soothed my uncle. "It is not as you say."

"It is as I say," she insisted. "And when I keep quiet you think I am enjoying it. So today I am telling you I am not happy. I am not happy any more in this house."

Babamukuru thought he had taken enough. "Then go where you will be happy," he snapped, and departed to his office.

"I don't think she will leave," Nyasha said as we lay in bed in the dark. "But you never know. She's never gone this far before." There was a note of awe in her voice that I had not heard before when she talked of her mother.

"But you can't want her to go," I whispered. "How will you manage without her?"

"I don't know," admitted the daughter, "but it would be good for her if she did."

I was silent. Nyasha knew nothing about leaving. She had only been taken to places—to the mission, to England, back to the mission. She did not know what essential parts of you stayed behind no matter how violently you tried to dislodge them in order to take them with you.

"You grow," said Nyasha, as though she had heard what I was thinking. "You grow and you compensate. You have to. There's no other way. We're all trying to do it, you know. All of us. But it's difficult when everything's laid out for you. It's difficult when everything's taken care of. Even the way you think."

To our surprise, Maiguru did leave, by bus, early the next morning. She did not slink away in the dark, but quite openly packed a suitcase, put on her travelling clothes, had her breakfast and left. Babamukuru was still feeling injured, which was why, I thought, he let her go, but Nyasha had a different theory. She thought Babamukuru simply did not believe that Maiguru would do it. Would do it, could do it. It made no difference, she said. The point was that he did not believe. Babamukuru, she said, expected his wife to get cold feet before she got to the bus-stop or, at the latest, before the bus pulled away. It would have been useful, Nyasha said, if things had turned out that way, because then Babamukuru would always have been able to remind his wife that she had tried to leave and had failed. Unfortunately, she told me, Babamukuru had to wait until Maiguru had boarded that bus and had gone to discover whether he was right or not, and by that time it was too late to do anything about it.

Whether this was the case or not, I remember that there was something large and determined about Maiguru in the way that she made up her mind and, making no fuss, carried out her plan. Even Nyasha was impressed. She went to hug her mother goodbye at the door, but Maiguru, wanting only to go, remained cold. Nyasha was hurt but big-hearted enough not to be jealous of her mother. "I guess it's a one-woman show," she said ruefully.

Personally, I thought Nyasha was a little unbalanced not to be distressed by being abandoned so abruptly. Nyasha, though, didn't know what I was talking about. She did not think her mother had deserted her. She thought there was a difference between people deserting their daughters and people saving themselves. Maiguru was doing the latter and would be available to her daughter when she was needed. "We'll survive," she assured me. "We'll manage somehow."

I was not so sure. Managing Babamukuru was not a child's job. Maiguru's departure was evidence of this. But Nyasha, who had still not tested the cast of Babamukuru's soul, thought that Babamukuru was, like her, flexible and would in the long run make a healthy adjustment. Consequently she thought only in terms of her mother's emancipation and was comforted by it.

"I'll tell you why, Tambu," she explained. "Sometimes I feel I'm trapped by that man, just like she is. But now she's done it, now she's broken out, I know it's possible, so I can wait." She sighed. "But it's not that simple, you know, really it isn't. It's not really him, you know. I mean not really the person. It's everything, it's everywhere. So where do you break out to? You're just one person and it's everywhere. So where do you break out to? I don't know, Tambu, really I don't know. So what do you do? I don't know."

It was true. It was a sad truth, tragic in Maiguru's case, because even if there had been somewhere to go, she would not have been able to, since her investment, in the form of her husband and two children, was all at the mission. We tried not to be discouraged by this knowledge, but it weighed heavily on our minds. We needed to be reassured, which we did for each other by inventing increasingly fantastic options for Maiguru.

"She'll go back to England. To study for another degree," said I.

"She'll teach at the University," Nyasha countered.

"She'll become a doctor."

"She'll start her own business," Nyasha suggested,

and sighed again. "Maybe she could have once. But now it's too late." Poor Nyasha. She could not conquer the hopelessness.

If Babamukuru was unhappy about Maiguru's disappearance, he made a good job of concealing it. He carried on as he normally did: up and out before we had eaten our breakfast, back for lunch and for supper, and then back to the office until we were in bed. I do not know what would have happened had Chido not telephoned in the evening, on the Thursday after my aunt's departure. Nyasha took the call. Maiguru was well, Chido told us. She had been to see him. She was spending some time with her brother and his family. She did not know how long. She would return when she felt strong enough to do so.

Nyasha was unhappy that Maiguru had gone to her brother. "A man! She always runs to men," she despaired. "There's no hope, Tambu. Really, there isn't." Nor did she want her mother to come back so soon. It was difficult to say whether she wanted her to come back at all. She thought Maiguru had not had enough of a break, that Babamukuru would appreciate her more if he were made to miss her a bit longer. For these reasons she was in two minds as to whether she should pass on Chido's message or not, but of course she had to, so she waited up for her father until he came home at one o'clock, which was a little later than usual, to tell him what Chido had said.

"Thank you," grunted the man when the girl had repeated the message, and passed on to his bedroom.

Nyasha came to bed, but before we were able to fall asleep, the green sedan roared down the drive, its lights flooding our bedroom for an instant before receding into the night. Babamukuru returned at eight o'clock the next morning, bringing his wife with him.

Maiguru had been away for only five days, but the change had done her good. She smiled more often and less mechanically, fussed over us less and was more willing or able to talk about sensible things. Although she still called Babamukuru her Daddy-sweet, most of her baby-talk had disappeared.

"It's such a waste," lamented Nyasha, noting the difference. "Imagine what she might have been with the right kind of exposure!" And then she confessed that she was having one of her rare pangs of guilt, because deep down she was glad that her mother had come home.

Chapter 9

One day, I remember it was late in the third term because it was just before our Grade Seven examinations, the nuns came to the mission. We were concentrating hard on our studies. Lessons had ended because, our teacher said, he had taught us the entire syllabus so it was up to us now to embed what he had taught us firmly in our memories. So instead of classes we had revision periods. Mr. Sanyati divided us up into groups and sent us outside with the life-cycle of the Anopheles mosquito, the dates of the Boer rebellions, the ordinary, comparative and superlative of irregular adjectives, and expected us to be able to recite them by rote when we came back into the classroom. With all this on our minds, we might not have paid much attention to the nuns when they drove up to the school in their sparkling Kombi. But ours was a Protestant mission. We had no knowledge of nuns except as spiritual, chaste beings who dedicated their pious, prayerful lives to the service of God. This, we knew, was why the Roman Catholic Church was superior to our own: it created such virtue. Thus, when the nuns came to the mission and we saw that instead of murmuring soft blessings and gliding seraphically over the grass in diaphanous habits, they wore smart blouses and skirts and walked, laughed and talked in low twanging tones very much like our own American missionaries did, we were very disappointed.

Seeing them close up like that, finding out how ordinary they were, exploded most of the myth about them, or at least the parts that mattered, since the question of sex was not an obsession with us, and anyway we had no way of judging their chastity. But it was not all disappointing. They lived up to part of their promise by smiling beatifically over us as Mr. Sanyati showed off our talents. Of course I was chosen first to recite a poem. "Hamelintown'sin-BrunswickbyfamousHanoverCity," I began, raising a gasp of admiration from my class, who knew I was bright but not quite that bright, not bright enough to have learnt such a long poem, one they had never heard of before, and recite it so well. I gabbled through the lines at a delirious pace, because the faster you recited things like that, the more fluent it meant you were. Then we danced for the nuns, in a circle, singing and clapping our hands. After that we subjected them to a play. They enjoyed it all tremendously.

They made us write a test, which we thought was unfair because we had not been warned and had not prepared. Mr. Sanyati said we should not worry because it was general knowledge and general ability, but this only confused us more. General knowledge was all right, but general ability was a subject we had not taken. It sounded foreign and sophisticated and ever so difficult. Mr. Sanyati told us that the nuns had come all the way from their own mission to have us write this test and herded all the girls in Grade Seven A into the classroom to answer questions about Louisa M. Alcott and *Little Women*, to multiply seven acorns by twenty-three acorns by forty-eight acorns by no acorns and to pick the odd item out in a set of gumboots, galoshes, snow shoes and bedroom slippers.

After the examination the nuns wanted to talk to us. One by one we were ushered in to see them. We were actually very impressed with them after that. We thought they were very kind and definitely holy to take such an interest in us, for interested they were, asking us all sorts of questions about our parents and our friends and what we liked to do in our free time.

I was delighted that people, white people for that matter, thought my background was interesting. I thought I should tell them about Babamukuru as well, to show them that my family had a progressive branch, but they were more interested in my own father and my life on the homestead.

As it turned out, the nuns had come to recruit us. There was much excited discussion when we found out that we had written an entrance examination. One or two girls knew some Catholics and they told us in hushed voices of the nuns' nefarious practices. Apparently what they did was this: they took you to school and after your Form Two they persuaded you to join the order. Their methods were not particularly subtle. Further scholarships were offered and it was made clear that refusal indicated a damnable lack of grace. In this position many of the girls thought it practical to slip into a novice's habit, but most of them found it did not suit them. The vows were even more compromising and the girls often got pregnant to avoid making them. These were the widespread accusations against the nuns, but they didn't do much to dispel the glamour that, in a most attractive manner, surrounded the prospect of going to school at a convent. And not just any convent, but a multiracial convent. A prestigious private school that manufactured guaranteed young ladies. At that convent, which was just outside town but on the other side, to the south, you wore pleated terylene skirts to school every day and on Sundays a tailor-made two-piece linen suit with gloves, yes, even with gloves! We all wanted to go. That was only natural. But only two places were on offer, two places for all the African Grade Seven girls in the country. The effect was drastic and dangerous. We stopped liking each other as much as we used to in case the other was offered the place and we had to suffer the pangs of jealousy while she rose in status and esteem. It wasn't fair, we thought, which was true; but then nothing about that examination had been fair. Nobody else had prepared for the test, whereas I had been preparing ever since I came to the mission. With Nyasha's various and exotic library to digest, with having to cope with her experimental disposition, her insistence on alternatives, her passion for transmuting the present into the possible; having to cope with all this, which I did at a purely intellectual level, not because I thought it was rational but because it was amusing and I loved my cousin and admired her, having coped with these intellectual challenges for close on two years, I was far ahead of my peers in both general knowledge and general ability. So it was not in the least surprising that I performed brilliantly in that entrance examination, thereby earning the privilege of associating with the elite of that time, the privilege of being admitted on an honorary basis into their culture.

Of course, I did not appreciate the gravity of my situation at that time, my only experience of those people having been with charitable Doris and the fervent missionaries on the mission. But Nyasha knew them and was alarmed. She could not hide, did not even try to hide, her disappointment when I told her how thrilled I was, what an experience I would have, what an opportunity it was, how I intended to put that opportunity to maximum use. She thought there were more evils than advantages to be reaped from such an opportunity. It would be a marvellous opportunity, she said sarcastically, to forget. To forget who you were, what you were and why you were that. The process, she said, was called assimilation, and that was what was intended for the precocious few who might prove a nuisance if left to themselves, whereas the others—well really, who cared about the others? So they made a little space into which you were assimilated, an honorary space in which you could join them and they could make sure that you behaved yourself. I would be comfortable in such a position, she remarked nastily, because look how well I had got on with Babamukuru. But, she insisted, one ought not to occupy that space. Really, one ought to refuse. In my case that meant not going to the nun's mission. "You'll fall for their tricks," she said, pointing out that I would obtain a much more useful education at the mission.

If she hadn't said that, that last bit about education at the mission, I might have believed her, but everybody knew that the European schools had better equipment, better teachers, better furniture, better food, better everything. The idea that anything about our mission could be better than theirs was clearly ridiculous. Besides, once you were given a place at one of their schools, you went on and on until you'd finished your "A" levels. You didn't have to worry about eliminating exams at every stage of the way. That was how it was. That was how it would be. If you were clever, you slipped through any loophole you could find. I for one was going to take any opportunity that came my way. I was quite sure about that; I was very determined. The latest opportunity was this one of going to the convent. I would go. I was sure of myself. I was not sceptical like Nyasha. How could I possibly forget my brother and the mealies, my mother and the latrine and the wedding? These were all evidence of the burdens my mother had succumbed to. Going to the convent was a chance to lighten those burdens by entering a world where burdens were light. I would take the chance. I would lighten my burdens. I would go. If Babamukuru would let me.

Still Nyasha was not impressed. "Really, Tambudzai," she said severely when I had finished glorifying my interests, "there'll always be brothers and mealies and mothers too tired to clean latrines. Whether you go to the convent or not. There's more to be done than that." This was typical of Nyasha, this obstinate idealism. But she could afford it, being my affluent uncle's daughter. Whereas I, I had to take whatever chances came my way.

Babamukuru was of the opinion that enough chances had come my way, and on another level he agreed with Nyasha that the experience would not be good for me. From his armchair opposite the fireplace he told me why I could not go to the convent.

"It is not a question of money," he assured me. "Although there would still be a lot of expense on my part, you have your scholarship, so the major financial burden would be lifted. But I feel that even that little money could be better used. For one thing, there is now the small boy at home. Every month I put away a little bit, a very little bit, a very little bit every month, so that when he is of school-going age everything will be provided for. As you know, he is the only boy in your family, so he must be provided for. As for you, we think we are providing for you quite well. By the time you have finished your Form Four you will be able to take your course, whatever it is that you choose. In time you will be earning money. You will be in a position to be married by a decent man and set up a decent home. In all that we are doing for you, we are preparing you for this future life of yours, and I have observed from my own daughter's behaviour that it is not a good thing for a young girl to associate too much with these white people, to have too much freedom. I have seen that girls who do that do not develop into decent women."

Marriage. I had nothing against it in principle. In an abstract way I thought it was a very good idea. But it was irritating the way it always cropped up in one form or another, stretching its tentacles back to bind me before I had even begun to think about it seriously, threatening to disrupt my life before I could even call it my own. Babamukuru had lost me with his talk of marriage. I inspected my dressing-gown for fluff, waiting for the session to end. "This," continued my uncle, "is what I shall tell your father: if he wishes to send you there to that school, he may do so if he can find the money. Myself, I would not consider it money well spent. Mai," he concluded, turning to my aunt, "is there anything that you would wish to say?"

"Yes, Baba," Maiguru spoke up softly from the sofa. My inspection came to an abrupt end. I listened incredulously.

"You do!" exclaimed Babamukuru and, recovering himself, invited her to continue. "Speak freely, Mai. Say whatever you are thinking."

There was a pause during which Maiguru folded her arms and leant back in the sofa. "I don't think," she began easily in her soft, soothing voice, "that Tambudzai will be corrupted by going to that school. Don't you remember, when we went to South Africa everybody was saying that we, the women, were loose." Babamukuru winced at this explicitness. Maiguru continued. "It wasn't a question of associating with this race or that race at that time. People were prejudiced against educated women. Prejudiced. That's why they said we weren't decent. That was in the fifties. Now we are into the seventies. I am disappointed that people still believe the same things. After all this time and when we have seen nothing to say it is true. I don't know what people mean by a loose woman—sometimes she is someone who walks the streets, sometimes she is an educated woman, sometimes she is a successful man's daughter or she is simply beautiful. Loose or decent, I don't know. All I know is that if our daughter Tambudzai is not a decent person now, she never will be, no matter where she goes to school. And if she is decent, then this convent should not change her. As for money, you have said yourself that she has a full scholarship. It is possible that you have other reasons why she should not go there, Babawa Chido, but these—the question of decency and the question of money—are the ones I have heard and so these are the ones I have talked of."

There was another pause during which Maiguru unfolded her arms and clasped her hands in her lap.

Babamukuru cleared his throat. "Er, Tambudzai," he asked tentatively, "do you have anything to say?"

The next day Babamukuru took me home for the Christmas vacation. My sisters were excited to see me because I was astonishing them with my academic prowess. "Mauya wekuchirungu," they greeted me, and I modestly declined the title, not because I did not want it but because Babamukuru had not granted it to me.

My uncle was not staying long that day. There was no time to discuss the question of my education. My father, who was always enthusiastic in Babamukuru's presence, congratulated Babamukuru on having moulded my mind so skilfully that even white people were impressed by the result, but Babamukuru refused to be drawn. "We have not decided what will be done about Tambudzai. We shall discuss it when I come to spend some time here at Christmas."

This gave me hope that Maiguru's speech had had some effect. I waited impatiently for Christmas, but when it came it did not bring our relatives to the homestead. Maiguru flatly refused to spend another Christmas catering for a family of two dozen. So, for ten days of the Christmas season, Babamukuru drove back and forth between the homestead and the mission, sometimes bringing Maiguru and Nyasha with him, more often coming alone. Chido we never saw, because he always had other engagements. My

mother was secretly pleased that Maiguru did not
want to stay on the homestead, although naturally she
had to make polite protestations, inviting them to
sleep over every time that my uncle and aunt left for
the mission. She was very proud of her house and
Dover Stove and could not bear the thought of their
being used by their original owner. Technically the
situation was that Maiguru no longer had a kitchen at
home, the promised house not yet having been built,
and this was probably why she had been so adamant
in her refusal to spend Christmas at home. Another
consequence of Maiguru's kitchenless state was that
the food could not be as appetising or as plentiful as
it was when she managed the catering. We would have
had a serious problem with shortages if Tete and
Babamunini Thomas had come to stay that year, but a
week or so before the festivities began they sent word
that they were not able to come. The foundations for
Maiguru's house were begun in the middle of January.

It was on New Year's Eve that my uncle and my
father discussed my future. The discussion took place
in the house. I was obliged to eavesdrop.

"It may change her character for the worse . . .
these Whites, you know . . . you never know," mused
Babamukuru.

"No," agreed my father. "How could you know
with these ones? You never know. With Whites! No.
You never know."

"On the other hand," continued my uncle, "she
would receive a first-class education."

"Ah, ya, Mukoma, first class. First class," my
father enthused.

"I did not want her to go to that school . . ." said
Babamukuru.

"What for, Mukoma? Why should she go there?
Your mission is first class."

". . . because of the reasons I have told you,"

continued my uncle. "But then, considering that this is a fine opportunity for the girl to receive the finest education in Rhodesia, I think she must not be denied the opportunity. I have decided to let her go."

My father went down on one knee. Bo-bo-bo. "We thank you, Chirandu, we thank you, *Muera bonga*, Chihwa" he intoned. "Truly, we would not survive without you. Our children would not survive without you. Head of the family, princeling, we thank you."

This is how it was settled. I was to take another step upwards in the direction of my freedom. Another step away from the flies, the smells, the fields and the rags; from stomachs which were seldom full, from dirt and disease, from my father's abject obeisance to Babamukuru and my mother's chronic lethargy. Also from Nyamarira that I loved.

The prospect of this freedom and its possible price made me dizzy. I had to sit down, there on the steps that led up to the house. Then I felt numb; then I felt better. The cost would balance. What I needed I would take with me, the rest I would discard. It would be worth it to dress my sisters in pretty clothes, feed my mother until she was plump and energetic again, stop my father making a fool of himself every time he came into Babamukuru's presence. Money would do all this for me. With the ticket I would acquire attending the convent, I would earn lots of it.

"No," Babamukuru was saying, his face beaming to compete with the paraffin flame, "do not thank me. It is Tambudzai who worked hard for that scholarship."

I did not listen any more but let my imagination take over. I saw myself smart and clean in a white blouse and dark-red pleated terylene skirt, with blazer and gloves and a hat. It was a pretty picture, so charming it had to be described to my mother immediately. She was in the kitchen because, in spite of her Dover Stove, she preferred her old hearth. She said she felt more comfortable beside it. So she sat there, often, as I found her this time, alone on her mat suckling Dambudzo, who was now nine months old, holding him on her lap with one hand and picking without interest with the other at her supper of *sadza* and sour milk.

"I thought you did not want food," she apologised for beginning without me. "You were so long taking the food to the house."

I washed my hands, sat down beside her and swallowed a few morsels of *sadza* without tasting them, moulding them much longer between my fingers than was necessary: my appetite had departed with the news I had heard. Hardly able to believe my luck, I told my mother of Babamukuru's decision.

"Ho-o-re," she sighed at length and bitterly when I was through. "Tell me, Tambudzai, does that man want to kill me, to kill me with his kindness, fattening my children only to take them away, like cattle are fattened for slaughter? Tell me, my daughter, what will I, your mother say to you when you come home a stranger full of white ways and ideas? It will be English, English all the time. He-e, Mummy this, he-e, Mummy that. Like that cousin of yours. I have seen it happen—we saw it happen here in our home. Truly that man is calling down a curse of bad luck on my head. You have survived the mission so now he must send you even further away. I've had enough, I tell you, I've had enough of that man dividing me from my children. Dividing me from my children and ruling my life. He says this and we jump. To wear a veil, at my age, to wear a veil! Just imagine—to wear a veil. If I were a witch I would enfeeble his mind, truly I would do it, and then we would see how his education and his money helped him."

My mother declined so rapidly after that it was as though she was the one who had been cursed. She ate less and less and did less and less, until within days she could neither eat nor do anything, not even change the dress she wore. She did not go to Nyamarira to wash, or to the garden. On the days that she did get up at all she rose late and did nothing but sit in the sun, feeding Dambudzo when he cried but otherwise reacting to nothing. Dambudzo developed diarrhoea, a horrendous watery stool that ran and ran. My mother said that he would die, that babies died when they had diarrhoea. My father was truly frightened and spent the few precious cents that he reserved for his beer on the bus-fare to the mission. When he came back he told us that the nurses thought my mother was bottle-feeding and that the diarrhoea had been caused by an insanitary teat. He thought the best thing to do was to take my mother to a medium. He knew a good one in the next village, but I was against it. I could not tell my father what curses my mother had wished on Babamukuru. Such things were not said lightly and I was truly frightened that she would devise some terrible mischief if she had the opportunity to engage the services of a medium. Besides, I knew what was worrying my mother. A medium could not help whereas I could, by not going to Sacred Heart. But this was asking too much of me, so I reminded my father that Babamukuru would not approve of such things as mediums and the like. My father was not concerned, because he said Babamukuru would not know, so I threatened that I would tell my uncle, whereupon my father gave in and sent for Lucia, who came immediately.

Takesure was very pleased with this development, but Lucia did not even see him. She went straight into a regime of what I can only call a sort of shock treatment. First Lucia made my mother walk to Nyamarira, quite simply by strapping Dambudzo to her back, grasping my mother round the waist and walking her there. Then she made my mother wash herself and the baby. "Sisi," she threatened, wading calf-high through the water and depositing Dumbudzo on a boulder, "watch me. I am putting him on this rock and leaving him there, right in the middle, in the middle of the river. If he slips into the water because you do nothing to save him then you will truly go mad, because this time you will be guilty." Dambudzo, because the rock was warm and smooth and because the water sparkled prettily at its edges, thought it was a jolly game. He gurgled at Lucia and crawled to the edge to splash. Babies are clever and do not crawl over edges, but mothers are anxious nevertheless.

"Lucia," my mother said, "Lucia, why are you doing this? Why? Why do you bother me? Why don't you just let me die?" And removing her dress she waded out to the rock to wash herself and her son. While mother was washing, Lucia washed my mother's dress for her, so that when my mother and Dambudzo were clean, they were forced to sit in the sun until the dress dried. Now, unlike a physical ailment of which everyone is told, an illness of this nature is kept quiet and secret, and so when other women came to wash or to draw water they saw my mother and Lucia and Dambudzo leisurely waiting for their clothes to dry, which is a normal sight at Nyamarira. In addition, they were all very pleased to see Lucia and so they were very lively and gay when they came over to greet my mother and Lucia, merrily scolding Lucia for having been away so long, laughing over how Dambudzo had grown, what a handsome young man he was becoming, how all the women in the neighbourhood would soon be falling in love with him. It was all very good medicine.

When they returned Lucia cooked the evening meal, making a thick stew out of some meat she had brought with her.

"Tambudzai," she instructed me in my father's presence, "make sure nobody touches this meat. Nobody besides your mother, who is ill and needs to regain her strength."

That night my mother and Lucia slept together in the kitchen, which annoyed Takesure, who had invited Lucia to the *hozi*. They talked most of the night. My mother slept in the early hours of the morning, waking at ten o'clock to find Lucia had prepared her porridge and had made it with milk to make it rich and sustaining. Lucia stayed two more days to see my mother well on her way to recovery before she returned to the mission. She could not stay longer as she, as we all, would have wished, because although it was vacation time she was officially on duty, and also because the Grade One class was writing examinations at the end of the month and she was studying hard. A week after Lucia left my mother felt strong enough to go back to her garden. Life resumed its normal round of hoeing and watering and visits to Nyamarira with our water-drums and laundry.

Early in the third week of January, Babamukuru sent word that he was busy with admissions, would not be able to fetch me as usual. I was to make my way to the mission alone that same week in order to prepare for my advent to the convent. Grumbling at the expense, my father gave me thirty cents for the bus-fare. My mother was sad, but I had seen that she was recovering and so could look forward to the new life I was moving into without feeling guilty. I felt so important on that trip, so grown up and responsible as I bought my ticket and selected my seat. I sat next to a woman my mother's age so that the young men would not bother me. Unable to restrain myself I proudly informed her that I was going to my uncle who was headmaster at the mission and would take me to Sacred Heart.

I had only one night at the mission before going on to the Young Ladies College of the Sacred Heart. One night was not long and there was much to say. I could hardly wait to see my cousin, who had come to the homestead infrequently that vacation. I was eager to discuss with her yet again and in detail the richness of people and self that I expected to find at the convent.

It was such a blow to find on arriving that she was not yet home from her lessons, and I was impatient even though there was not long to wait before classes ended for the day. Lessons at the secondary school ended at four o'clock, which meant forty minutes to wait and then maybe twenty more to give Nyasha time to pack away her books, have a word with her classmates and walk down to the house. But half-past four went by without bringing Nyasha, then five o'clock and half past. Maiguru came but could not say where her daughter was. "Perhaps playing netball," she suggested, so I walked up to the netball field, where I found a group of girls whiling away the time between the end of lessons and supper by shooting into the ring.

From a distance I recognised Jocelyn and Maidei but there was no sign of Nyasha. This was disappointing, but still it was good to see my friends, especially Maidei, whom I had not expected to see again. It had been fairly certain that Jocelyn would be back for Form One, because she had been good in Grade Seven, always in the top dozen, whereas Maidei had hardly ever managed to scrape more than 50 per cent in the tests. So it was a surprise, a pleasant surprise, to see her there, shooting the ball into the ring. It was especially good to see them now after six weeks of vacation, for that was a long time to spend without seeing either your friends, or the old familiar places, or your friends in the old familiar places. Almost as bad, it had been six weeks without netball, six weeks with none of the camaraderie and closeness of friendly competition in which there are no stakes. Itching to get my hands on that ball, I ran over to the pitch. They all saw me coming. To this day I can swear that Maidei saw me first. I saw her stop with the ball in her hands to point me out to the others, but as I ran on to the field they were cool and silent. They ignored me. It hurt to have my friends behave so cruelly and I was naïve enough not to know why I deserved it, so I joined the game anyway, jumping into the ring to catch the ball as it fell and scoring a clean goal. As luck would have it—I was not a particularly good shooter—the ball did not even graze the rim. That broke the ice.

"She has been practising," Jocelyn joked as I caught the ball again since nobody else appeared inclined to. Balancing it in my hand I took careful aim. This annoyed Maidei so much that she knocked the ball out of my hand.

"Don't waste our time," she snapped. "We're practising for the team. They don't play netball where you're going, do they? So what are you doing here? Basketball," she chanted, bouncing the ball about in a professional way, "and hockey and tennis and swimming. That's what you'll be doing. With your Whites. Knowing you, the next thing we'll hear is that you've gone to the Olympics." She giggled loudly into the awkward silence that greeted her words, then illogically took offence at the sound of her own voice. "What's the matter with you?" she snapped at the rest of the girls. "Have you had enough of netball today? It's suppertime. Who's coming?" she asked, and left without waiting for an answer. Jocelyn stayed long enough to say goodbye.

"Write to us when you get there," she said. "We'll reply to all your letters."

"Yes," said the others, leaving also, "make sure you don't forget us."

Sadly, thoughtfully, I watched them go. Don't forget, don't forget, don't forget. Nyasha, my mother, my friends. Always the same message. But why? If I forgot them, my cousin, my mother, my friends, I might as well forget myself. And that, of course, could not happen. So why was everybody so particular to urge me to remember? These questions buzzed about in my head as I walked to the Form Four A classroom to look for my cousin; questions, questions, questions, but not a single answer.

Nyasha was at her desk studying, so intent on her work that she did not notice me until I stood beside her and said hello. She returned my greeting abruptly, hardly looking up from her books and not even bothering to ask after my family. It was a saddening reception I received from Nyasha that day, reminding me of the closed girl who had come from England in a pink mini-dress, not the cousin and friend she had mellowed into in the years since then. She did not want me there, it seemed, but I had not seen her for three whole weeks, had been looking forward to seeing her so much during those weeks, did not have much time before I went away to Sacred Heart. I could not leave. I sat down and waited, pulling my hair, cleaning my fingernails and finding a spot on my knee that I could squeeze to pass the time. When I had finished with the spot I looked up to find Nyasha regarding me very sadly. She looked down in confusion and applied herself to her books once more. She did not stop writing but she began to talk.

"I shall miss you, Tambu," she said, frowning in her effort to concentrate on her notes and so avoid saying more than was useful. In the end she gave up and faced me directly. "It's been good having you around," she said, "and . . ." There was a lot more to be said, we could feel it hanging in the air, a thread between us that we both wanted to grasp but were too clumsy to be able to. ". . . and I shall miss you," was all she managed to say.

"I shall miss you too," I told her.

"It's suppertime. We'd better go," she said, packing her books away in the desk. We walked down to the house in silence. The sadness of parting hung over us so heavily that even the prospect of Sacred Heart, the novelty, the excitement, the glamour I expected to find there, not even these seemed worth talking about.

Baba and Maiguru were already at table by the time we reached the house. Babamukuru was not in a good mood.

"Er, Nyasha," he asked, cutting her greeting short and not even seeing me, "can you tell me why you are only coming in at this time, at a quarter to seven?"

"I was working," she replied, seating herself, "in the classroom."

"Until this hour? I have told you to be home by six o'clock. That is a decent hour for a decent girl to come home."

"There were no boys there, if that's what you're worried about," Nyasha volunteered recklessly.

"Nyasha, try to be quiet," advised Maiguru.

"What did you say?" Babamukuru asked his daughter, his voice rising in annoyance.

"Nothing," said Nyasha. "May I be excused from the table?"

"You aren't going anywhere," her father told her. "Where do you think you are going?"

"I'm not hungry," Nyasha explained.

"You will eat that food," commanded the man. "Your mother and I are not killing ourselves working just for you to waste your time playing with boys and then come back and turn up your nose at what we offer. Sit and eat that food. I am telling you. Eat it!"

Nyasha took a few mouthfuls.

"She has had enough, Baba," Maiguru said, but

Babamukuru was adamant. He was very upset.

"She must eat her food, all of it. She is always doing this, challenging me. I am her father. If she doesn't want to do what I say, I shall stop providing for her— fees, clothes, food, everything."

"Nyasha, eat your food," her mother advised.

"Christ!" Nyasha breathed and with a shrug picked up her fork and began to eat, slowly at first, then gobbling the food down without a break. The atmosphere lightened with every mouthful she took.

"You may go now," her father said when she had emptied her plate.

She went straight to the bathroom, spent a long time there. Excusing myself from the table, I waited in the bedroom. I could hear her gagging and choking.

"Are you ill?" I asked when she came in.

She sat heavily on her bed, shook her head. "No," she answered at length. "I did it myself. With my toothbrush. Don't ask me why. I don't know." She was quiet for a minute, not looking at me, and when she turned to me again her eyes were distressed.

"You know, Tambu," she began again painfully, "I guess he's right, right to dislike me. It's not his fault, it's me. But I can't help it. Really, I can't. He makes me so angry. I can't just shut up when he puts on his God act. I'm just not made that way. Why not? Why can't I just take it like everybody else does? I ought to take it, but really, I can't."

There was nothing I could say that was true that would have helped, so I said nothing but sat down beside her and put my arm round her.

"It was better," she went on, "when you were here because we could laugh about it, so it looked silly and funny and we could carry on that way. But now that you're going, there won't be anyone to laugh with. It won't be funny any more. We'll all take these things much too seriously. But they are silly, you know, really they are. Imagine all that fuss over a plateful of food. But it's more than that really, more than just food. That's how it comes out, but really it's all the things about boys and men and being decent and indecent and good and bad. He goes on and on with the accusations and the threats, and I'm just not coping very well. Sometimes I look at things from his point of view, you know what I mean, traditions and expectations and authority, that sort of thing, and I can see what he means and I try to be considerate and patient and obedient, really I do. But then I start thinking that he ought to look at things from my point of view and be considerate and patient with me, so I start fighting back and off we go again. I suppose it's all right really," she said, attempting to smile. "I'll just have to try harder to be better, that's all. I'm sorry I was nasty when you came into the classroom. It's just that . . . just that . . . well, as I said, I'll miss you."

Then we talked about other things, mainly about Sacred Heart and what I would do there, until it was time to sleep.

Chapter 10

Excitement. Anticipation. Elation and exultation. It was all very much the same as it had been on that first day that I went to the mission, the day that I began my new life. Yes, it had begun so thoroughly that January afternoon two years ago when I went to the mission, and it was continuing. Everything was coming together. All the things that I wanted were tying themselves up into a neat package which presented itself to me with a flourish. There should have been trumpets, truly there should have been. For was I—I Tambudzai, lately of the mission and before that the homestead—was I Tambudzai, so recently a peasant, was I not entering, as I had promised myself I would, a world where burdens lightened with every step, soon to disappear altogether? I had an idea that this would happen as I passed through the school gates, those gates that would declare me a young lady, a member of the Young Ladies College of the Sacred Heart. I was impatient to get to those gates. The drive was too long. The car had to go faster to get me there in time.

We were all in the car, all four of us, Babamukuru, Maiguru, Nyasha and me. Babamukuru was not happy about the arrangement, thinking Nyasha ought not to miss her classes just to take me to mine, but she had free periods that afternoon and her form-master had given her permission to miss the prep that usually took up the time. Maiguru must have talked to Babamukuru as well because though he looked annoyed when Nyasha climbed into the car beside me, he did not tell her to get out.

Maiguru, who had not fussed for a long time, could not resist the temptation on this occasion. A marvellous chicken lunch had been prepared in my honour, with chocolate cake afterwards so deliciously rich and sticky with icing that even Nyasha had forgotten her figure long enough to put away two slices of it. Somehow the question of tuck had escaped Maiguru's maternal attention and although I insisted to her that I did not need chocolate biscuits and potato crisps and orange juice, she insisted that I did, and so we stopped in town to buy these things, adding twenty endless minutes to the time I had calculated the journey would take. Maiguru bought enough tuck to feed a small colony for several months. Nyasha warned me that if I ate all of it, even over the course of a term, I would end up unable to see past my stomach to admire my dainty new uniform shoes. We had a rather wild laugh at this even though it wasn't very funny. But we needed to laugh to forget that this was the end of our closeness and to that extent our friendship. So we giggled foolishly as we piled the packets and bottles and tins into the car. There was jam, tomato sauce, all sorts of things besides the biscuits and squash and crisps. Then, just as Babamukuru started the engine, Maiguru remembered that I would need a tumbler to drink my orange juice out of and went back to buy it. Eventually we arrived at Sacred Heart.

None of us had been there before, except Babamukuru. He had been several times to discuss my admission with Sister Emmanuel, who was both Mother Superior and Principal, and to pay her the only expenditure, the cost of my uniform, which, he told me dourly, would have paid for my whole year's board and tuition at his mission. Because I had not seen the place before, I was infatuated when we turned into the school gates. The grounds were majestically spacious. I never did discover how many hectares of land those nuns owned, but to the eye it looked like hundreds. We drove, slowly because there were humps, up past the hockey pitches, four of them neatly laid out side by side, past the tennis courts and the netball, yes, netball courts, to a thicket of conifers that seemed to signify that within this rich kingdom we had left the province of the physical and entered the realm of mental activity, because beyond the trees was a roundabout at the top of which stood the school buildings. The dormitories, bright and shimmering white in the clear summer sun, stretched towards us on one side of the roundabout, the classrooms stretched down on the other. Between them was an archway, supported by ornate plaster pillars in, I was to be told, the Greek style, not the Roman, and above this long archway rose the dining-room and chapel. The roundabout itself was serenely green with a lavish, permanently moist lawn, the latter relieved in places carefully selected so that the green would not be too monotonous, by flowering shrubs. Delicate mimosa fluffed puffs of yellow and silvery white, robust poinsettia splashed patches of crimson and peach against the green. Two swans cruised elegantly across a pond in the middle of the lawn and later I found there shoals of goldfish, goldfish which were not a pale imitation but definitely gold. Their rich, ruddy glow flicked in and out of water weeds in the company of more exotic species that shot flashes of red and blue and silver through the gold. I was enchanted, so obviously so that Nyasha thought she ought to remind me that I had come to school and not on holiday. Reluctantly I remembered.

Ours was not the only car on the wide tarmac drive complete with road markings. Dozens of cars were winding their way up one arm of the roundabout, stopping at the top for whatever period of time it took to get daughter settled, and then winding away again down the other side. There were more cars in the parking area at the top of the roundabout than I had ever seen in one place in my life. I imagined that every girl, every single one of the three hundred pupils at Sacred Heart must have brought with her her very own car. And what cars they were, long, lean and gleaming. I sent up a little prayer of thanksgiving that Babamukuru had seen fit to drive the green Ford, but I noticed that he always arrived in the Rover after that. Nyasha accurately perceived that all this affluence was dazzling me. Delicately she cleared her throat. "Excuse me," she murmured in cultured tones, "but are you sure this is the right place?"

"What do you mean?" growled my uncle. "Of course this is the place!" His foot pressed down, certainly unconsciously, on the accelerator, sending us swinging over a hump which left our stomachs behind and caused Maiguru and me to catch our breath sharply, while Nyasha let out a sharp yelp. Perhaps Babamukuru was worrying about the cost of my uniform. Maybe that was why his nerves were so sharply on edge that afternoon, making it a bad day for both the man and his daughter. "Nyasha," he snapped, "stop that. What's the matter with you? Why can't you keep quiet like Tambudzai there?"

We found a parking space, though this was not easy, and disembarking, walked, taking the general direction of the stream of parents and pupils ahead of us, over crazy-paving of geometrically cut stone, through a corridor of creamy-white roses to the door that appeared to be the main entrance. Anticipation. Disappointment. I looked and looked and searched carefully through the crowd, but I could not find a single black face which did not belong to our party, except of course for the porters. The porters were carrying trunks, but none of them offered to carry mine.

At the door a nun, smiling beatifically, made us

welcome by shaking our hands and asking us "Which one is this?" before taking us up steps and down corridors to a room at the end of a long hallway.

"All the first-formers live on this corridor," she explained as she led the way. "And the Africans live in here," she announced, triumphantly flinging the door to my new life wide open. The room was empty. I was, it seemed, the first black first-former to have arrived. It was not a small room but then neither was it large. It certainly was not large enough for the six beds that stood in it, three along one wall and three along the other, all of necessity so closely arranged that there was barely space to walk between them.

"This is your room," the nun said, smiling first at Nyasha and then at me, and then confessing her confusion. "Mr. See-ga-ookey," she smiled, "you have only one coming. Which one is it?" She had forgotten already although we had been introduced at the door. I wished I had been wearing uniform like the other girls I had seen. Then she would have known who I was. But I was getting my uniform second-hand. The nuns would give it to me later.

"I have been wondering, Sister," began Babamukuru politely. "I was under the impression that the girls sleep four to a room, but I see there are six beds here."

"Ah, yes," agreed the Sister, proud of the fact. "We have more Africans here than usual this year and so we had to put them all in here."

"There are only four wardrobes," objected my uncle.

"It is inconvenient, isn't it?" sympathised Sister. "The youngest will have to share. We've got a sixth-former in here and a fourth-former as well. They have to have their own."

Babamukuru turned to me. "Come Tambudzai, let us help you get settled."

Baba and Maiguru made my bed for me, Nyasha,

wanting to help but not having anything to do, only tweaking a sheet once or twice. While they made the bed, I unpacked. With my uniform still to be provided I had brought with me, besides the bedding, only toiletries, underwear and the two casual dresses that the uniform list stipulated, so I was soon through. When we had finished, we said our goodbyes. These were stern and exhortatory on my uncle's part, briskly cheerful from Maiguru, determinedly gay from Nyasha. We walked down to the car. In the courtyard Nyasha hugged me. "Have a good time, you African," she grinned. We parted with laughter and requests and promises to write and reply and to visit.

Term began and progressed but Nyasha did not come to visit. I hardly noticed the omission. You will say again that I was callous but I was not, only overwhelmed. It was all so heady and affluent and new that I was sure I was on the path of progress. I did not want to be left behind, so I threw myself into everything: exotic languages, like Latin and French and Portuguese, with unfamiliar sentence structures that told of brave legionnaires the enemy laying waste and pupils who wrote with the pen of their aunts. I wondered a while at such strange constructions, and then remembered that I was no longer writing in English, finding on closer inspection that the structures were quite similar to our own. Still, I mused, those foreign people had strange things on their minds: it did not seem likely that you could hold normal conversations in those languages. There were new games to play too, basketball, tennis and hockey, with interesting rules and intricate scoring procedures to be learnt. There were nuns to be observed and classified according to whether they were human or not, lay-teachers whose idiosyncracies had to be identified so that you did not fall prey to them. The white students needed careful study to decide whether they were different or similar to me, whether they were likeable or not and what their habits were. Most importantly, most wonderfully, there was the library, big, bright, walled in glass on one side and furnished with private little cubicles where you could do your homework, or simply lose yourself in any one of the hundreds of tantalising books whose glossy covers never seemed to get dirty or torn. The sheer number of books in that library made me deeply ashamed of my ignorance. I resolved to read every single one of those informative volumes from the first page to the last.

With all those new books, reading took up so much of my time that there was none left in which to miss Nyasha, or my uncle and aunt; and if I had ever really missed my home, I had long since stopped doing that during my stay with Babamukuru. Besides, although Nyasha did not visit, she wrote often. She wrote long, expansive, entertaining letters full of lucid, irreverent detail: my father's latest method of extorting money from Babamukuru; the most recent gossip gleaned from the girls' hostel (Josie and Maidei were no longer speaking); Maiguru's progress with respect to her emancipation and the way Babamukuru was coping with his more adamant wife; that Lucia had passed her Grade One so well that they were moving her into Grade Three; news about my mother—she was well. This was the bulk of her news. She did not write much about herself until one day I received a serious letter from her.

"I am missing you badly," she wrote, "as I knew I would and told you so, but I did not want to worry you with it because I know about your guilts, and I did not want guilt over your luck to stop you enjoying it. But the fact is I am missing you and missing you badly. In many ways you are very essential to me in bridging some of the gaps in my life, and now that you are away, I feel them again. I find it more and more difficult to speak with the girls at school. I try, Tambu, but there is not much to speak of between us. They resent the fact that I do not read their romance stories and if I do not read them, then of course I cannot talk about them. If only they knew that when I was ten my mother used to scold me very severely indeed for sneaking them down from the bookshelf. But I was ten six years ago and that is a long time to have grown out of such habits. I should, I suppose, have acquired more useful habits instead. I should have learnt to be light-hearted and gay, but it's difficult, you know. Besides, I am convinced that they have other reasons for disapproving of me. They do not like my language, my English, because it is authentic and my Shona, because it is not! They think that I am a snob, that I think I am superior to them because I do not feel that I am inferior to men (if you can call the boys in my class men). And all because I beat the boys at math! I know that I should not complain, but I very much would like to belong, Tambu, but I find I do not. I spend a lot of time reading and studying now that you are not here for us to distract each other, but I must admit I long for those distractions—it's not virtue that keeps me so busy! I think, though, that your uncle is pleased with the quieter environment and I have discovered that it is restful to have him pleased, and so these days I am doing my best not to antagonise him. You can imagine how difficult that is. Impossible, it seems. I cannot help thinking that what antagonises is the fact that I am me—hardly, I admit, the ideal daughter for a hallowed headmaster, a revered patriarch. I have asked him several times if we may come to see you (through my mother, of course—it's always best to be quiet in his presence), but he believes it will spoil you."

This letter did cause a pang of guilt. I believed I was being irresponsible. Folding the pages away in my desk where I would see it often and be reminded to write, I resolved to reply as soon as I had a spare moment. But the pang of guilt was no more than a pang which dissolved quickly in the stream of novelty and discovery I had plunged into. No spare moment came my way, nor did I find the time to make one, before I received my cousin's next letter. This letter was of the usual kind. Bubbly and bouncy, Nyasha updated me on the mission gossip and announced that she had embarked on a diet "to discipline my body and occupy my mind. When you come back you will find a svelte, sensuous me."

That was one of the last letters I received from her. During the second half of the term her letters became less regular and eventually stopped altogether. Again I must confess that I did not really notice. The thirteen weeks of term galloped by so quickly that while I was still wondering when she would write next, Babamukuru came to fetch me. Preoccupied and tense, he came alone, informing me that Nyasha was keeping to her books. There was no conversation during the ride home, no enquiries from my uncle about the lessons, the dormitories, my friends or the food, and when I asked about Maiguru and the mission, he grunted so distractedly that I gave up the attempt. I was disappointed because Nyasha's letters had led me to believe that his disposition had improved, but I did not dwell on disappointment. If not Babamukuru, there was Nyasha to turn an attentive ear to the torrent of news about the goings on at Sacred Heart that was positively bursting to be told.

Nyasha was indeed looking svelte when she dashed out to hug me, flinging her arms round me almost before I had stepped out of the car. In fact too svelte. By my standards she had grown definitely thin, but I knew that she preferred bones to bounce and so I said nothing.

I did not stay at the mission long that vacation. Babamukuru drove me home the very next day. Nor did I pass through the mission on my way back to Sacred Heart at the beginning of the second term, so I did not see my cousin again until the August holiday. Three months had passed. In those three months she had grown skeletal. She was pathetic to see, but when she hugged me hello I was surprised at the strength in her arms, so frail they looked, as though they would snap if she so much as picked up a pen. She hugged me briefly, hoped that my second term had been as interesting as the first and disappeared into the house with a suitcase while I unloaded the rest of my luggage and followed her to our bedroom. There I found her absorbed in a history text. She did not speak when I entered—a brief smile informed me she was busy. She worked until suppertime. When Anna called she put away her books and came to the table. She sat down very quietly and that was the beginning of a horribly weird and sinister drama. Babamukuru dished out a large helping of food for his daughter and set it before her, watching her surreptitiously as he picked casually at his own meal to persuade us that he was calm. Nyasha regarded her plate malevolently, darting anguished glances at her father, drained two glasses of water, then picked up her fork and shovelled the food into her mouth, swallowing without chewing and without pause except to sip between mouthfuls from a third glass of water. Maiguru ate steadily and fussed over me, placing another chunk of meat, another spoonful of vegetables on my plate and making cheerful conversation about my lessons, my friends and the food at Sacred Heart. When Nyasha's plate was empty they both relaxed and the atmosphere returned almost to normal. Nyasha excused herself immediately. I thought she had gone to the bedroom to read but when I followed her there the room was empty. I could hear retching and gagging from the bathroom.

She returned silently to her books, a mathematics exercise this time, and was still working when I rolled over to sleep at eleven o'clock. In the early hours of the morning something prodded me awake. It was Nyasha.

"Can you help me?" she asked timidly. "I can't get the right answer. I ought to be able to, but I keep getting it wrong." It was not a difficult problem. She had made a careless mistake. "Silly me," she said when I found her mistake. "I'm not concentrating hard enough."

Babamukuru wanted to take me home the next day, the day after I arrived. He told Maiguru to tell me at breakfast to be sure to be ready by lunchtime. I did not want to go, I felt I could not. I could not leave my cousin in that state. You know how it is when something that has been a cornerstone of your security begins to crumble. You start worrying about yourself. For that reason alone, even if others were less selfish, I knew I could not leave. So my uncle had to be told. I had to tell him that I would not go, but how was that to be done? I might have been becoming a young lady and being educated at the convent, but what use were educated young ladies on the homestead? Or at the mission? I was and would remain Tambudzai, the daughter. Babamukuru was still and would always be the closest thing a human being could get to God. So although I knew I had to talk to him, I had no idea how that could be done.

I thought I would telephone him at his office, went so far as to dial the number and wait for a reply, but he was not there. The phone rang and rang. I grew more relieved with every buzz: I would not have to talk to him after all. I thought I would write a letter instead, then thought again and decided that since he would return for lunch I would take my courage in both hands, close my ears to my daughterly conscience and confront him then. And while I made these plans I knew all the time that it couldn't be done.

So I wasn't surprised when I nearly backed down. Babamukuru was angry at lunchtime because Nyasha refused to leave her bedroom. He was all for going in there himself to drag her to the table, but Maiguru managed to dissuade him. His daughter was so fragile, she said, the shock might do her serious harm. "And starving herself," he cried, "you mean starving herself does her no harm?" Eventually he allowed himself to be pacified. "Perhaps you are right," he conceded to Maiguru. "She does eat her supper when I have time to supervise her properly. Yes, I think you are right, Mai. It is not so serious. What she needs is to rest."

Yet it was serious. Nyasha was losing weight steadily, constantly, rapidly. It dropped off her body almost hourly and what was left of her was grotesquely unhealthy from the vital juices she flushed down the toilet. Did he not know? Did he not see? I could not ask him these questions. The most I could do was ask in a small, timid voice to be allowed to stay, with Nyasha, I specified, for a few more days. Nobody was more surprised by my audacity than I was. Babamukuru did not answer, but I was not taken home. I did not take it as a victory though. I took it as proof that Babamukuru was good.

Nyasha grew weaker by the day. She weaved when she walked and every night was the same. Although we were on vacation she studied fourteen hours a day to make sure that she passed her "O" levels. She worked late into the night to wake me up regularly and punctually at three o'clock with a problem—a chemical equation to balance, the number of amperes in a circuit to be calculated or an irregular Latin verb to be conjugated, although I was only in Form One and could not often help her. "I have to get it right," she would whisper with an apologetic smile. It was truly alarming, but nobody commented, nobody acted; we were all very frightened. One evening, at supper, she passed out into her plate. It didn't last long, only a minute or two, but it was enough to overtax her father's precarious patience. Babamukuru, who thought she was making a scene, ordered her to her bedroom, where she lay open-eyed and quiet all night. At three o'clock she woke me up.

"Can I get into bed with you, Tambu?" she whispered, but when I rolled over to make room for her to climb in she shook her head and smiled. "It's all right," she said. "I just wanted to see if you would let me." Then she sat on her bed and looked at me out of her sunken eyes, her bony knees pressed together so that her nightdress fell through the space where her thighs had been, agitated and nervous and picking her skin. "I don't want to do it, Tambu, really I don't, but it's coming, I feel it coming." Her eyes dilated. "They've done it to me," she accused, whispering still. "Really, they have." And then she became stern. "It's not their fault. They did it to them too. You know they did," she whispered. "To both of them, but especially to him. They put him through it all. But it's not his fault, he's good." Her voice took on a Rhodesian accent. "He's a good boy, a good munt. A bloody good kaffir," she informed in sneering sarcastic tones. Then she was whispering again. "Why do they do it, Tambu," she hissed bitterly, her face contorting with rage, "to me and to you and to him? Do you see what they've done? They've taken us away. Lucia. Takesure. All of us. They've deprived you of you, him of him, ourselves of each other. We're grovelling. Lucia for a job, Jeremiah for money. Daddy grovels to them. We grovel to him." She began to rock, her body quivering tensely. "I won't grovel.

Oh no, I won't. I'm not a good girl. I'm evil. I'm not a good girl." I touched her to comfort her and that was the trigger. "I won't grovel, I won't die," she raged and crouched like a cat ready to spring.

The noise brought Babamukuru and Maiguru running. They could do nothing, could only watch. Nyasha was beside herself with fury. She rampaged, shredding her history book between her teeth ("Their history. Fucking liars. Their bloody lies."), breaking mirrors, her clay pots, anything she could lay her hands on and jabbing the fragments viciously into her flesh, stripping the bedclothes, tearing her clothes from the wardrobe and trampling them underfoot. "They've trapped us. They've trapped us. But I won't be trapped. I'm not a good girl. I won't be trapped." Then as suddenly as it came, the rage passed. "I don't hate you, Daddy," she said softly. "They want me to, but I won't." She lay down on her bed. "I'm very tired," she said in a voice that was recognisably hers. "But I can't sleep. Mummy, will you hold me?" She curled up in Maiguru's lap looking no more than five years old. "Look what they've done to us," she said softly. "I'm not one of them but I'm not one of you." She fell asleep.

The next morning she was calm, but she assured me it was an illusion, the eye of a storm. "There's a whole lot more," she said. "I've tried to keep it in but it's powerful. It ought to be. There's nearly a century of it," she added, with a shadow of her wry grin. "But I'm afraid," she told me apologetically. "It upsets people. So I need to go somewhere where it's safe. You know what I mean? Somewhere where people won't mind."

Nyasha's kamikazi behaviour jolted my uncle and aunt into action. Even as she was speaking to me in the bedroom, Babamukuru was on the telephone to

Maiguru's brother in Salisbury. By ten o'clock we were on our way to the city, arriving there before twelve because Babamukuru drove like an August wind. Maiguru and I talked to Nyasha constantly all the way, to keep her with us, to prevent her mind from wandering too far. In the city Maiguru's brother immediately made an appointment with a psychiatrist. We felt better—help was at hand. But the psychiatrist said that Nyasha could not be ill, that Africans did not suffer in the way we had described. She was making a scene. We should take her home and be firm with her. This was not a sensible thing to say in front of my uncle, who found these words vastly reassuring and considered going back to Umtali at once, turning a deaf ear to Nyasha when she begged to see an African psychiatrist. Nyasha's uncle though, with the authority of seven years of learning to recognise suffering when he saw it, was able to persuade my uncle to wait.

There were no black psychiatrists, but she was persuaded to see a white one. This man was human. She needed to rest, he said. So Nyasha was put into a clinic, where she stayed for several weeks. Slowly, with the aid of doses of Largactil and the practical attention of her aunts who lived in the city, my cousin's condition improved, but I did not stay to see her improvement. Babamukuru, having a school to keep in order, was anxious to be back in Umtali and in three weeks' time I would have to be back at school, so I had to go back with him. I was upset. I felt Nyasha needed me but it was true: I had to go to school.

We did not talk on the drive back to Umtali, Babamukuru and I, and this was as things should be. Babamukuru's age alone merited the respect of silence. His education made him almost an elder. You simply could not talk. It would not have mattered if this had been my first car-ride along that road, but sophistication is acquired quickly. The vast rippling fields of maize and tobacco between Rusapi and Marandellas no longer impressed me, nor did Gomore Mhanda, whose stony baldness had been so intriguing on the outward journey. There was nothing to distract me. Although we had left at nine o'clock in the morning I forced myself to sleep; there was nothing to keep me awake except thoughts of Nyasha and these were thoughts I preferred to ignore. If Nyasha who had everything could not make it, where could I expect to go? I could not bear to think about it, because at that time we were not sure whether she would survive. All I knew was that the doctor would not commit himself. Nyasha's progress was still in the balance, and so, as a result, was mine.

With this knowledge disturbing my mind, I was not unhappy when Babamukuru took me straight to the homestead. I did not want to stay at the mission, where there was too much that reminded me of Nyasha, and where she was. It was difficult to accept that this thing had happened, particularly difficult because I had no explanation. If you had asked me before it all began, I would have said it was impossible. I would have said it was impossible for people who had everything to suffer so extremely.

I may have had no explanation, but my mother had. She was very definite.

"It's the Englishness," she said. "It'll kill them all if they aren't careful," and she snorted. "Look at them. That boy Chido can hardly speak a word of his own mother's tongue, and you'll see, his children will be worse. Running around with that white one, isn't he, the missionary's daughter? His children will disgrace us. You'll see. And himself, to look at him he may look all right, but there's no telling what price he's paying." She wouldn't say much about Nyasha. "About that one we don't even speak. It's speaking for itself. Both of them, it's the Englishness. It's a wonder it hasn't affected the parents too."

She went on like this for quite a while, going on about how you couldn't expect the ancestors to stomach so much Englishness. She didn't mention Nhamo, but I was beginning to follow her trend of thought. I knew she was thinking about him and I could see she considered me a victim too: "The problem is the Englishness, so you just be careful!"

It was a warning, a threat that would have had disastrous effects if I had let it. When you're afraid of something it doesn't help to have people who know more than you do come out and tell you you're quite right. Mother knew a lot of things and I had regard for her knowledge. Be careful, she had said, and I thought about Nyasha and Chido and Nhamo, who had all succumbed, and of my own creeping feelings of doom. Was I being careful enough? I wondered. For I was beginning to have a suspicion, no more than the seed of a suspicion, that I had been too eager to leave the homestead and embrace the "Englishness" of the mission; and after that the more concentrated "Englishness" of Sacred Heart. The suspicion remained for a few days, during which time it transformed itself into guilt, and then I had nightmares about Nhamo and Chido and Nyasha two nights in a row. That should tell you how much my mother's words disturbed me: I had not had a nightmare since the first time I went to the mission. But term-time was fast approaching and the thought of returning to Sacred Heart filled me with pleasure. The books, the games, the films, the debates—all these things were things that I wanted. I told myself I was a much more sensible person than Nyasha, because I knew what could or couldn't be done. In this way, I banished the suspicion, buried it in the depths of my subconscious, and happily went back to Sacred Heart.

I was young then and able to banish things, but

seeds do grow. Although I was not aware of it then, no longer could I accept Sacred Heart and what it represented as a sunrise on my horizon. Quietly, unobtrusively and extremely fitfully, something in my mind began to assert itself, to question things and refuse to be brainwashed, bringing me to this time when I can set down this story. It was a long and painful process for me, that process of expansion. It was a process whose events stretched over many years and would fill another volume, but the story I have told here, is my own story, the story of four women whom I loved, and our men, this story is how it all began.

Related Readings

CONTENTS

Professions for Women

by Virginia Woolf

As Tambudzai grows up, she becomes increasingly aware of the expectation in her society that women will serve the needs of men and suppress their own interests, ambitions, and abilities. In this speech, delivered to a group of professional women more than 50 years ago, Virginia Woolf addresses similar attitudes in her society.

When your secretary invited me to come here, she told me that your Society is concerned with the employment of women and she suggested that I might tell you something about my own professional experiences. It is true I am a woman; it is true I am employed; but what professional experiences have I had? It is difficult to say. My profession is literature; and in that profession there are fewer experiences for women than in any other, with the exception of the stage—fewer, I mean, that are peculiar to women. For the road was cut many years ago—by Fanny Burney, by Aphra Behn, by Harriet Martineau, by Jane Austen, by George Eliot—many famous women, and many more unknown and forgotten, have been before me, making the path smooth, and regulating my steps. Thus, when I came to write, there were very few material obstacles in my way. Writing was a reputable and harmless occupation. The family peace was not broken by the scratching of a pen. No demand was made upon the family purse. For ten and sixpence one can buy paper enough to write all the plays of Shakespeare—if one has a mind that way. Pianos and models, Paris, Vienna and Berlin, masters and mistresses, are not needed by a writer. The cheapness of writing paper is, of course, the reason why women have succeeded as writers before they have succeeded in the other professions.

But to tell you my story—it is a simple one. You have only got to figure to yourselves a girl in a bedroom with a pen in her hand. She had only to move that pen from left to right—from ten o'clock to one. Then it occurred to her to do what is simple and cheap enough after all—to slip a few of those pages into an envelope, fix a penny stamp in the corner, and drop the envelope into the red box at the corner. It was thus that I became a journalist; and my effort was rewarded on the first day of the following month—a very glorious day it was for me—by a letter from an editor containing a cheque for one pound ten shillings and sixpence. But to show you how little I deserve to be called a professional woman, how little I know of the struggles and difficulties of such lives, I have to admit that instead of spending that sum upon bread and butter, rent, shoes and stockings, or butcher's bills, I went out and bought a cat—a beautiful cat, a Persian cat, which very soon involved me in bitter disputes with my neighbours.

What could be easier than to write articles and to buy Persian cats with the profits? But wait a moment. Articles have to be about something. Mine, I seem to remember, was about a novel by a famous man. And while I was writing this review, I discovered that if I were going to review books I should need to do battle with a certain phantom. And the phantom was a woman, and when I came to know her better I called her after the heroine of a famous poem, The Angel in the House. It was she who used to come between me and my paper when I was writing reviews. It was she who bothered me and wasted my time and so tormented me that at last I killed her. You who come of a younger and happier generation may not have heard of her—you may not know what I mean by the Angel in the House. I will describe her as shortly as I can. She was intensely sympathetic. She was immensely charming. She was utterly unselfish. She excelled in the difficult arts of family life. She sacrificed herself daily. If there was chicken, she took the leg; if there was a draught she sat in it—in short she was so constituted that she never had a mind or a wish of her own, but preferred to sympathise always with the minds and wishes of others. Above all—I need not say it—she was pure. Her purity was supposed to be her chief beauty—her blushes, her great grace. In those days—the last of Queen Victoria—every house had its Angel. And when I came to write I encountered her with the very first words. The shadow of her wings fell on my page; I heard the rustling of her skirts in the room. Directly, that is to say, I took my pen in hand to review that novel by a famous man, she slipped behind me and whispered: "My dear, you are a young woman. You are writing about a book that has been written by a man. By sympathetic; be tender; flatter; deceive; use all the arts and wiles of our sex. Never let anybody guess that you have a mind of your own. Above all, be pure." And she made as if to guide my pen. I now record the one act for which I take some credit to myself, though the credit rightly belongs to some excellent ancestors of mine who left me a certain sum of money—shall we say five hundred pounds a year?—so that it was not necessary for me to depend solely on charm for my living. I turned upon her and caught her by the throat. I did my best to kill her. My excuse, if I were to be had up in a court of law, would be that I acted in self-defence. Had I not killed her she would have killed me. She would have plucked the heart out of my writing. For, as I found, directly I put pen to paper, you cannot review even a novel without having a mind of your own, without expressing what you think to be the truth about human relations, morality, sex. And all these questions, according to the Angel in the House, cannot be dealt with freely and openly by women; they must charm, they must conciliate, they must—to put it bluntly—tell lies if they are to succeed. Thus, whenever I felt the shadow of her wing or the radiance of her halo upon my page, I took up the inkpot and flung it at her. She died hard. Her fictitious nature was of great assistance to her. It is far harder to kill a phantom than a reality. She was always creeping back when I thought I had despatched her. Though I flatter myself that I killed her in the end, the struggle was severe; it took much time that had better have been spent upon learning Greek grammar; or in roaming the world in search of adventures. But it was a real experience; it was an experience that was bound to befall all women writers at that time. Killing the Angel in the House was part of the occupation of a woman writer.

But to continue my story. The Angel was dead; what then remained? You may say that what remained was a simple and common object—a young woman in a bedroom with an inkpot. In other words, now that she had rid herself of falsehood, that young woman had only to be herself. Ah, but what is "herself"? I mean, what is a woman? I assure you, I do not know. I do not believe that you know. I do not believe that anybody can know until she has expressed herself in all the arts and professions open to human skill. That indeed is one of the reasons why I have come here— out of respect for you, who are in process of showing us by your experiments what a woman is, who are in process of providing us, by your failures and successes, with that extremely important piece of information.

But to continue the story of my professional experiences. I made one pound ten and six by my first review; and I bought a Persian cat with the proceeds. Then I grew ambitious. A Persian cat is all very well, I said; but a Persian cat is not enough. I must have a motor car. And it was thus that I became a novelist—for it is a very strange thing that people will give you a motor car if you will tell them a story. It is a still stranger thing that there is nothing so delightful in the world as telling stories. It is far pleasanter than writing reviews of famous novels. And yet, if I am to obey your secretary and tell you my professional experiences as a novelist, I must tell you about a very strange experience that befell me as a novelist. And to understand it you must try first to imagine a novelist's state of mind. I hope I am not giving away professional secrets if I say that a novelist's chief desire is to be as unconscious as possible. He has to induce in himself a state of perpetual lethargy. He wants life to proceed with the utmost quiet and regularity. He wants to see the same faces, to read the same books, to do the same things day after day, month after month, while he is writing, so that nothing may break the illusion in which he is living—so that nothing may disturb or disquiet the mysterious nosings about, feelings round, darts, dashes and sudden discoveries of that very shy and illusive spirit, the imagination. I suspect that this state is the same both for men and women. Be that as it may, I want you to imagine me writing a novel in a state of trance. I want you to figure to yourselves a girl sitting with a pen in her hand, which for minutes, and indeed for hours, she never dips into the inkpot. The image that comes to my mind when I think of this girl is the image of a fisherman lying sunk in dreams on the verge of a deep lake with a rod held out over the water. She was letting her imagination sweep unchecked round every rock and cranny of the world that lies submerged in the depths of our unconscious being. Now came the experience, the experience that I believe to be far commoner with women writers than with men. The line raced through the girl's fingers. Her imagination had rushed away. It had sought the pools, the depths, the dark places where the largest fish slumber. And then there was a smash. There was an explosion. There was foam and confusion. The imagination had dashed itself against something hard. The girl was roused from her dream. She was indeed in a state of the most acute and difficult distress. To speak without figure she had thought of something, something about the body, about the passions which it was unfitting for her as a woman to say. Men, her reason told her, would be shocked. The consciousness of what men will say of a woman who speaks the truth about her passions had roused her from her artist's state of unconsciousness. She could write no more. The trance was over. Her imagination could work no longer. This I believe to be a very common experience with women writers—they are impeded by the extreme conventionality of the other sex. For though men sensibly allow themselves great freedom in these respects, I doubt that they realise or can control the extreme severity with which they condemn such freedom in women.

These then were two very genuine experiences of my own. These were two of the adventures of my professional life. The first—killing the Angel in the House—I think I solved. She died. But the second, telling the truth about my own experiences as a body, I do not think I solved. I doubt that any woman has solved it yet. The obstacles against her are still immensely powerful—and yet they are very difficult to define. Outwardly, what is simpler than to write books? Outwardly, what obstacles are there for a woman rather than for a man? Inwardly, I think, the case is very different; she has still many ghosts to fight, many prejudices to overcome. Indeed it will be a long time still, I think, before a woman can sit down to write a book without finding a phantom to be slain, a rock to be dashed against. And if this is so in literature, the freest of all professions for women, how is it in the new professions which you are now for the first time entering?

Those are the questions that I should like, had I time, to ask you. And indeed, if I have laid stress upon these professional experiences of mine, it is because I believe that they are, though in different forms, yours also. Even when the path is nominally open—when there is nothing to prevent a woman from being a doctor, a lawyer, a civil servant—there are many phantoms and obstacles, as I believe, looming in her way. To discuss and define them is I think of great value and importance; for thus only can the labour be shared, the difficulties be solved. But besides this, it is necessary also to discuss the ends and the aims for which we are fighting, for which we are doing battle with these formidable obstacles. Those aims cannot be taken for granted; they must be perpetually questioned and examined. The whole position, as I see it—here in this hall surrounded by women practising for the first time in history I know not how many different professions—is one of extraordinary interest and importance. You have won rooms of your own in the house hitherto exclusively owned by men. You are able, though not without great labour and effort, to pay the rent. You are earning your five hundred pounds a year. But this freedom is only a beginning; the room is your own, but it is still bare. It has to be furnished; it has to be decorated; it has to be shared.

How are you going to furnish it, how are you going to decorate it? With whom are you going to share it, and upon what terms? These, I think are questions of the utmost importance and interest. For the first time in history you are able to ask them; for the first time you are able to decide for yourselves what the answers should be. Willingly would I stay and discuss those questions and answers—but not tonight. My time is up; and I must cease.

Back to School

by Andrea Lee

*When Tambudzai goes to the mission
school and then to the convent school,
she is full of anticipation and dreams. She
quickly has to adjust, however, to second-
class treatment and condescension. In
the following personal essay, an African-
American woman describes the discrimination she experienced during the 1960s as
a black student in a white school and the
changes that have occurred in the school
since then.*

A couple of weeks ago, I paid a visit to the girls'
preparatory school outside Philadelphia where, about
thirty years ago, I enrolled as one of the first two
black students. It wasn't my first return trip, but it
was one that had a peculiarly definitive feeling: this
time, I was going back to look at classes with my
daughter, who is eleven—exactly the age I was when I
first put on a blue-and-white uniform and walked in
the front entrance of an institution where black people
had always used the back door. My daughter, who
was born in Europe, and who views the civil-rights
struggles of the sixties as an antique heroic cycle not
much removed in drama and time frame from the
Iliad, sees her mother's experience as a singularly tame
example of integration. There were, after all, no
jeering mobs, no night riders, no police dogs or fire
hoses—just a girl going to school and learning with
quiet thoroughness the meaning of isolation.

The air inside the schoolhouse smelled exactly as it used to on rainy April days—that mysterious school essence of damp wood and ancient chalk dust and pent-up young flesh. For an instant, I relived precisely what it felt like to walk those halls with girls who never included me in a social event, with teachers and administrators who regarded me with bemused incomprehension—halls where the only other black faces I saw were those of maids and cooks, and where I never received the slightest hint that books had been written and discoveries made by people whose skin wasn't white. I remembered the defensive bravado that I once used as a cover for a constant and despairing sense of worthlessness, born and reinforced at school.

As I delivered my daughter to the sixth-grade classroom where she would spend the day, I saw that in the intervening time not only had the school sprouted a few glossy modern additions—an art wing, science and computer facilities, and a new lower school—but the faculty and the student body had also been transformed. Black and Asian girls mingled in the crowd of students rushing back and forth between classrooms and playing fields, giddy with excitement over the impending Easter and Passover weekend. A black teacher with braids strode out of the room where long ago I'd conjugated Latin verbs. Posters celebrating African-American artists and scientists hung on the walls, and the school's curriculum included dozens of works by black, Native American, and Hispanic writers. The director of the middle school was, miracle of miracles, a young black woman—a woman who combined an old-fashioned headmistress's unflappable good sense with a pre-ternatural sensitivity to the psychology of culture and identity. She explained to me that she herself had once been a student at a mostly white East Coast prep school. When I asked who on her staff, in particular, was responsible for the self-esteem of minority students, she said firmly, "Every person who works here."

That day, I finally forgave my old school. I'd held a touchy rancor toward it through much of my adult life, like someone heaping blame on a negligent parent, and had taken the institution rather churlishly to task during a Commencement address I gave there some years ago. The changes I saw now disarmed and delighted me. Watching my daughter run by with a group of girls, I realized with envy how different her experience would be from mine if she were enrolled there. "Just think, I used to dream of burning the place down," I remarked to her, as we drove away, along the school's winding drive. She looked at me impatiently. "Can't you just forget all that?" she asked. The sound of her voice—half childish and half adolescent—made it clear to me that I wouldn't do any such thing. Wounds that have healed bring a responsibility to avoid repeating the past. The important thing is to pardon, even with joy, when the time comes—but never, I thought, driving on in silence, to forget.

from Hunger of Memory

by Richard Rodriguez

*When Nyasha and Tambudzai first meet
after Nyasha's return from England,
Tambudzai is disappointed by Nyasha's
aloofness and puzzled by her use of
English instead of Shona. Later, when
Tambudzai goes to the mission school, she
herself experiences the tensions of living in
two cultures. In this excerpt from his
autobiography, Richard Rodriguez writes
with eloquence of his childhood in a
working-class immigrant family in
California and of the role of language—
Spanish and English—in shaping his world.*

I remember to start with that day in Sacramento—
a California now nearly thirty years past—when I first
entered a classroom, able to understand some fifty
stray English words.

The third of four children, I had been preceded to a
neighborhood Roman Catholic school by an older
brother and sister. But neither of them had revealed
very much about their classroom experiences. Each
afternoon they returned, as they left in the morning,
always together, speaking in Spanish as they climbed
the five steps of the porch. And their mysterious
books, wrapped in shopping-bag paper, remained on
the table next to the door, closed firmly behind them.

An accident of geography sent me to a school where
all my classmates were white, many the children of
doctors and lawyers and business executives. All my

classmates certainly must have been uneasy on that first day of school—as most children are uneasy—to find themselves apart from their families in the first institution of their lives. But I was astonished.

The nun said, in a friendly but oddly impersonal voice, "Boys and girls, this is Richard Rodriguez." (I heard her sound out: *Rich-heard Road-ree-guess.*) It was the first time I had heard anyone name me in English. "Richard," the nun repeated more slowly, writing my name down in her black leather book. Quickly I turned to see my mother's face dissolve in a watery blur behind the pebbled glass door. . . .

In the early years of my boyhood, my parents coped very well in America. My father had steady work. My mother managed at home. They were nobody's victims. Optimism and ambition led them to a house (our home) many blocks from the Mexican south side of town. We lived among *gringos* and only a block from the biggest, whitest houses. It never occurred to my parents that they couldn't live wherever they chose. Nor was the Sacramento of the fifties bent on teaching them a contrary lesson. My mother and father were more annoyed than intimidated by those two or three neighbors who tried initially to make us unwelcome. ("Keep your brats away from my sidewalk!") But despite all they achieved, perhaps because they had so much to achieve, any deep feeling of ease, the confidence of "belonging" in public was withheld from them both. They regarded the people at work, the faces in crowds, as very distant from us. They were the others, *los gringos.* That term was interchangeable in their speech with another, even more telling, *los americanos.*

I grew up in a house where the only regular guests were my relations. For one day, enormous families of relatives would visit and there would be so many people that the noise and the bodies would spill out to the backyard and front porch. Then, for weeks, no one came by. (It was usually a salesman who rang the doorbell.) Our house stood apart. A gaudy yellow in a row of white bungalows. We were the people with the noisy dog. The people who raised pigeons and chickens. We were the foreigners on the block. A few neighbors smiled and waved. We waved back. But no one in the family knew the names of the old couple who lived next door; until I was seven years old, I did not know the names of the kids who lived across the street.

In public, my father and mother spoke a hesitant, accented, not always grammatical English. And they would have to strain—their bodies tense—to catch the sense of what was rapidly said by *los gringos*. At home they spoke Spanish. The language of their Mexican past sounded in counterpoint to the English of public society. The words would come quickly, with ease. Conveyed through those sounds was the pleasing, soothing, consoling reminder of being at home.

During those years when I was first conscious of hearing, my mother and father addressed me only in Spanish; in Spanish I learned to reply. By contrast, English (*inglés*), rarely heard in the house, was the language I came to associate with *gringos*. I learned my first words of English overhearing my parents speak to strangers. At five years of age, I knew just enough English for my mother to trust me on errands to stores one block away. No more.

I was a listening child, careful to hear the very different sounds of Spanish and English. Wide-eyed with hearing, I'd listen to sounds more than words. First, there were English (*gringo*) sounds. So many words were still unknown that when the butcher or the lady at the drugstore said something to me, exotic polysyllabic sounds would bloom in the midst of their sentences. Often, the speech of people in public seemed to me very loud, booming with confidence. The man behind the counter would literally ask, "What can I do for you?" But by being so firm and so clear, the sound of his voice said that he was a *gringo*; he belonged in public society.

I would also hear then the high nasal notes of middle-class American speech. The air stirred with sound. Sometimes, even now, when I have been traveling abroad for several weeks, I will hear what I heard as a boy. In hotel lobbies or airports, in Turkey or Brazil, some Americans will pass, and suddenly I will hear it again—the high sound of American voices. For a few seconds I will hear it with pleasure, for it is now the sound of *my* society—a reminder of home. But inevitably—already on the flight headed for home—the sound fades with repetition. I will be unable to hear it anymore.

When I was a boy, things were different. The accent of *los gringos* was never pleasing nor was it hard to hear. Crowds at Safeway or at bus stops would be noisy with sound. And I would be forced to edge away form the chirping chatter above me.

I was unable to hear my own sounds, but I knew very well that I spoke English poorly. My words could not stretch far enough to form complete thoughts. And the words I did speak I didn't know well enough to make into distinct sounds. (Listeners would usually lower their heads, better to hear what I was trying to say.) But it was one thing for *me* to speak English with difficulty. It was more troubling for me to hear my parents speak in public: their high-whining vowels and guttural consonants; their sentences that got stuck with "eh" and "ah" sounds; the confused syntax; the hesitant rhythm of sounds so different from the way *gringos* spoke. I'd notice, moreover, that my parents' voices were softer than those of *gringos* we'd meet.

I am tempted now to say that none of this mattered.

In adulthood I am embarrassed by childhood fears. And, in a way, it didn't matter very much that my parents could not speak English with ease. Their linguistic difficulties had no serious consequences. My mother and father made themselves understood at the county hospital clinic and at government offices. And yet, in another way, it mattered very much—it was unsettling to hear my parents struggle with English. Hearing them, I'd grow nervous, my clutching trust in their protection and power weakened.

There were many times like the night at a brightly lit gasoline station (a blaring white memory) when I stood uneasily, hearing my father. He was talking to a teenaged attendant. I do not recall what they were saying, but I cannot forget the sounds my father made as he spoke. At one point his words slid together to form one word—sounds as confused as the threads of blue and green oil in the puddle next to my shoes. His voice rushed through what he had left to say. And, toward the end, reached falsetto notes, appealing to his listener's understanding. I looked away to the lights of passing automobiles. I tried not to hear anymore. But I heard only too well the calm, easy tones in the attendant's reply. Shortly afterward, walking toward home with my father, I shivered when he put his hand on my shoulder. The very first chance that I got, I evaded his grasp and ran on ahead into the dark, skipping with feigned boyish exuberance.

But then there was Spanish. *Español:* my family's language. *Español:* the language that seemed to me a private language. I'd hear strangers on the radio and in the Mexican Catholic church across town speaking in Spanish, but I couldn't really believe that Spanish was a public language, like English. Spanish speakers, rather, seemed related to me, for I sensed that we shared—through our language—the experience of feeling apart from *los gringos.* It was thus a ghetto

Spanish that I heard and I spoke. Like those whose lives are bound by a barrio, I was reminded by Spanish of my separateness from *los otros, los gringos* in power. But more intensely than for most barrio children—because I did not live in a barrio—Spanish seemed to me the language of home. (Most days it was only at home that I'd hear it.) It became the language of joyful return.

A family member would say something to me and I would feel myself specially recognized. My parents would say something to me and I would feel embraced by the sounds of their words. Those sounds said: *I am speaking with ease in Spanish. I am addressing you in words I never use with* los gringos. *I recognize you as someone special, close, like no one outside. You belong with us. In the family.*

(*Ricardo.*)

At the age of five, six, well past the time when most other children no longer easily notice the difference between sounds uttered at home and words spoken in public, I had a different experience. I lived in a world magically compounded of sounds. I remained a child longer than most; I lingered too long, poised at the edge of language—often frightened by the sounds of *los gringos,* delighted by the sounds of Spanish at home. I shared with my family a language that was startlingly different from that used in the great city around us.

For me there were none of the gradations between public and private society so normal to a maturing child. Outside the house was public society; inside the house was private. Just opening or closing the screen door behind me was an important experience. I'd rarely leave home all alone or without reluctance. Walking down the sidewalk, under the canopy of tall trees, I'd warily notice the—suddenly—silent neighborhood kids who stood warily watching me. Nervously, I'd arrive at the grocery store to hear there the sounds of the *gringo*—foreign to me—reminding me that in this world so big, I was a foreigner. But then I'd return. Walking back toward our house, climbing the steps from the sidewalk, when the front door was open in summer, I'd hear voices beyond the screen door talking in Spanish. For a second or two, I'd stay, linger there, listening. Smiling, I'd hear my mother call out, saying in Spanish (words): "Is that you, Richard?" All the while her sounds would assure me: *You are home now; come closer; inside. With us.*

"*Sí*," I'd reply.

Once more inside the house I would resume (assume) my place in the family. The sounds would dim, grow harder to hear. Once more at home, I would grow less aware of that fact. It required, however, no more than the blurt of the doorbell to alert me to listen to sounds all over again. The house would turn instantly still while my mother went to the door. I'd hear her hard English sounds. I'd wait to hear her voice return to soft-sounding Spanish, which assured me, as surely as did the clicking tongue of the lock on the door, that the stranger was gone.

Plainly, it is not healthy to hear such sounds so often. It is not healthy to distinguish public words from private sounds so easily. I remained cloistered by sounds, timid and shy in public, too dependent on voices at home. And yet it needs to be emphasized: I was an extremely happy child at home. I remember many nights when my father would come back from work, and I'd hear him call out to my mother in Spanish, sounding relieved. In Spanish, he'd sound light and free notes he never could manage in English. Some nights I'd jump up just at hearing his voice. With *mis hermanos* I would come running into the room where he was with my mother. Our laughing (so deep was the pleasure!) became screaming. Like others who know the pain of public alienation, we transformed the knowledge of our public separateness and made it consoling—the reminder of intimacy. Excited, we joined our voices in a celebration of sounds. *We are speaking now the way we never speak out in public. We are alone—together,* voices sounded, surrounded to tell me. Some nights, no one seemed willing to loosen the hold sounds had on us. At dinner, we invented new words. (Ours sounded Spanish, but made sense only to us.) We pieced together new words by taking, say, an English verb and giving it Spanish endings. My mother's instructions at bedtime would be lacquered with mock-urgent tones. Or a word like *sí* would become, in several notes, able to convey added measures of feeling. Tongues explored the edges of words, especially the fat vowels. And we happily sounded that military drum roll, the twirling roar of the Spanish *r.* Family language: my family's sounds. The voices of my parents and sisters and brother. Their voices insisting: *You belong here. We are family members. Related. Special to one another. Listen!* Voices singing and sighing, rising, straining, then surging, teeming with pleasure that burst syllables into fragments of laughter. At times it seemed there was steady quiet only when, from another room, the rustling whispers of my parents faded and I moved closer to sleep.

Losing a Language

by W.S. Merwin

*What do you think it would be like to feel
your native language slipping away as you
learn a new language and move into a new
culture? Do you think this process would
affect people of different generations in
different ways? This poem speaks to both
the pain and the relentlessness of such an
experience.*

A breath leaves the sentences and does not
    come back
yet the old still remember something that they
    could say

but they know now that such things are no
    longer believed
and the young have fewer words

5   many of the things the words were about
no longer exist

the noun for standing in mist by a haunted
    tree
the verb for I

the children will not repeat
10 the phrases their parents speak

somebody has persuaded them
that it is better to say everything differently

so that they can be admired somewhere
farther and farther away

15   where nothing that is here is known
we have little to say to each other

we are wrong and dark
in the eyes of the new owners

the radio is incomprehensible
20   the day is glass

when there is a voice at the door it is foreign
everywhere instead of a name there is a lie

nobody has seen it happening
nobody remembers

25   this is what the words were made
to prophesy

here are the extinct feathers
here is the rain we saw

Points of View

by Lucinda Roy

*One of the most loved places in
Tambudzai's homeland is the river,
Nyamarira. In this poem by Roy, born in
England to a Jamaican father and an
English mother, the speaker evokes the
close relationship of women to water in
many cultures and times.*

Even now, women bend to rivers
Or to wells; they scoop up life and offer it
To men or to their children, to their elders,
To blistered cooking-pots. Heavy with light,
5   And the brief mosaics of the world,
Water is carried home. Even now,
Women bend to see themselves in rivers
Or catch unsteady faces in buckets drawn
From wells. And water sucks them in,
10 Catching the wild geometry of the soul
Tossing it onto a plane. The wells
Are brimming with women's fluid faces;
The rivers are alive with women's hands.
Reflections savoured for a while, then gone.

15 From up here, what can I know of water?
I catch it tamed from metal spouts encased
In quiet glass, contoured in porcelain.
I compartmentalize the beast in ice,
Then serve it, grinning, to distant friends.
20 What do I know of water? Tomorrow
I must go again to find it. I will swim
In rivers thick with time, permanent as eyes

Of sleepy crocodiles. I will watch women
In slow genuflections ease water
25 Into round bowls. The river-blinded boys
With jellied eyes transparent in the sun
Will look at me. Children will jump from ele-
    ment
To element making paths through air to
    water,
Shooting diamond-drops along trajectories
30 Too long for me to measure. "This is water,"
They will tell me. This intense immersion.
A new baptism free of metaphor
Will be mine. Water will be water,
And I, a newly-evolved fish, will hear
35 The aquabatic rippling of gills.

The Old Chief Mshlanga

by Doris Lessing

Tambudzai describes from a black perspective the injustices the Shona people suffer as a result of colonization of their country by the British. This story, written earlier in the century, portrays the prejudice of colonization from an opposite perspective—that of a young white girl, the daughter of colonists, who gradually realizes the intolerance and cruelty of her own culture.

They were good, the years of ranging the bush over her father's farm which, like every white farm, was largely unused, broken only occasionally by small patches of cultivation. In between, nothing but trees, the long sparse grass, thorn and cactus and gully, grass and outcrop and thorn. And a jutting piece of rock which had been thrust up from the warm soil of Africa unimaginable eras of time ago, washed into hollows and whorls by sun and wind that had travelled so many thousands of miles of space and bush, would hold the weight of a small girl whose eyes were sightless for anything but a pale willowed river, a pale gleaming castle—a small girl singing: "Out flew the web and floated wide, the mirror cracked from side to side . . ."

Pushing her way through the green aisles of the mealie stalks, the leaves arching like cathedrals veined with sunlight far overhead, with the packed red earth underfoot, a fine lace of red starred witchweed would summon up a black bent figure croaking premonitions: the Northern witch, bred of cold Northern forests, would stand before her among the mealie fields, and it was the mealie fields that faded and fled, leaving her among the gnarled roots of an oak, snow falling thick and soft and white, the woodcutter's fire glowing red welcome through crowding tree trunks.

A white child, opening its eyes curiously on a sun-suffused landscape, a gaunt and violent landscape, might be supposed to accept it as her own, to take the msasa trees and the thorn trees as familiars, to feel her blood running free and responsive to the swing of the seasons.

This child could not see a msasa tree, or the thorn, for what they were. Her books held tales of alien fairies, her rivers ran slow and peaceful, and she knew the shape of the leaves of an ash or an oak, the names of the little creatures that lived in English streams, when the words "the veld" meant strangeness, though she could remember nothing else.

Because of this, for many years, it was the veld that seemed unreal; the sun was a foreign sun, and the wind spoke a strange language.

The black people on the farm were as remote as the trees and the rocks. They were an amorphous black mass, mingling and thinning and massing like tadpoles, faceless, who existed merely to serve, to say "Yes, Baas," take their money and go. They changed season by season, moving from one farm to the next, according to their outlandish needs, which one did not have to understand, coming from perhaps hundreds of miles North or East, passing on after a few months—where? Perhaps even as far away as the fabled gold mines of Johannesburg, where the pay was so much better than the few shillings a month and the double handful of mealie meal twice a day which they earned in that part of Africa.

The child was taught to take them for granted: the servants in the house would come running a hundred yards to pick up a book if she dropped it. She was called "Nkosikaas"—Chieftainess, even by the black children her own age.

Later, when the farm grew too small to hold her curiosity, she carried a gun in the crook of her arm and wandered miles a day, from vlei to vlei, from *kopje* to *kopje*, accompanied by two dogs: the dogs and the gun were an armour against fear. Because of them she never felt fear.

If a native came into sight along the kaffir paths half a mile away, the dogs would flush him up a tree as if he were a bird. If he expostulated (in his uncouth language which was by itself ridiculous) that was cheek. If one was in a good mood, it could be a matter for laughter. Otherwise one passed on, hardly glancing at the angry man in the tree.

On the rare occasions when white children met together they could amuse themselves by hailing a passing native in order to make a buffoon of him; they could set the dogs on him and watch him run; they could tease a small black child as if he were a puppy— save that they would not throw stones and sticks at a dog without a sense of guilt.

Later still, certain questions presented themselves in the child's mind; and because the answers were not easy to accept, they were silenced by an even greater arrogance of manner.

It was even impossible to think of the black people who worked about the house as friends, for if she talked to one of them, her mother would come running anxiously: "Come away; you mustn't talk to natives."

It was this instilled consciousness of danger, of something unpleasant, that made it easy to laugh out loud, crudely, if a servant made a mistake in his

English or if he failed to understand an order—there is a certain kind of laughter that is fear, afraid of itself.

One evening, when I was about fourteen, I was walking down the side of a mealie field that had been newly ploughed, so that the great red clods showed fresh and tumbling to the vlei beyond, like a choppy red sea; it was that hushed and listening hour, when the birds send long sad calls from tree to tree, and all the colours of earth and sky and leaf are deep and golden. I had my rifle in the curve of my arm, and the dogs were at my heels.

In front of me, perhaps a couple of hundred yards away, a group of three Africans came into sight around the side of a big antheap. I whistled the dogs close in to my skirts and let the gun swing in my hand, and advanced, waiting for them to move aside, off the path, in respect for my passing. But they came on steadily, and the dogs looked up at me for the command to chase. I was angry. It was "cheek" for a native not to stand off a path, the moment he caught sight of you.

In front walked an old man, stooping his weight on to a stick, his hair grizzled white, a dark red blanket slung over his shoulders like a cloak. Behind him came two young men, carrying bundles of pots, assegais, hatchets.

The group was not a usual one. They were not natives seeking work. These had an air of dignity, of quietly following their own purpose. It was the dignity that checked my tongue. I walked quietly on, talking softly to the growling dogs, till I was ten paces away. Then the old man stopped, drawing his blanket close.

"Morning, Nkosikaas," he said, using the customary greeting for any time of the day.

"Good morning," I said. "Where are you going?" My voice was a little truculent.

The old man spoke in his own language, then one of the young men stepped forward politely and said in careful English: "My Chief travels to see his brothers beyond the river."

A Chief! I thought, understanding the pride that made the old man stand before me like an equal— more than an equal, for he showed courtesy, and I showed none.

The old man spoke again, wearing dignity like an inherited garment, still standing ten paces off, flanked by his entourage, not looking at me (that would have been rude) but directing his eyes somewhere over my head at the trees.

"You are the little Nkosikaas from the farm of Baas Jordan?"

"That's right," I said.

"Perhaps your father does not remember," said the interpreter for the old man, "but there was an affair with some goats. I remember seeing you when you were . . ." The young man held his hand at knee level and smiled.

We all smiled.

"What is your name?" I asked.

"This is Chief Mshlanga," said the young man.

"I will tell my father that I met you," I said.

The old man said: "My greetings to your father, little Nkosikaas."

"Good morning," I said politely, finding the politeness difficult, from lack of use.

"Morning, little Nkosikaas," said the old man, and stood aside to let me pass.

I went by, my gun hanging awkwardly, the dogs sniffing and growling, cheated of their favourite game of chasing natives like animals.

Not long afterwards I read in an old explorer's book the phrase: "Chief Mshlanga's country." It went like this: "Our destination was Chief Mshlanga's country, to the north of the river; and it was our desire to ask his permission to prospect for gold in his territory."

The phrase "ask his permission" was so extraordinary to a white child, brought up to consider all natives as things to use, that it revived those questions, which could not be suppressed: they fermented slowly in my mind.

On another occasion one of those old prospectors who still move over Africa looking for neglected reefs, with their hammers and tents, and pans for sifting gold from crushed rock, came to the farm and, in talking of the old days, used that phrase again: "This was the Old Chief's country," he said. "It stretched from those mountains over there way back to the river, hundreds of miles of country." That was his name for our district: "The Old Chief's Country"; he did not use our name for it—a new phrase which held no implication of usurped ownership.

As I read more books about the time when this part of Africa was opened up, not much more than fifty years before, I found Old Chief Mshlanga had been a famous man, known to all the explorers and prospectors. But then he had been young; or maybe it was his father or uncle they spoke of—I never found out.

During that year I met him several times in the part of the farm that was traversed by natives moving over the country. I learned that the path up the side of the big red field where the birds sang was the recognised highway for migrants. Perhaps I even haunted it in the hope of meeting him: being greeted by him, the exchange of courtesies, seemed to answer the questions that troubled me.

Soon I carried a gun in a different spirit; I used it for shooting food and not to give me confidence. And now the dogs learned better manners. When I saw a native approaching, we offered and took greetings; and slowly that other landscape in my mind faded, and my feet struck directly on the African soil, and I saw the shapes of tree and hill clearly, and the black people moved back, as it were, out of my life: it was as if I stood aside to watch a slow intimate dance of landscape and men, a very old dance, whose steps I could not learn.

But I thought: this is my heritage, too; I was bred here; it is my country as well as the black man's country; and there is plenty of room for all of us, without elbowing each other off the pavements and roads.

It seemed it was only necessary to let free that respect I felt when I was talking with old Chief Mshlanga, to let both black and white people meet gently, with tolerance for each other's differences: it seemed quite easy.

Then, one day, something new happened. Working in our house as servants were always three natives: cook, houseboy, garden boy. They used to change as the farm natives changed: staying for a few months, then moving on to a new job, or back home to their kraals. They were thought of as "good" or "bad" natives; which meant: how did they behave as servants? Were they lazy, efficient, obedient, or disrespectful? If the family felt good-humoured, the phrase was: "What can you expect from savages?" If we were angry, we said: "We would be much better off without them."

One day, a white policeman was on his rounds of the district, and he said laughingly: "Did you know you have an important man in your kitchen?"

"What!" exclaimed my mother sharply. "What do you mean?"

"A Chief's son." The policeman seemed amused.

"He'll boss the tribe when the old man dies."

"He'd better not put on a Chief's son act with me," said my mother.

When the policeman left, we looked with different eyes at our cook: he was a good worker, but he drank too much at week-ends—that was how we knew him.

He was a tall youth, with very black skin, like black polished metal, his tightly-growing black hair parted white man's fashion at one side, with a metal comb from the store stuck into it; very polite, very distant, very quick to obey an order. Now that it had been pointed out, we said: "Of course, you can see. Blood always tells."

My mother became strict with him now she knew about his birth and prospects. Sometimes, when she lost her temper, she would say: "You aren't the Chief yet, you know." And he would answer her very quietly, his eyes on the ground: "Yes, Nkosikaas."

One afternoon he asked for a whole day off, instead of the customary half-day, to go home next Sunday.

"How can you go home in one day?"

"It will take me half an hour on my bicycle," he explained.

I watched the direction he took; and the next day I went off to look for this kraal; I understood he must be Chief Mshlanga's successor: there was no other kraal near enough our farm.

Beyond our boundaries on that side the country was new to me. I followed unfamiliar paths past kopjes that till now had been part of the jagged horizon, hazed with distance. This was Government land, which had never been cultivated by white men; at first I could not understand why it was that it appeared, in merely crossing the boundary, I had entered a completely fresh type of landscape. It was a wide green valley, where a small river sparkled, and vivid water-birds darted over the rushes. The grass was thick and soft to my calves, the trees stood tall and shapely.

I was used to our farm, whose hundreds of acres of harsh eroded soil bore trees that had been cut for the mine furnaces and had grown thin and twisted, where the cattle had dragged the grass flat, leaving innumerable criss-crossing trails that deepened each season into gullies, under the force of the rains.

This country had been left untouched, save for prospectors whose picks had struck a few sparks from the surface of the rocks as they wandered by; and for migrant natives whose passing had left, perhaps, a charred patch on the trunk of a tree where their evening fire had nestled.

It was very silent: a hot morning with pigeons cooing throatily, the midday shadows lying dense and thick with clear yellow spaces of sunlight between and in all that wide green park-like valley, not a human soul but myself.

I was listening to the quick regular tapping of a woodpecker when slowly a chill feeling seemed to grow up from the small of my back to my shoulders, in a constricting spasm like a shudder, and at the roots of my hair a tingling sensation began and ran down over the surface of my flesh, leaving me goosefleshed and cold, though I was damp with sweat. Fever? I thought; then uneasily, turned to look over my shoulder; and realised suddenly that this was fear. It was extraordinary, even humiliating. It was a new fear. For all the years I had walked by myself over this country I had never known a moment's uneasiness; in the beginning because I had been supported by a gun and the dogs, then because I had learnt an easy friendliness for the Africans I might encounter.

I had read of this feeling, how the bigness and

silence of Africa, under the ancient sun, grows dense and takes shape in the mind, till even the birds seem to call menacingly, and a deadly spirit comes out of the trees and the rocks. You move warily, as if your very passing disturbs something old and evil, something dark and big and angry that might suddenly rear and strike from behind. You look at groves of entwined trees, and picture the animals that might be lurking there; you look at the river running slowly, dropping from level to level through the vlei, spreading into pools where at night the bucks come to drink, and the crocodiles rise and drag them by their soft noses into underwater caves. Fear possessed me. I found I was turning round and round, because of that shapeless menace behind me that might reach out and take me; I kept glancing at the files of *kopjes* which, seen from a different angle, seemed to change with every step so that even known landmarks, like a big mountain that had sentinelled my world since I first became conscious of it, showed an unfamiliar sunlit valley among its foothills. I did not know where I was. I was lost. Panic seized me. I found I was spinning round and round, staring anxiously at this tree and that, peering up at the sun which appeared to have moved into an eastern slant, shedding the sad yellow light of sunset. Hours must have passed! I looked at my watch and found that this state of meaningless terror had lasted perhaps ten minutes.

The point was that it was meaningless. I was not ten miles from home: I had only to take my way back along the valley to find myself at the fence; away among the foothills of the *kopjes* gleamed the roof of a neighbour's house, and a couple of hours' walking would reach it. This was the sort of fear that contracts the flesh of a dog at night and sets him howling at the full moon. It had nothing to do with what I thought or felt; and I was more disturbed by the fact that I could become its victim than of the physical sensation itself: I walked steadily on, quietened, in a divided mind, watching my own pricking nerves and apprehensive glances from side to side with a disgusted amusement. Deliberately I set myself to think of this village I was seeking, and what I should do when I entered it—if I could find it, which was doubtful, since I was walking aimlessly and it might be anywhere in the hundreds of thousands of acres of bush that stretched about me. With my mind on that village, I realised that a new sensation was added to the fear: loneliness. Now such a terror of isolation invaded me that I could hardly walk; and if it were not that I came over the crest of a small rise and saw a village below me, I should have turned and gone home. It was a cluster of thatched huts in a clearing among trees. There were neat patches of mealies and pumpkins and millet, and cattle grazed under some trees at a distance. Fowls scratched among the huts, dogs lay sleeping on the grass, and goats friezed a *kopje* that jutted up beyond a tributary of the river lying like an enclosing arm round the village.

As I came close I saw the huts were lovingly decorated with patterns of yellow and red and ochre mud on the walls; and the thatch was tied in place with plaits of straw.

This was not at all like our farm compound, a dirty and neglected place, a temporary home for migrants who had no roots in it.

And now I did not know what to do next. I called a small black boy, who was sitting on a lot playing a stringed gourd, quite naked except for the strings of blue beads round his neck, and said: "Tell the Chief I am here." The child stuck his thumb in his mouth and stared shyly back at me.

For minutes I shifted my feet on the edge of what seemed a deserted village, till at last the child scuttled off, and then some women came. They were draped in bright cloths, with brass glinting in their ears and on their arms. They also stared, silently; then turned to chatter among themselves.

I said again: "Can I see Chief Mshlanga?" I saw they caught the name; they did not understand what I wanted. I did not understand myself.

At last I walked through them and came past the huts and saw a clearing under a big shady tree, where a dozen old men sat cross-legged on the ground, talking. Chief Mshlanga was leaning back against the tree, holding a gourd in his hand, from which he had been drinking. When he saw me, not a muscle of his face moved, and I could see he was not pleased: perhaps he was afflicted with my own shyness, due to being unable to find the right forms of courtesy for the occasion. To meet me, on our own farm, was one thing; but I should not have come here. What had I expected? I could not join them socially: the thing was unheard of. Bad enough that I, a white girl, should be walking the veld alone as a white man might: and in this part of the bush where only Government officials had the right to move.

Again I stood, smiling foolishly, while behind me stood the groups of brightly-clad, chattering women, their faces alert with curiosity and interest, and in front of me sat the old men, with old lined faces, their eyes guarded, aloof. It was a village of ancients and children and women. Even the two young men who knelt beside the Chief were not those I had seen with him previously: the young men were all away working on the white men's farms and mines, and the Chief must depend on relatives who were temporarily on holiday for his attendants.

"The small white Nkosikaas is far from home," remarked the old man at last.

"Yes," I agreed, "it is far." I wanted to say: "I have come to pay you a friendly visit, Chief Mshlanga." I could not say it. I might now be feeling an urgent helpless desire to get to know these men and women as people, to be accepted by them as a friend, but the truth was I had set out in a spirit of curiosity: I had wanted to see the village that one day our cook, the reserved and obedient young man who got drunk on Sundays, would one day rule over.

"The child of Nkosi Jordan is welcome," said Chief Mshlanga.

"Thank you," I said, and could think of nothing more to say. There was a silence, while the flies rose and began to buzz around my head; and the wind shook a little in the thick green tree that spread its branches over the old men.

"Good morning," I said at last. "I have to return now to my home."

"Morning, little Nkosikaas," said Chief Mshlanga.

I walked away from the indifferent village, over the rise past the staring amber-eyed goats, down through the tall stately trees into the great rich green valley where the river meandered and the pigeons cooed tales of plenty and the woodpecker tapped softly.

The fear had gone; the loneliness had set into stiff-necked stoicism; there was now a queer hostility in the landscape, a cold, hard, sullen indomitability that walked with me, as strong as a wall, as intangible as smoke; it seemed to say to me: you walk here as a destroyer. I went slowly homewards, with an empty heart: I had learned that if one cannot call a country to heel like a dog, neither can one dismiss the past with a smile in an easy gush of feeling, saying: I could not help it, I am also a victim.

I only saw Chief Mshlanga once again.

One night my father's big red land was trampled down by small sharp hooves, and it was discovered that the culprits were goats from Chief Mshlanga's kraal. This had happened once before, years ago.

My father confiscated all the goats. Then he sent a message to the old Chief that if he wanted them he would have to pay for the damage.

He arrived at our house at the time of sunset one evening, looking very old and bent now, walking stiffly under his regally-draped blanket, leaning on a big stick. My father sat himself down in his big chair below the steps of the house; the old man squatted carefully on the ground before him, flanked by his two young men.

The palaver was long and painful, because of the bad English of the young man who interpreted, and because my father could not speak dialect, but only kitchen kaffir.

From my father's point of view, at least two hundred pounds' worth of damage had been done to the crop. He knew he could not get the money from the old man. He felt he was entitled to keep the goats. As for the old Chief, he kept repeating angrily: "Twenty goats! My people cannot lose twenty goats! We are not rich, like the Nkosi Jordan, to lose twenty goats at once."

My father did not think of himself as rich, but rather as very poor. He spoke quickly and angrily in return, saying that the damage done meant a great deal to him, and that he was entitled to the goats.

At last it grew so heated that the cook, the Chief's son, was called from the kitchen to be interpreter, and now my father spoke fluently in English, and our cook translated rapidly so that the old man could understand how very angry my father was. The young man spoke without emotion, in a mechanical way, his eyes lowered, but showing how he felt his position by a hostile uncomfortable set of the shoulders.

It was now in the late sunset, the sky a welter of colours, the birds singing their last songs, and the cattle, lowing peacefully, moving past us towards their sheds for the night. It was the hour when Africa is most beautiful; and here was this pathetic, ugly scene, doing no one any good.

At last my father stated finally: "I'm not going to argue about it. I am keeping the goats."

The old Chief flashed back in his own language: "That means that my people will go hungry when the dry season comes."

"Go to the police, then," said my father, and looked triumphant.

There was, of course, no more to be said.

The old man sat silent, his head bent, his hands dangling helplessly over his withered knees. Then he rose, the young men helping him, and he stood facing my father. He spoke once again, very stiffly; and turned away and went home to his village.

"What did he say?" asked my father of the young man, who laughed uncomfortably and would not meet his eyes.

"What did he say?" insisted my father.

Our cook stood straight and silent, his brows knotted together. Then he spoke. "My father says: All this land, this land you call yours, is his land, and belongs to our people."

Having made this statement, he walked off into the bush after his father, and we did not see him again.

Our next cook was a migrant from Nyasaland, with no expectations of greatness.

Next time the policeman came on his rounds he was told this story. He remarked: "That kraal has no right to be there; it should have been moved long ago. I don't know why no one has done anything about it. I'll have a chat with the Native Commissioner next week. I'm going over for tennis on Sunday, anyway."

Some time later we heard that Chief Mshlanga and his people had been moved two hundred miles east, to a proper Native Reserve; the Government land was going to be opened up for white settlement soon.

I went to see the village again, about a year afterwards. There was nothing there. Mounds of red mud, where the huts had been, had long swathes of rotting thatch over them, veined with the red galleries of the white ants. The pumpkin vines rioted everywhere, over the bushes, up the lower branches of trees so that the great golden balls rolled underfoot and dangled overhead: it was a festival of pumpkins. The bushes were crowding up, the new grass sprang vivid green.

The settler lucky enough to be allotted the lush warm valley (if he chose to cultivate this particular section) would find, suddenly, in the middle of a mealie field, the plants were growing fifteen feet tall, the weight of the cobs dragging at the stalks, and wonder what unsuspected vein of richness he had struck.

Young Africa's Plea

by Dennis Osadebay

*As Tambudzai moves between Shona
culture and Westernized culture, she has
conflicting responses to both societies—
sometimes criticizing, sometimes
questioning, sometimes admiring. In this
poem by a Nigerian tribal chief, the
speaker acknowledges the clash of
cultures and asserts his worth.*

Don't preserve my customs
As some fine curios
To suit some white historian's tastes.
There's nothing artificial
5   That beats the natural way,
In culture and ideals of life.
Let me play with the white man's ways.
Let me work with the black man's brains,
Let my affairs sort themselves out.
10 Then in sweet re-birth
I'll rise a better man,
Not ashamed to face the world.
Those who doubt my talents
In secret fear my strength;
15 They know I am no less a man.
Let them bury their prejudice,
Let them show their noble sides,
Let me have untrammelled growth.
My friends will never know regret
20 And I, I never once forget.

Acknowledgments

(*continued from page ii*)

David R. Godine, Publisher, Inc.: Excerpts from *Hunger of Memory: The Education of Richard Rodriguez* by Richard Rodriguez. Copyright © 1982 by Richard Rodriguez. Reprinted by permission of David R. Godine, Publisher, Inc.

Alfred A. Knopf, Inc.: "Losing a Language," from *The Rain in the Trees* by W. S. Merwin. Copyright © 1988 by W. S. Merwin. Reprinted by permission of Alfred A. Knopf, Inc., a division of Random House, Inc.

Lucinda Roy: "Points of View," from *Wailing the Dead to Sleep* by Lucinda Roy. Copyright © 1988 by Lucinda Roy. Reprinted by permission of the author.

Simon & Schuster, Inc.: "The Old Chief Mshlanga," from *African Stories* by Doris Lessing. Copyright © 1951, renewed 1981 by Doris Lessing. Reprinted with the permission of Simon & Schuster, Inc.